The Definitive Guide to Apache MyFaces and Facelets

Zubin Wadia, Martin Marinschek,
Hazem Saleh, and Dennis Byrne

Contributing Authors: Bruno Aranda, Mario Ivankovits, Cagatay Civici,
Arvid Hülsebus, Detlef Bartetzko, and Allan Lykke Christensen

Apress®

The Definitive Guide to Apache MyFaces and Facelets

ISBN-13 (pbk): 978-1-59059-737-8

ISBN-10 (pbk): 1-59059-737-0

ISBN-13 (electronic): 978-1-4302-0344-5

9 8 7 6 5 4 3 2 1

Lead Editor: Steve Anglin
Technical Reviewer: Dr. Sarang Poornachandra
Editorial Board: Clay Andres, Steve Anglin, Ewan Buckingham, Tony Campbell, Gary Cornell, Jonathan Gennick, Matthew Moodie, Joseph Ottinger, Jeffrey Pepper, Frank Pohlmann, Ben Renow-Clarke, Dominic Shakeshaft, Matt Wade, Tom Welsh
Project Manager: Sofia Marchant
Copy Editor: Heather Lang
Associate Production Director: Kari Brooks-Copony
Production Editor: Kelly Winquist
Compositor: Linda Weidemann, Wolf Creek Press
Proofreader: Martha Whitt
Indexer: John Collin
Artist: April Milne
Cover Designer: Kurt Krames
Manufacturing Director: Tom Debolski

Distributed to the book trade worldwide by Springer-Verlag New York, Inc., 233 Spring Street, 6th Floor, New York, NY 10013. Phone 1-800-SPRINGER, fax 201-348-4505, e-mail orders-ny@springer-sbm.com, or visit http://www.springeronline.com.

For information on translations, please contact Apress directly at 2855 Telegraph Avenue, Suite 600, Berkeley, CA 94705. Phone 510-549-5930, fax 510-549-5939, e-mail info@apress.com, or visit http://www.apress.com.

Apress and friends of ED books may be purchased in bulk for academic, corporate, or promotional use. eBook versions and licenses are also available for most titles. For more information, reference our Special Bulk Sales–eBook Licensing web page at http://www.apress.com/info/bulksales.

The source code for this book is available to readers at http://www.apress.com.

My parents, Rustom and Avan,
whose guidance and encouragement mean the world.
—Zubin Wadia

For the prophet Muhammad,
from whom I learnt all the good things in my life.
—Hazem Saleh

Ainhoa, my wife,
whose support and patience made this book possible.
—Bruno Aranda

Contents at a Glance

Contents

About the Authors

ZUBIN WADIA has seven years of experience in JEE and .NET technologies. His experiences with enterprise content management, workflow, imaging, compression, and security allow him to appreciate a powerful framework that offers a high degree of flexibility and efficiency. In 2005, Zubin designed and deployed an award-winning solution for a criminal justice agency in the government space, leveraging next-generation technologies such as Ajax, Hibernate, Spring, BPEL, and, of course, MyFaces. His current focus is on architecting an enterprisewide contract management platform for the New York City Department of Health. Zubin is CTO at ImageWork Technologies, a leading government systems integrator on the East Coast.

MARTIN MARINSCHEK has eight years of experience in Java EE and open source technologies. He is a MyFaces PMC member and a popular speaker at major open source events such as JavaPolis and ApacheCon. Martin brings dynamism, experience, and innovation to the MyFaces project. Martin is a CEO of Irian, a fast-growing consulting company focused on providing JSF solutions to customers.

HAZEM SALEH has four years of experience in Java EE and open source technologies and is a MyFaces committer. He is the initiator of many components in the MyFaces Tomahawk sandbox such as CAPTCHA, pdfExport, media, and passwordStrength. He is also a yui4jsf committer. He is now working at IBM Egypt as a staff engineer.

DENNIS BYRNE works for ThoughtWorks, a global consultancy with a focus on end-to-end agile software development of mission-critical systems. Dennis is a committer and PMC member for Apache MyFaces. He is also an experienced public speaker and a committer for JBoss JSFUnit.

About the Technical Reviewer

POORNACHANDRA SARANG, PHD, in his long tenure of over 20 years, has worked in various capacities in the IT industry. Dr. Sarang provides consulting and training in enterprise architecting, solution architecting, design, and development to a large number of clients worldwide. He has been a consultant to Sun Microsystems for several years, and his recent engagements include Director, Architecture for Kynetia (a Spanish-origin MNC). He has been a recipient of Microsoft's Most Valuable Professional (MVP) award for two consecutive years. He has spoken in several international conferences on Java, CORBA, XML, and .NET organized by O'Reilly, SYS-CON, WROX, SUN, and Microsoft in various countries such as India, the United States, the United Kingdom, Switzerland, Singapore, and so on. He has been invited to deliver keynote speeches at highly acclaimed Microsoft Architect Summits and several other prestigious events. He has several research papers, journal articles, and books to his credit.

Dr. Sarang has been a visiting professor of computer engineering at University of Notre Dame and currently holds an adjunct faculty position at the Department of Computer Science at the University of Mumbai, where he teaches postgraduate courses, provides project guidance to postgraduate students, and guides PhD students. His current research interests include distributed systems, mobile computing, and algorithm development. He may be reached at `profsarang@gmail.com`.

Acknowledgments

This book would not have been possible without the MyFaces project founders—Manfred Geiler and Thomas Spiegl. Additionally, Jacob Hookom's seminal work with Facelets was a prime driver to increasing JSF adoption in the Java developer community. Without their vision, this comprehensive book would not have an audience.

Additionally, we would like to acknowledge the contributions of Simon Kitching, who is a regular committer to MyFaces and the Orchestra projects. His insight and attention to detail have been valuable to the continuing growth and applicability of Orchestra. Arash Rajaeeyan also provided valuable input, contributions, and insight into Tomahawk and the IDE setup. We are grateful for their inputs.

Finally, we would like to thank the MyFaces and JSF community as a whole for their tireless support and contributions to a variety of subprojects. Without this anarchic collaboration, MyFaces would cease to be competitively differentiated against the Sun Reference Implementation.

Introduction

In the four years that the Sun, IBM, and MyFaces implementations have been available, the MyFaces project has arguably been the front-runner when it comes to innovation and dexterity. It also is the most responsive to user issues and has a vibrant community that ensures progression (you can always find free support on the mailing lists). With JavaServer Faces (JSF) 2.0 around the corner, preparation is already under way as the committers quickly review the early access draft and plan for MyFaces 2.0.

This "anarchic collaboration," a term coined by Roy Fielding, is the essence of the Apache MyFaces project: many talented people share information with a single-minded objective to make JSF a pleasurable developer experience for all. The Tomahawk, Trinidad, Tobago, Orchestra, and MyFaces implementations have been downloaded over a million times. Before the Sun JSF 1.2 implementation was released, we could safely say the MyFaces implementation was the only reliable way to build production JSF applications. Even today, many developers are happy with simply using MyFaces 1.1.x and Facelets to form a potent combination.

This book assumes you are interested in JSF and component-oriented development. It takes you through a journey beginning with the unique aspects of JSF, introduces you to the MyFaces specification, and continues with building your first application. Once you've mastered that, this book advances your skill set further by taking you into the world of the Tomahawk component library. Here, you learn the power of componentization in JSF (you will be able to build a complex application with a few lines of code) and see the advantages of having a vibrant community like MyFaces continually developing new components into the sandbox like CAPTCHA-, media-, exporter-, and AJAX-enabled UI widgets.

Next, we take you into one of the most important chapters in the book—learning to leverage Facelets's powerful view-definition capabilities within your JSF application. After absorbing the material in this chapter, you will be able to write JSF view tiers with greater efficiency and yield more performance out of your applications, as compared to similar applications leveraging classic JSP. The patterns we encourage in this chapter are a result of our more than ten years of cumulative experience with JSF across two of the major Reference Implementations: Sun and MyFaces.

The second half of this book focuses on smaller but equally critical projects to the future of MyFaces: Trinidad, Tobago, and Orchestra. Trinidad and Tobago offer high-quality component libraries that are particularly adept at custom rendition, themes, and layouts. Trinidad's presence is also a testament to the commercial support of MyFaces by Oracle for its Application Development Framework (ADF). Although a relatively young project, Orchestra offers powerful functionality like conversation scope for persistence-rich JSF applications.

The final chapter weaves together all your newfound knowledge and shows how to avoid some of the common antipatterns new JSF developers often end up pursuing. JSF is a complex specification augmented by a significant number of support frameworks to assist with development. We make sure the details in this book allow you to make educated decisions on which ones to leverage.

Finally, be sure to take advantage of the book's modular nature. We tried to strike a natural balance between this book being a *guide* and a *reference*. Refreshing your memory on a particular topic is extremely easy because of the atomic nature of each chapter. Enjoy!

CHAPTER 1

An Introduction to JavaServer Faces

Welcome to the world of JavaServer Faces. In this chapter, we will explain the core architecture of JavaServer Faces (JSF) and how the technology has evolved over the last few years. This chapter will make you aware of the ingredients of any JSF application and of the critical features added in JSF's major releases (1.0, 1.1, and 1.2). It will also explain the JSF life cycle and how a Struts developer can become a JSF developer.

The chapter will introduce the Apache MyFaces platform and some of the key differentiating features and competitive advantages it presents over the standard Sun Reference Implementation (RI).

The Evolution of Java Web Frameworks

Java web application development today is within a unique period in its history. Hundreds of frameworks, a dynamic open source community, rapidly evolving web development standards, and a thirst for dynamic interfaces make the developer's job simpler and more difficult simultaneously. Choices made six months ago that seemed graced with genius now feel outdated, as new approaches and versions have already superceded them. A seemingly difficult problem that might have taken weeks to crack has been permanently resolved by a colleague halfway around the world. Developing for the web is demanding. It requires an astute understanding of the history behind HTML, JavaScript, and other web development tools and some of the overarching trends that figure as central themes. Modern Java web applications tend to have the following characteristics:

- Complex functionality as core business processes become web enabled
- Increased interactivity with the user for validation, verification, and notification
- A simple and consistent user interface
- Adherence to web standards such as CSS and XHTML

Java web development began with the Servlet specification in 1996 and was progressively enhanced and refactored for ease of use with the advent of JavaServer Pages (JSP) in 1999, the Struts Action Framework in 2001, and finally JavaServer Faces in 2004 (see Figure 1-1).

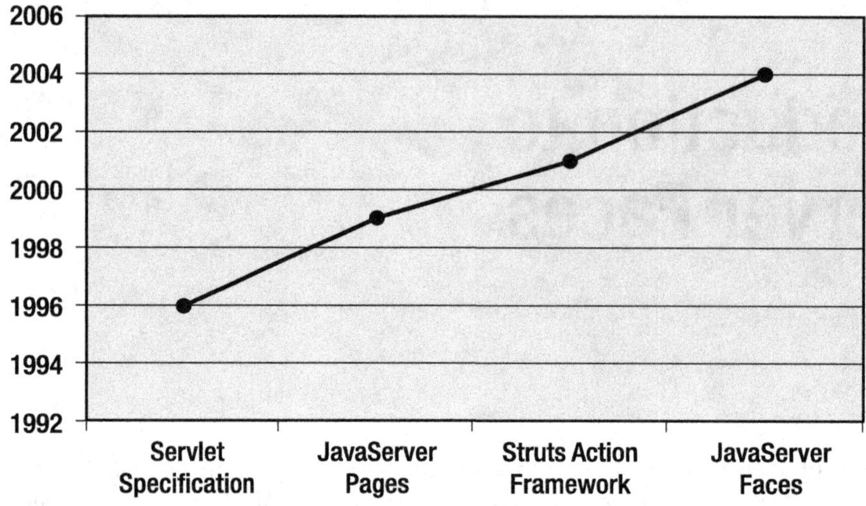

Figure 1-1. *The evolution of Java web frameworks*

Servlets

The Servlet specification is significant, because it is still at the core of all Java web development specifications. Understanding its internal working offers insight into the low-level pipelining occurring within your abstracted web application. Listing 1-1 shows a simple servlet.

Listing 1-1. *The Hello World Servlet Example*

```
import java.io.PrintWriter;
import java.io.IOException;

import javax.servlet.ServletException;

import javax.servlet.http.HttpServlet;
import javax.servlet.http.HttpServletRequest;
import javax.servlet.http.HttpServletResponse;

public class HelloWorldServlet extends HttpServlet {

  protected void doGet(HttpServletRequest request,
                       HttpServletResponse response)
                       throws ServletException, IOException {
    PrintWriter writer = response.getWriter();

    writer.println("<html>");
    writer.println("<head><title>Hello World Example</title></head>");
    writer.println("<body>Hello World!</body>");
    writer.println("</html>");
    writer.close();
  }
```

```
  protected void doPost(HttpServletRequest request,
                        HttpServletResponse response)
                        throws ServletException, IOException {
    doGet(request, response);
  }
}
```

Listing 1-1 shows the servlet program structure. The servlet's class should extend the `HttpServlet` class and override `doGet()`, `doPost()`, or both depending on whether the data is sent using `GET` or `POST` requests. These methods have two parameters: `HttpServletRequest` and `HttpServletResponse`. The `HttpServletRequest` parameter allows you to get the incoming request data, while the `HttpServletResponse` parameter allows outputting the response to the client.

Classical servlet programming mixes HTML with Java code, which leads to complex development and maintainability concerns for both web designers and developers.

JavaServer Pages

The JSP specification further addressed the logic-markup interlacing issue. The Java code can be separated from the markup in three ways:

- Encapsulating Java code with standard HTML tags around it
- Using beans
- Using JSP tags that employ Java code behind the scenes

JSP made the web application code base easier to maintain and gave developers more freedom in terms of the way they organized the content of their pages—though encapsulating Java code in the page is now frowned upon because it doesn't really separate the Java code from the markup. Listing 1-2 is an example of JSP and shows why JSP tags are preferred.

Listing 1-2. *The Hello World JSP Example*

```
<html>
  <head>
    <title>Hello World JSP</title>
  </head>
  <body>
    <% out.println("Hello World!"); %>
  </body>
</html>
```

Listing 1-2 achieves the same output as the previous servlet example but is better organized, as the HTML markup is not part of the Java code. It's still not an ideal situation, however.

■ **Note** Of course, we could have used `<%= "Hello World!" %>` to write the message, but the point is the same: using Java code in any way in the page is not a good idea.

Struts and Web Development Patterns

When the Struts Application Framework 1.0 became popular post-2001, a new architectural pattern became the de facto standard for Java web development: the Model, View, Controller (MVC) pattern. In a typical MVC implementation, often called Model 2, the servlet acts as a controller for incoming requests from the client, routing requests to a JavaBean (model) to fetch data and then handing it over to the related JSP (view) to render the appropriate markup, update the model, and issue a response to the client. Figure 1-2 shows these MVC architectural pattern steps, which together form the Model 2 architecture.

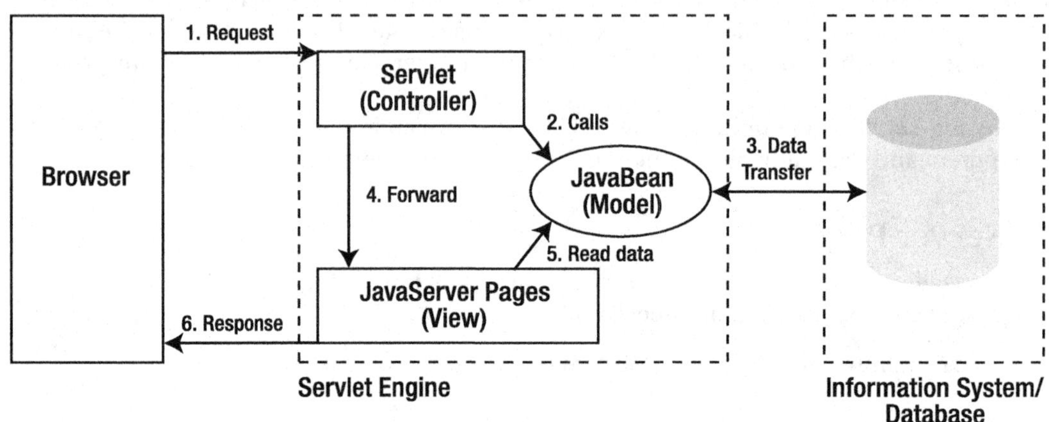

Figure 1-2. *Model 2 architectural pattern*

Struts 1.0 and 2.0 and a host of other frameworks like Spring MVC, Stripes, and Tapestry followed this pattern. The problem with having so many frameworks is that each one ends up implementing unique and widely desired features within their stacks. Developers then tried to make two or more frameworks work together or extend each other to meet their design objectives. This approach resulted in a magnification of the inherent complexity of a web project and ended up being a futile quest. In other words, there was no unified standard for Java web development and no standardized API existed for building web components.

These difficulties gave birth to JavaServer Faces (JSF), a standard developed by Sun Microsystems under the Java Community Process to provide a powerful component-based, event-driven platform for web application development in Java.

A Brief History of JSF

When Sun released JSF 1.0 in 2004, it offered a significant evolution in the way the web tier was implemented. Along with this significant advance came equally significant shortcomings that would limit developer adoption. The Sun Expert Group worked hard on the specification and, in 2005, released version 1.1, which eliminated some of JSF's greatest performance issues and made it usable within next-generation web applications. After the release of version 1.1, the Apache MyFaces implementation came to the fore due to its extensibility, real-world feedback, and large community. Some major enterprise applications use Apache MyFaces within their web tiers today, proving the real-world viability of JSF 1.1.

With JSF 1.1, the Sun Expert Group had achieved most of the early goals they set out to achieve in Java Specification Request (JSR) 127. These goals were related to creation of a standard GUI component framework that can be supported by development tools that allowed JSF developers to create custom components by extending base framework components, defining APIs for input validation and conversion, and specifying a model for GUI localization and internationalization. You can read the complete JSR 127 at `http://jcp.org/en/jsr/detail?id=127`.

In May 2006, JSF 1.2 was released with Java Enterprise Edition 5.0. JSF 1.2 might sound like a point release on paper, but it has significant enhancements to address some of the user community's real-world issues with JSF 1.1. By all accounts, this is a feature release of JSF with enhancements to security, standardization, and Expression Language (EL). JSR 252 is the JSF 1.2 specification; you can read it at `http://jcp.org/en/jsr/detail?id=252`.

With JSF 1.2, Sun has a release that not only brings the component-oriented vision to life but also offers a more developer-friendly way of implementing JSF at the web tier. Lastly, JSF 1.2 offers a significant degree of future proofing by being in full concert with the Java EE 5.0 stack. JSF 1.2 requires JSP 2.1 and Servlet 2.4 to run. JSF 2.0, due for release in late 2008, will bring with it enhancements to tooling, validation, and an extended component library with support for JSR 227 (Standard Data Binding and Data Access).

JSF Features

JSF, in a nutshell, is a standardized, component-based, event-driven framework for Java web applications with a strong focus on rapid development and best practices. It allows web designers or UI engineers to create simple templates for a given application. It allows Java developers to write the backend code independently of the web tier. And lastly, it allows third-party vendors to develop tools and component libraries that are compliant with the specification.

JSF components can be embedded inside JSP pages and can render the appropriate markup for HTML or any other output for which a render kit is provided. In other words, the render kit transforms the JSF markup into markup that is suitable for the client, such as HTML for a web browser.

Take, for example, the following JSF markup that uses JSF tags:

```
<h:form id="myForm">
  <h:inputText id="myText" />
</h:form>
```

This would render in HTML 4.0.1 as:

```
<input type="text" id="myForm:myText" />
```

Components in JSF generate events. Each event triggers a method call with action and event handlers. The state of a web application changes due to a given event.

JSF offers developers

- A set of standard converters and validators likely to be used in a web application
- A set of standard components likely to be used in a web application

- A basic component architecture that can be extended by creating custom converters, validators, and components
- Ability to build a layout with a set of subviews
- Java EE 5.0 compatibility
- IDE support for Sun, Eclipse, Oracle, and more
- Several implementations of the standard (Sun RI, Apache MyFaces, etc.)
- Extended component libraries like MyFaces Tomahawk, MyFaces Tobago, MyFaces Trinidad (formerly Oracle ADF), and Backbase
- Extended frameworks like Facelets, Shale, and Seam
- Classic Struts integration with the Struts Integration Library
- Struts Action Framework 2.0 integration with FacesInterceptors

As with a standard MVC framework, the JSF model contains the objects and properties of a given application. The model can also be called the business tier binding. The view handles the rendering via render kits. The controller in JSF is the FacesServlet, which defines and handles the flow of the application.

The JSF Life Cycle

The key differentiating factor between JSF and other frameworks like Spring MVC, Struts, and Stripes is the life cycle (see Figure 1-3). JSF has a very different request processing life cycle with six phases:

1. Restore view.
2. Apply request values; process events.
3. Process validations; process events.
4. Update model values; process events.
5. Invoke application; process events.
6. Render response.

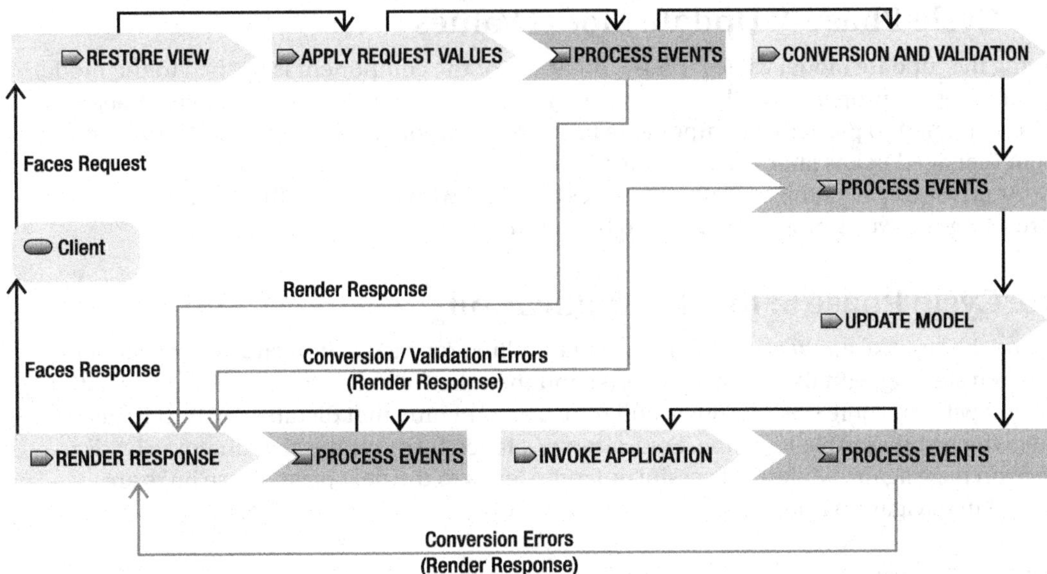

Figure 1-3. *The JSF life cycle*

Life Cycle Phase 1: Restore View

The primary purpose of the "restore view" phase is to build the component tree. On the first nonpostback request, the restore view goes directly to the render response phase. It then uses the template and creates the initial tree by parsing the request. Lastly, it saves the tree state in the `FacesContext` object. On subsequent postback requests, it creates the tree from state and proceeds to execute the rest of the life cycle.

Life Cycle Phase 2: Apply Request Values

In the second phase, JSF takes each component in the tree starting with the root and creates or retrieves it from the `FacesContext` object. Every component in the tree manages its own values and takes them from the HTTP request parameters, cookies, and headers.

Life Cycle Phase 3: Process Validations

In the "process validations" phase, JSF performs conversion and validation on all the components starting with the root, all of which constitutes event handling. The submitted value of each component is converted to an object and validated by calling the registered validator. Lastly, JSF saves the submitted value (or local value). If an error occurs during conversion or validation, the life cycle skips directly to the "render response" phase.

Life Cycle Phase 4: Update Model Values

During the "update model values" phase, the value of the component is pushed to the model by updating the properties of the backing beans. Backing beans are called managed beans in JSF and are tied to particular components using JSF component attributes. You'll see more about managed beans later in the chapter.

At this stage, all of the component values are valid with respect to the form. In other words, they are well formed according to the input validators.

Life Cycle Phase 5: Invoke Application

During the "invoke application" phase, event handling for each action and action listener is executed starting with the action listener(s) and then the calling action method. Each action method will run some business logic and return an outcome that dictates the next logical view, which you are able to define. For example, a failed form submission outcome leads to the form page again, while a successful outcome leads to the next page. These links are defined in navigation rules.

Life Cycle Phase 6: Render Response

During the "render response" phase, a navigation handler determines the next view, and then the view handler takes over. In the case of a JSP page, the JSP view handler takes over and enforces a forward. The JSP page gets parsed by the JSP container by performing a lookup for each component. Finally, the renderer is invoked, resulting in an HTML page.

Moving from Struts Frameworks to JSF

Many developers entering the JSF world for the first time come from action-oriented frameworks, of which the most popular is Struts. Applying Struts's action-oriented patterns to JSF's component-oriented architecture will induce massive amounts of stomach acid to your development experience.

The Struts core mainly leverages the Front Controller and Command patterns. JSF, however, is a far more complex component-oriented superstructure with Decorator, Template, Singleton, Filter, and Observer patterns in play.

■ **Note** For more on design patterns, see *Design Patterns: Elements of Reusable Object-Oriented Software* by Erich Gamma, Richard Helm, Ralph Johnson, and John M. Vlissides (Addison-Wesley Professional, 1994).

It is also important to choose the right time to introduce JSF to your project. If you already have an established code base built on Struts, extending it with JSF is probably not a good idea. Your team will have to compensate for too many architectural mismatches to make it a viable partnership. You are better off keeping the architecture homogenous.

If you want to execute on a Struts-JSF hybrid, it is possible using the Struts-Faces integration library. Just remember that one of the basic techniques of standard enterprise architecture—abstraction—can become an overhead cost if overused. Abstraction at a given tier may deliver improved configurability, but it usually brings with it a performance hit.

If you have the opportunity to begin a new project and have selected JSF as your primary technology, then congratulations. You have two excellent options to begin your journey with:

- Plain JSF with no supporting frameworks
- JSF++ with frameworks such as Facelets

Whichever method you choose, your approach to developing web applications will have to change. Switching from Struts to JSF is like switching from procedural to object-oriented programming: you have to change the way you see, model, and implement the problem.

Struts is a pure implementation of the classical MVC pattern. When you are developing with Struts or similar frameworks, you see the application as a set of pages, each of which may interact with the user and require the system to conduct an action. Therefore, you must recognize user commands and system actions in response to those inputs. You would then write the code for each action. The action may change the model state and forward it to a view. Finally, the view reads data from the model and proceeds to display it to the user.

With actions, you have full responsibility for updating the model and redirecting the user to the correct view. Struts actions are like partial servlets; they interact with request/response objects and process `GET`/`POST` requests. For Struts, the view is usually written in JSP or another templating language that generates the HTML. In Struts, request and session objects are used for transferring data between different parts of the application.

On the other hand, this kind of low-level manipulation of HTTP and JSP facilities would be a mistake with JSF. JSF works more like Swing, where you can drag and drop component sets onto the canvas, define necessary model objects, relate those objects to your form components, assign event handlers to component actions, and so on.

If you try processing the request objects yourself, you are forcing yourself to experience the dreaded JSP-JSF life cycle mismatch. The coexistence of JSP and JSF allows you, the developer, to easily fall into such traps. For JSF 2.0, the JSP syntax is likely to be dropped altogether and superceded by one single Unified Expression Language and Tag Library (taglib)—no more life cycle mismatches or overhead.

Until then, there is a way to use JSF without a dependency on the JSP taglib. That option is Facelets, which allows you to use just JSF and XHTML tags in your view, removing the dependency on JSP. We will discuss Facelets in more detail in Chapter 3.

Another common pitfall from the Struts world is to redirect the view. In Struts, you can return the name of the view from your action, while in JSF your navigation graph is a state machine where each action method in the managed bean returns an object (`String` in version 1.x of JSF), which is used as input to this state machine, and the state machine can decide what to do with this input. This method makes modeling state diagrams in UML a much more intuitive process allowing for simpler committee reviews and validation.

The following list of recommendations summarizes the best practices and approaches for JSF developers transitioning from an action-oriented background:

- Design your application with components in mind; use JSF component objects for the view and managed beans for the model objects.
- The JSF framework does all controller work. Use navigation rules mechanism to define your navigation graph, but keep in mind that they don't return the view name directly, they just return one object that will be used by navigation mechanism.
- Try writing your JSF pages using only JSF tags or leverage Facelets to blend XHTML into the mix.
- Don't embed Java code in your JSF pages.
- Don't put your objects in Request and Session; use managed beans with different scopes instead.
- Use methods in managed beans as action handlers.
- Use managed beans as the model of your application (you can delegate business logic to lower layers, like EJB, web services, etc.).
- Use the JSF configuration for dependency injection between managed beans instead of passing objects in Session and Request.

JSF Shortcomings

Like any framework, JSF has some shortcomings; a few of these follow:

- JSF has no templating support before JSF 1.2. You can overcome this shortcoming by using Facelets (see Chapter 3 for instructions).
- Creating custom components is difficult, as every component should contain tag handler, renderer, and component classes. You can overcome this shortcoming by using Facelets, which enables the user to easily create custom components (which will be illustrated in Chapter 3).
- JSF lacks a conversion scope that can be synchronized with the database session. You can overcome this shortcoming by using Orchestra (will be illustrated in Chapter 5).
- JSF lacks advanced components such as tabbed panes, menus, and trees. You can overcome this shortcoming by using either Tomahawk or Trinidad or Tobago (will be illustrated in Chapters 2, 4, and 6).
- Mixing HTML with JSF tags may lead to unexpected rendering results. You can overcome this shortcoming by usingshortcomings Facelets (will be illustrated in Chapter 3).

Apache MyFaces

In 1999, Sun Microsystems released the first reference implementation (RI) for the JSF standard. In Austria, two developers, Manfred Geiler and Thomas Spiegl, rapidly grasped the practicality of JSF's component-oriented approach and decided to create an open source implementation called MyFaces (`http://myfaces.apache.org`). Geiler and Spiegl got to work on MyFaces, and before long, many like-minded developers joined the initiative to create the world's first free, open source JSF implementation.

Its rapidly growing stature gained it membership to the Apache Software Foundation in 2001, where it has become a top-level project. With over 250,000 downloads and over 10,000 visits a month to the web site, MyFaces is a proven JSF implementation with a wide variety of solutions utilizing it due to its open nature.

Over the last few years, the key advantage of MyFaces over other implementations has been the active community and its ability to circumvent any shortcomings of the standard JSF implementation by elegantly extending the RI. To this day, Apache MyFaces's core implementation passes all of Sun's JSF TCK test suites and remains 100 percent compliant.

In addition to compatibility with the Sun RI, Apache MyFaces offers a host of extension components through a library called Tomahawk. This library is immensely popular among JSF developers due to its large portfolio of ready-to-use components that aid rapid development. The standards-based nature of Apache MyFaces means that most Tomahawk components will run directly with the JSF RI itself, circumventing the MyFaces core altogether.

MyFaces also offers the developer a substantial array of integration options. Applications can be developed in conjunction with popular frameworks such as Spring, Hibernate, Tiles, Facelets, and Dojo using various integration libraries that are widely available today.

MyFaces is compatible with the Java Development Kit (JDK) versions 1.4.x and 1.5.x and with the following servlet containers:

- Tomcat 4.x, 5.x, and 6.x
- JRun 4
- JBoss 3.2.x and 4.x
- BEA WebLogic 8.1
- Jonas 3.3.6
- Resin 2.1.x
- Jetty 4.2.x
- WebSphere 6.x
- WebSphere Community Edition
- Geronimo
- Oracle Containers for Java EE (OC4J)

MyFaces Installation

Here you are, a Java developer looking to delve into the JSF world and build a real-world application—so how do you get MyFaces set up on your machine? Beyond some minor considerations, installation of MyFaces is straightforward and causes very little stress.

First of all, download the latest MyFaces core release (1.2.3) and the latest Tomahawk release (1.1.6) from `http://myfaces.apache.org/download.html`. Extract the binaries and copy all the (*.jar) files to your WEB-INF/lib directory. If you like to run lean and mean, you'll need to understand the purpose of each JAR.

Table 1-1 shows some important MyFaces JARs and the functionality they enable.

Table 1-1. *Important MyFaces JARs*

JAR Name	Function
commons-beanutils.jar	Provides services for collections of beans
commons-codec.jar	Provides implementations of common encoders and decoders such as Base 64, Hexadecimal, Phonetic, and URL
commons-collections.jar	The recognized standard for collection handling in Java
commons-digester.jar	Provides rules-based processing of arbitrary XML documents
commons-logging.jar	Providing a wrap-around for common Logging APIs
myfaces-api.jar and myfaces-impl.jar	The core MyFaces library
tomahawk.jar	The MyFaces extended component library
commons-discovery.jar	Used for locating classes that implement a given Java interface
commons-el.jar	Interpreter for the Expression Language defined by the JSP 2.0 specification
jstl.jar	JSP Standard Template Library (JSTL)

After downloading the necessary packages and setting up your project hierarchy, make sure that the files jsf-api.jar and jsf-impl.jar (i.e., Sun's RI implementation) are not in the classpath or in one of your container's shared library directories (e.g., common/lib or shared/lib for Tomcat).

Configuring MyFaces

To set up MyFaces, you need to configure your web application's web.xml file. See Listing 1-3.

Listing 1-3. *The MyFaces Application web.xml File*

```
<?xml version="1.0"?>
<web-app version="2.4" xmlns="http://java.sun.com/xml/ns/j2ee"
                       xmlns:xsi="http://www.w3.org/2001/XMLSchema-instance"
                       xsi:schemaLocation="http://java.sun.com/xml/ns/j2ee
                       http://java.sun.com/xml/ns/j2ee/web-app_2_4.xsd">
  <display-name>BasicExamples</display-name>
  <context-param>
    <param-name>javax.faces.STATE_SAVING_METHOD</param-name>
    <param-value>server</param-value>
  </context-param>
```

```
  <listener>
    <listener-class>
      org.apache.myfaces.webapp.StartupServletContextListener
    </listener-class>
  </listener>
  <!-- Faces Servlet -->
  <servlet>
    <servlet-name>Faces Servlet</servlet-name>
    <servlet-class>javax.faces.webapp.FacesServlet</servlet-class>
    <load-on-startup>1</load-on-startup>
  </servlet>
  <!-- Faces Servlet Mapping -->
  <servlet-mapping>
    <servlet-name>Faces Servlet</servlet-name>
    <url-pattern>*.jsf</url-pattern>
  </servlet-mapping>
</web-app>
```

This sets up the FacesServlet controller that will process the requests and implement the JSF life cycle. One thing to note is that the `*.jsf` extension maps to the `*.jsp` extension, unless you define the `javax.faces.DEFAULT_SUFFIX` context parameter. This means that your JSP pages containing MyFaces components should be accessed with the `*.jsf` extension.

To use MyFaces in your JSP pages, add the following lines, which include the MyFaces tags:

```
<%@ taglib uri="http://java.sun.com/jsf/html" prefix="h"%>
<%@ taglib uri="http://java.sun.com/jsf/core" prefix="f"%>
```

Caution The configuration steps in this section are for the Tomcat servlet container only. In our experience, various application servers have their own quirky class loader behaviors and conflicts. Application servers such as IBM's WebSphere 6.0 require specific JAR mixes and classloader settings to run Apache MyFaces. For more information about configuration requirements for particular application servers, visit `http://myfaces.apache.org/impl/dependencies.html`.

Writing Your First MyFaces Application

Before writing our first JSF application, let's go over the ingredients of any MyFaces application:

- *JSP files*: Each JSP file contains two basic tag declarations: one for defining the MyFaces HTML components and the other for defining the MyFaces core components.
- *Java beans*: A single Java bean usually represents the page data.
- *Configuration file*: The configuration file for the application lists the managed beans (the Java beans used by the MyFaces application) and the navigation rules. By default, this file is called `faces-config.xml`.

Let's write our first MyFaces application (and by implication our first JSF application). The application simply allows its users to enter their information in one page and to view their entered information in another page; see Figure 1-4.

Figure 1-4. *The information entry screen*

The file that describes the information entry page is essentially an HTML file with the two basic tag declarations; see Listing 1-4.

Listing 1-4. *Information Entry Page (pages/enterInformation.jsp)*

```
<html>
  <%@ taglib uri="http://java.sun.com/jsf/html" prefix="h" %>
  <%@ taglib uri="http://java.sun.com/jsf/core" prefix="f" %>
  <f:loadBundle basename="org.apache.myfaces.book.bundle.Messages" var="message"/>
  <head> <title>Your first JSF Application</title> </head>
  <body bgcolor="white">
    <f:view>
      <h1><h:outputText value="#{message.inputname_header}"/></h1>
      <h:form id="enterInformationForm">

        <h:panelGrid columns="3">
          <h:outputText value="#{message.name_prompt}"/>
          <h:inputText id="userName" value="#{person.name}" required="true">
            <f:validateLength minimum="2" maximum="30"/>
          </h:inputText>
          <h:message style="color: red" for="userName" />

          <h:outputText value="#{message.sex_prompt}"/>
          <h:selectOneMenu id="userSex" value="#{person.sex}">
            <f:selectItem itemLabel="male" itemValue="male"/>
            <f:selectItem itemLabel="female" itemValue="female"/>
          </h:selectOneMenu>
          <h:message style="color: red" for="userSex" />
```

```
            <h:outputText value="#{message.address_prompt}"/>
            <h:inputTextarea id="userAddress" value="#{person.address}"
                             required="true"></h:inputTextarea>
            <h:message style="color: red" for="userAddress" />
          </h:panelGrid>

          <h:commandButton id="submit" action="#{person.viewDetails}"
                           value="View my information" />
        </h:form>
      </f:view>
    </body>
</html>
```

Listing 1-4 is a simple JSF page containing the following:

- The page contains standard HTML tags like `<body>`, `<title>`, and `<head>`.
- Two tag libraries' declarations are included. The first represents the HTML tags that generate HTML markup:

  ```
  <%@ taglib uri="http://java.sun.com/jsf/html" prefix="h" %>
  ```

  The second represents the JSF core tags that are independent of any rendering technology, including validators, converters, bundle loader, and so on:

  ```
  <%@ taglib uri="http://java.sun.com/jsf/core" prefix="f" %>
  ```

- JSF tags like `<h:inputText>`, `<h:inputTextarea>`, and `<h:commandButton>`, which correspond to the text field, text area, and submit button, are included.
- The input fields included in this page are linked to Java object properties and methods. For example, the attribute `value="#{person.name}"` tells the JSF to link the text field with the `name` property of the `person` object, which we can define in the JSF configuration file, shown in Listing 1-5. And the attribute `action="#{person.viewDetails}"` tells JSF to link the `commandButton` action with the `viewDetails()` method of the `person` object.
- There are also required field validators. We simply made the input components' values required by just adding the `required="true"` attribute to our JSF input components.
- We used the `<f:loadBundle>` tag, which is used for loading resource bundles inside JSF pages, and linked the bundle's keys with the JSF components in the same way we linked the input fields to Java object properties and methods using `#{...}`.

Tip If you look, you will find all the JSF tags are contained inside an `<f:view>` tag, and instead of using the HTML `<form>` tag, we contained all the JSF components inside the `<h:form>` tag. Instead of using the HTML `<input>` tag, we use `<h:inputText>`, `<h:inputTextarea>`, and `<h:commandButton>`.

Let's see the bean that manages personal data (name, sex, and address). See Listing 1-5.

Listing 1-5. *The Person Bean (PersonBean.java)*

```
public class PersonBean {
  String name;
  String sex;
  String address;

  public String getName() {
    return name;
  }

  public void setName(String name) {
    this.name = name;
  }

  public String getAddress() {
    return address;
  }

  public void setAddress(String address) {
    this.address = address;
  }

  public String getSex() {
    return sex;
  }

  public void setSex(String email) {
    this.sex = email;
  }

  public String viewDetails() {
    return "success";
  }
}
```

Listing 1-5 is a basic `person` bean that contains the properties' getters and setters. The `person` bean also contains a `viewDetails()` action method that returns a string that will be used to determine the next page to go to. In this case, we simply return `"success"`.

■ **Tip** If you want the action method to go to the current page, you should make the action method return `null`.

Let's look at the faces-config.xml file in Listing 1-6.

Listing 1-6. *faces-config.xml*

```
<faces-config>
  <managed-bean>
    <description>Person Bean</description>
    <managed-bean-name>person</managed-bean-name>
    <managed-bean-class>PersonBean</managed-bean-class>
    <managed-bean-scope>session</managed-bean-scope>
  </managed-bean>

  <navigation-rule>
    <from-view-id>/pages/enterInformation.jsp</from-view-id>
    <navigation-case>
      <from-outcome>success</from-outcome>
      <to-view-id>/pages/welcome.jsp</to-view-id>
      <redirect/>
    </navigation-case>
  </navigation-rule>
  <navigation-rule>
    <from-view-id>/pages/welcome.jsp</from-view-id>
    <navigation-case>
      <from-outcome>back</from-outcome>
      <to-view-id>/pages/enterInformation.jsp</to-view-id>
      <redirect/>
    </navigation-case>
  </navigation-rule>
</faces-config>
```

Listing 1-6 is a simple JSF application's configuration file; it contains the basic JSF configuration elements:

- *The managed beans' declarations*: The managed bean root element <managed-bean> contains the following subelements:
  - <description>: An optional element that contains the managed bean description
  - <managed-bean-name>: A mandatory element that contains the managed bean name that will be used inside the JSP pages
  - <managed-bean-class>: A mandatory element that contains the managed bean fully qualified class name
  - <managed-bean-scope>: A mandatory element that determines the lifetime of the managed bean using one of the following four values: application, session, request, and none

- *The navigation rules*: The single navigation rule root element `<navigation-rule>` contains the following subelements:
    - `<from-view-id>`: An element that contains the starting page from which the navigation will start
    - `<navigation-case>`: A container element that defines the navigation case.

Also, note that the `<navigation-case>` container includes the following subelements:

- `<from-outcome>`: If this element's value matches an action (could be a `commandButton` or a `commandLink` or any `actionSource` action) outcome then the navigation case will be executed.
- `<to-view-id>`: An element that contains the next page to go to.
- `<redirect>`: An element that tells JSF to perform page redirection instead of page forwarding. If this element is not used then page forwarding will be used by default.

Now that you are aware of the basic ingredients of any JSF application, let's look at the other application page, which displays the user information; see Figure 1-5.

You entered the following information :

Your name :	Hazem Saleh
Your sex :	male
Your address :	24 xyz street Giza Egypt

Back

Figure 1-5. *The information viewing screen*

The file that describes the information viewing screen is not different from the `enterInformation.jsp` page in terms of the page structure. See Listing 1-7.

Listing 1-7. *Information Viewing Page (pages/welcome.jsp)*

```
<%@ taglib uri="http://java.sun.com/jsf/html" prefix="h" %>
<%@ taglib uri="http://java.sun.com/jsf/core" prefix="f" %>
<f:loadBundle basename="org.apache.myfaces.book.bundle.Messages" var="message"/>
<html>
  <head>
    <title>Your first JSF Application</title>
  </head>
  <body>
    <f:view>
      <h1><h:outputText value="#{message.result_text}"/></h1>
      <h:form id="informationViewForm">
```

```
        <h:panelGrid columns="2" border="1">
          <h:outputText value="#{message.name_prompt}"/>
          <h:outputText value="#{person.name}" />

          <h:outputText value="#{message.sex_prompt}"/>
          <h:outputText value="#{person.sex}" />

          <h:outputText value="#{message.address_prompt}"/>
          <h:outputText value="#{person.address}" />
        </h:panelGrid>

        <h:commandLink value="Back" action="back"></h:commandLink>

      </h:form>
    </f:view>
  </body>
</html>
```

To view the application, go to `http://localhost:8080/<webappname>/pages/enterInformation.jsf`. We've also supplied this example with this book's source code files. To run it, you should do the following:

1. Make sure that you have installed Tomcat 5.x or later. For the sake of simplicity, we will use Tomcat as the servlet container (both the Sun RI and Apache MyFaces work well on Tomcat, the leading open source servlet container). You can download it at `http://tomcat.apache.org`.
2. Place the `BasicExamples.war` file under the `TOMCAT_INSTALLATION_DIRECTORY/webapps` folder.
3. Start your Tomcat web container by executing the following commands (you can find the startup files in the `TOMCAT_INSTALLATION_DIRECTORY/bin` folder):
   a. `startup.bat` for Windows
   b. `startup.sh` for Unix
4. Type the following URL in your browser: `http://localhost:8080/BasicExamples/index.jsp`.
5. Enjoy the application.

Summary

In this chapter, we focused on preparing you for the rest of the book by examining the forces behind the creation of JSF and the design philosophies that govern it. In addition to JSF's unique features, we also introduced the MyFaces and some of the drivers behind its own formation and why it remains the most innovative platform for JSF development today. We also focused on the practical part of MyFaces by creating and deploying a simple MyFaces application.

CHAPTER 2

The Tomahawk Project

MyFaces Tomahawk is a tag library providing a series of JSF components that go well beyond the JSF specification and other goodies. These components are compatible with the Sun JSF 1.1 and 1.2 Reference Implementation (RI) or any other compatible JSF 1.1 or 1.2 implementations. The Tomahawk family of components also includes converters, validators, and a set of attributes added to the standard JSF components.

There's also a MyFaces Tomahawk sandbox subproject, which includes experimental components and goodies that may or may not be included in future Tomahawk releases. You can use these components in your projects, but there is no guarantee that the component code will be stable. In this chapter, we show some of the popular Tomahawk components that are embraced by the community today and exhibit the extensibility of JSF and how a dynamic community around it can make the difference.

Tomahawk Setup

Use the following steps to set up the Tomahawk tag library:

1. Download the MyFaces Tomahawk binary distribution (`tomahawk-x.x.x-bin.zip`) from `http://myfaces.apache.org/download.html`.

2. Unzip the downloaded file.

3. Copy `lib/tomahawk-x.x.x.jar` from the unzipped file to the `WEB-INF/lib` folder of the web application that will be using the library.

4. Install the MyFaces Extensions Filter by declaring it in the `web.xml` file of the web application. See Listing 2-1.

5. Add the tag library declarations to the JSP page where the Tomahawk components will be used:

   ```
   <%@ taglib uri="http://myfaces.apache.org/tomahawk" prefix="t"%>
   ```

   If you wish to use sandbox components, you need to add the following declaration as well:

   ```
   <%@ taglib uri="http://myfaces.apache.org/sandbox" prefix="s"%>
   ```

■ **Note** There is no release of the Tomahawk sandbox project. Therefore, if you want to use it in your project, you need to build it from the source code or download a nightly build from `http://people.apache.org/builds/myfaces/nightly/`.

You can build both the Tomahawk and the sandbox libraries from source code using Maven2. To download the source code, check the steps at `http://myfaces.apache.org/tomahawk/source-repository.html` (for Tomahawk) and at `http://myfaces.apache.org/sandbox/source-repository.html` (for the sandbox).

Listing 2-1. *The MyFaces Extensions Filter in web.xml*

```
<web-app>

<filter>
  <filter-name>extensionsFilter</filter-name>
  <filter-class>org.apache.myfaces.webapp.filter.ExtensionsFilter</filter-class>
</filter>

<!-- extension mapping for adding <script/>, <link/>, and other resource tags
     to JSF-pages
-->
<filter-mapping>
  <filter-name>extensionsFilter</filter-name>
  <url-pattern>*.jsf</url-pattern>
</filter-mapping>

<!-- extension mapping for serving page-independent resources
     (javascript, stylesheets, images, etc.)
-->
<filter-mapping>
  <filter-name>extensionsFilter</filter-name>
  <url-pattern>/faces/myFacesExtensionResource/*</url-pattern>
</filter-mapping>

</web-app>
```

Tomahawk Features

The MyFaces Tomahawk tag library offers an extended version of the standard JSF components (`inputText`, `outputText`, `commandLink`, and so on) and a set of components for rapidly creating advanced user interfaces (`calendar`, `dataScroller`, `jscookMenu`, `newspaperTable`, `tabbedPane`, `validateRegExpr`, `dataList`, `tree2`, and so on).

The extension of the standard JSF components by the Tomahawk tag library keeps the features as they are while supporting the following additional attributes, each of which is described in its own section:

- `forceId`
- `displayValueOnly`

The forceId Attribute

The `forceId` attribute forces the JSF framework to generate an ID equal to the one specified in the attribute. Let's illustrate this with an example.

```
<h:form id="myForm">
  <t:commandLink  id="myButton" value="Home" action="home"/>
</h:form>
```

This would be rendered as follows:

```
<a id="myForm:myButton">Home</a>
```

whereas the following code:

```
<h:form id="myForm">
  <t:commandLink forceId="true" id="myButton" value="Home" action="home"/>
</h:form>
```

would be rendered as

```
<a id="myButton">Home</a>
```

This feature can be useful if you want to use (or reuse preexisting) JavaScript libraries or CSS styles for the component.

The displayValueOnly Attribute

The `displayValueOnly` attribute switches the Tomahawk component from input to output and vice versa. The following example illustrates this:

```
<h:form id="myForm" />
  <t:inputHtml id="myText" value="Hello World" />
</h:form>
```

The example would be rendered as shown in Figure 2-1.

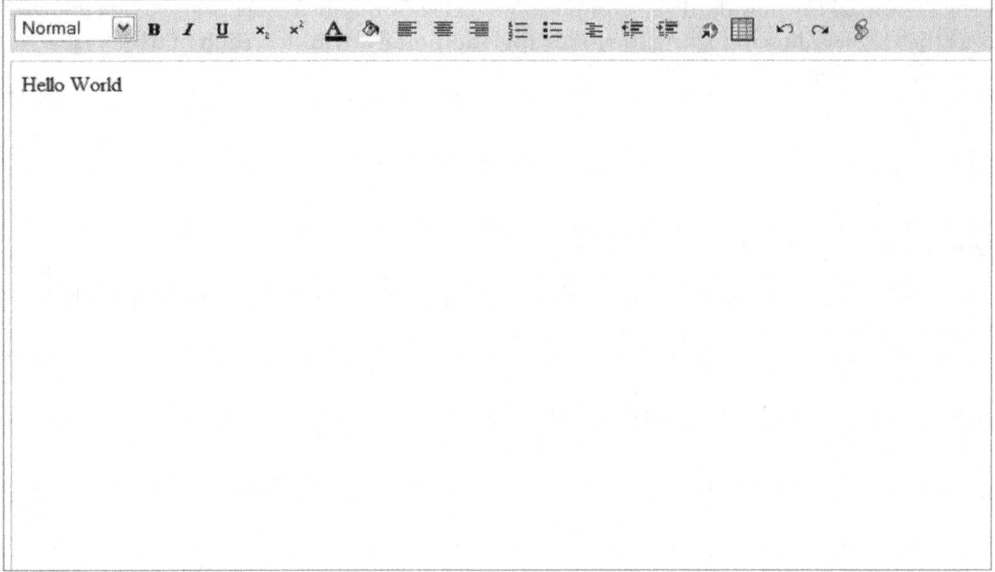

Figure 2-1. *The inputHTML tag output*

Now look at the following snippet:

```
<h:form id="myForm" />
  <t:inputHtml id="myText" value="Hello World" displayValueOnly="true" />
</h:form>
```

It would be rendered as shown in Figure 2-2.

Hello World

Figure 2-2. *The inputHTML tag output with displayValueOnly set to true*

Tomahawk's Major Components

Table 2-1 shows the major components of Tomahawk.

Table 2-1. *Major Components of Tomahawk*

Component Name	Component Usage
Calendar	Allows the user to choose a date from a month view.
DataScroller	Provides pagination and data scrolling for DataTable components.
DataList	Data-bound component displaying data entries in a list rather than a table.
NewspaperTable	Data-bound component displaying data entries in columns to optimize the screen display.
JsCookMenu	Generates and displays a JavaScript-based menu similar to the menu bar of a desktop application, useful for implementing sitewide navigation.

Component Name	Component Usage
TabbedPane	Organizes components by tabs.
ValidateRegExpr	General purpose validator that uses a regular expression to validate the input. The regular expression validator can represent an e-mail address, zip code, URL, or any other kind of user input that you might need inside the web site pages.
Schedule	Generates a daily, weekly, or monthly schedule containing events and appointments similar to desktop applications such as Microsoft Outlook and iCal.
Tree2	Provides an HTML-based tree that can expand and collapse on the client or server side.
SubForm	Although this powerful component is still in the sandbox (until Tomahawk 1.1.6), it allows the execution of model validation and update for only a part of the form page, for those components that are inside the `subForm` tag. You can also execute model validation and update for several subforms in the page using the `actionFor` attribute of the Tomahawk `commandButton` or `commandLink` components.

Component Examples

All examples in this chapter can be found in the `chapter2` directory available for download in the Source Code/Download page of the Apress web site. Table 2-2 shows the layout of this application.

Table 2-2. *File Structure of the Sample Components*

Folder Name	Contains
`css`	Cascading style sheets (CSS) used in the examples
`images`	Images used in the examples
`template`	Templates used to decorate the header and footer of the examples
`components`	Individual component examples
`WEB-INF/classes`	Managed beans of the component examples

For every component example, there is a managed bean class (model) and the JSP page (view). Let's start by looking at the Calendar component.

The Calendar Component

The Tomahawk Calendar component can be an inline or pop-up calendar. You'll see an example of both here.

Creating an Inline Calendar

To implement an inline calendar, first, we need a managed bean, as shown in Listing 2-2.

Listing 2-2. *The Calendar Managed Bean Class (CalendarBean.java)*

```
import java.io.Serializable;
import java.util.Date;

public class CalendarBean implements Serializable {
  private Date date;

  public Date getDate() {
    return date;
  }

  public void setDate(Date date) {
    this.date = date;
  }

  public String submit() {
    return null;
  }
}
```

Second we need to configure our managed bean in the JSF configuration file:

```
  <managed-bean>
    <managed-bean-name>calendar</managed-bean-name>
    <managed-bean-class>org.apache.myfaces.book.beans.CalendarBean</managed-bean-➥
class>
    <managed-bean-scope>request</managed-bean-scope>
  </managed-bean>
```

Finally in the JSP page, we should use the `<t:inputCalendar>` tag with the following attributes :

- `value` for binding the date attribute of the managed bean with the inline calendar component input
- `monthYearRowClass`, `weekRowClass`, and `currentDayCellClass` for styling the inline calendar

Listing 2-3 shows the inline Calendar example JSP page.

Listing 2-3. *The Inline Calendar Page (inLineCalendar.jsp)*

```
<%@ taglib uri="http://java.sun.com/jsf/core" prefix="f"%>
<%@ taglib uri="http://java.sun.com/jsf/html" prefix="h"%>
<%@ taglib uri="http://myfaces.apache.org/tomahawk" prefix="t"%>

<f:view>
  <h:form>
    <h:outputText value="Select your birth date : " />
```

```
    <t:outputText id="birthDate" value="#{calendar.date}" />

    <br />

    <t:inputCalendar monthYearRowClass="yearMonthHeader"
                     weekRowClass="weekHeader" currentDayCellClass="currentDayCell"
                     value="#{calendar.date}" />
  </h:form>
</f:view>
```

Figure 2-3 shows the output of the example.

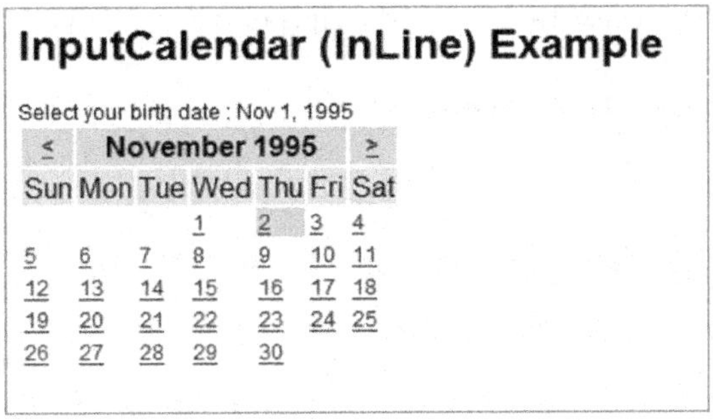

Figure 2-3. *The inline calendar*

Creating a Pop-Up Calendar

To implement a pop-up calendar, we should use additional attributes of the `<t:inputCalendar>` tag, which are:

- `renderAsPopup`: Renders the calendar as a JavaScript pop-up on the client
- `popupDateFormat`: Defines the date format used by the JavaScript pop-up
- `renderPopupButtonAsImage`: Defines if the button to open the pop-up calendar should be rendered as an image or as an HTML button

---

Tip Looking at the calendar examples, you will find the selected date days decreased by one. This behavior is not actually a bug, as the default JSF DateTime converter always uses UTC as described in the JSF specification. If you are not working with the UTC time zone, we suggest you write your own DateTime converter or use the `<s:convertDateTime>` converter from the sandbox.

Listing 2-4 shows the Pop-Up Calendar example JSP page.

Listing 2-4. *The Pop-Up Calendar Page (inputCalendar.jsp)*

```
<%@ taglib uri="http://java.sun.com/jsf/core" prefix="f"%>
<%@ taglib uri="http://java.sun.com/jsf/html" prefix="h"%>
<%@ taglib uri="http://myfaces.apache.org/tomahawk" prefix="t"%>
<html>
  <body>
    <f:view>
      <t:saveState value="#{calendar}" />
      <h:form id="myForm">

        <t:outputLabel for="calendar" value="Select your birth date : " />
        <t:inputCalendar id="calendar" monthYearRowClass="yearMonthHeader"
                         weekRowClass="weekHeader"
                         currentDayCellClass="currentDayCell"
                         value="#{calendar.date}"
                         renderAsPopup="true"
                         popupDateFormat="MM/dd/yyyy"
                         renderPopupButtonAsImage="true">
        </t:inputCalendar>
        <br />

        <h:commandButton value="Submit" action="#{calendar.submit}" />
        <br />

        <h:outputText id="birthDate" value="#{calendar.date}" />
      </h:form>
    </f:view>
  </body>
</html>
```

The example also uses the `<t:saveState>` tag. This tag keeps beans alive between requests. To use this tag, the JSF managed beans must implement the `java.io.Serializable` interface so that they can be saved in the JSF component tree. Figure 2-4 shows the output of the example.

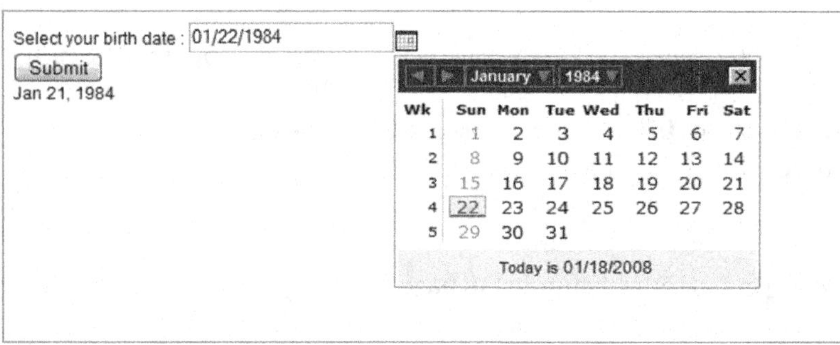

Figure 2-4. *The pop-up calendar*

The Main Attributes of the Calendar Component

Table 2-3 shows the most important attributes of the Calendar component.

Table 2-3. *Main Attributes of the Calendar Component*

Component Attribute Name	Component Attribute Explanation
`monthYearRowClass`	The CSS class to be used for the header row showing the month and year.
`weekRowClass`	The CSS class to be used for the header row showing the weekdays.
`dayCellClass`	The CSS class to be used for the cells showing days.
`currentDayCellClass`	The CSS class to be used for the cell of the currently selected date.
`renderAsPopup`	Renders the calendar as a JavaScript pop-up on the client if set to `true`.
`addResources`	Automatically adds the calendar scripts and CSS files to the header if set to `true`. Set the attribute value to `false` to provide the scripts manually.
`popupDateFormat`	Defines the date format used by the JavaScript pop-up.
`popupButtonString`	Defines the string displayed on the button that leads to the calendar pop-up window (`"..."` by default).
`popupButtonStyle`	Defines the CSS style for the button that leads to the calendar pop-up window.
`popupButtonStyleClass`	Defines the CSS style class for the button that leads to the calendar pop-up window.
`popupGotoString`	Sets the string for `"Go To Current Month"`.
`popupTodayString`	Sets the string for `"Today is"`.
`popupWeekString`	Sets the string for `"Wk"`.
`popupScrollLeftMessage`	Sets the string for scrolling to the left.
`popupScrollRightMessage`	Sets the string for scrolling to the right.
`popupSelectMonthMessage`	Sets the string for `"Click to select a month"`.
`popupSelectYearMessage`	Sets the string for `"Click to select a year"`.
`popupSelectDateMessage`	Sets the string for `"Select [date] as date"` (do not replace `[date]`, it will be replaced by the current date).
`renderPopupButtonAsImage`	Renders a calendar icon instead of the button to make the calendar pop up if set to `true`. The default is `false`.

The DataScroller Component

The DataScroller component provides pagination and data scrolling for the DataTable components.

Using the DataScroller Component

In this example, we'll show a data scroller that displays details of courses; see Figure 2-5.

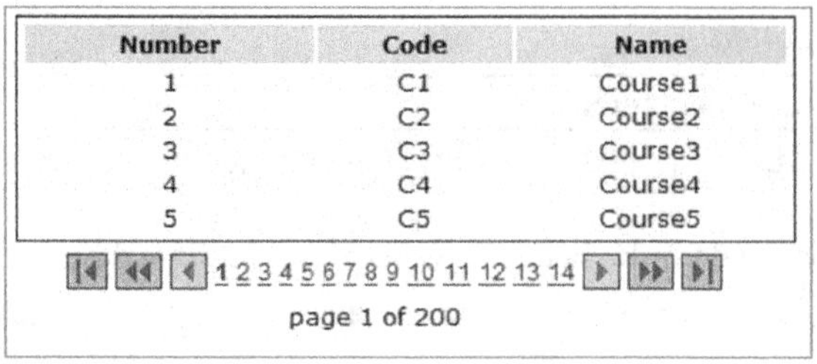

Number	Code	Name
1	C1	Course1
2	C2	Course2
3	C3	Course3
4	C4	Course4
5	C5	Course5

1 2 3 4 5 6 7 8 9 10 11 12 13 14

page 1 of 200

Figure 2-5. *The DataScroller component*

For this example, we need two managed beans. The first is `DataScrollerBean`, shown in Listing 2-5, and the second is `Course`, a simple bean that we won't show but is easy enough to implement. Remember to configure these beans in the JSF configuration file.

Listing 2-5. *The DataScroller Managed Bean Class (DataScrollerBean.java)*

```
import java.util.List;
import java.util.ArrayList;

public class DataScrollerBean {
  private List list = new ArrayList();

  public DataScrollerBean() {
    for (int i = 1; i < 1000; i++) {
      list.add(new Course("Course" + i, "C" + i, i + ""));
    }
  }

  public List getData() {
    return list;
  }
}
```

To implement a dataScroller, the following attributes should be used with the `<t:dataScroller>` tag:

- `for` links the DataScroller with the DataTable.
- `fastStep` indicates the value of the fast step. The effect of the `fastStep` attribute appears when clicking the `fastrewind` and `fastforward` facets.
- `paginator` indicates whether to display page numbers.
- `paginatorMaxPages` indicates the maximum number of paginator pages.

- `pageIndexVar` is a parameter name under which the actual page index is set into the request scope.
- `pageCountVar` is a parameter name under which the actual page count is set into the request scope.
- DataScroller's style attributes like `styleClass`, `paginatorTableClass`, and `paginatorActiveColumnStyle`.

For showing pagination, we need to add child facets to the `<t:dataScroller>`. The child facets' IDs should be:

- `first` represents a link to the first page.
- `last` represents a link to the last page.
- `previous` represents a link to the previous page.
- `next` represents a link to the next page.
- `fastforward` represents a link to the fast forward page whose index is the current page index plus `fastStep`.
- `fastrewind` represents a link to the fast rewind page whose index is the current page index minus `fastStep`.

Listing 2-6 shows the DataScroller example JSP page.

Listing 2-6. *The DataScroller Page (dataScroller.jsp)*

```
<%@ taglib uri="http://java.sun.com/jsf/core" prefix="f"%>
<%@ taglib uri="http://java.sun.com/jsf/html" prefix="h"%>
<%@ taglib uri="http://myfaces.apache.org/tomahawk" prefix="t"%>
<html>
  <body>
    <f:view>
      <h:form>
        <t:dataTable id="dataTable" styleClass="scrollerTable"
                     headerClass="standardTable_Header"
                     footerClass="standardTable_Header"
                     rowClasses="standardTable_Row1,standardTable_Row2"
                     columnClasses="standardTable_ColumnCentered"
                     var="course" value="#{dataScroller.data}" rows="5">
          <h:column>
            <f:facet name="header">
              <h:outputText value="Number" />
            </f:facet>
            <h:outputText value="#{course.number}" />
          </h:column>
```

```
  <h:column>
    <f:facet name="header">
      <h:outputText value="Code" />
    </f:facet>
    <h:outputText value="#{course.code}" />
  </h:column>

  <h:column>
    <f:facet name="header">
      <h:outputText value="Name" />
    </f:facet>
    <h:outputText value="#{course.name}" />
  </h:column>
</t:dataTable>

<h:panelGrid columns="1" styleClass="scrollerTable2"
             columnClasses="standardTable_ColumnCentered">

  <t:dataScroller id="pagination" for="dataTable" fastStep="20"
                  pageCountVar="pageCount" pageIndexVar="pageIndex"
                  styleClass="scroller" paginator="true"
                  paginatorMaxPages="14"
                  paginatorTableClass="paginator"
                  paginatorActiveColumnStyle="font-weight:bold;">

    <f:facet name="first">
      <t:graphicImage url="images/arrow-first.gif" border="1" />
    </f:facet>

    <f:facet name="last">
      <t:graphicImage url="images/arrow-last.gif" border="1" />
    </f:facet>

    <f:facet name="previous">
      <t:graphicImage url="images/arrow-previous.gif" border="1" />
    </f:facet>

    <f:facet name="next">
      <t:graphicImage url="images/arrow-next.gif" border="1" />
    </f:facet>

    <f:facet name="fastforward">
      <t:graphicImage url="images/arrow-ff.gif" border="1" />
    </f:facet>

    <f:facet name="fastrewind">
      <t:graphicImage url="images/arrow-fr.gif" border="1" />
    </f:facet>
```

```
        </t:dataScroller>

        <t:dataScroller id="paginationSummary" for="dataTable"
                        pageCountVar="pageCount" pageIndexVar="pageIndex">

          <h:outputFormat value="page #{pageIndex} of #{pageCount}"
                          styleClass="standard" />

        </t:dataScroller>
      </h:panelGrid>
    </h:form>
  </f:view>
</body>
</html>
```

The example uses two scrollers: pagination and paginationSummary. pagination is used for showing the pagination, while paginationSummary is used for showing the current page index of the total pages.

In paginationSummary, the pageCountVar and pageIndexVar attributes are used to display the current page index and total pages.

The Main Attributes of the DataScroller Component

Table 2-4 shows the most important attributes of the DataScroller component.

Table 2-4. *Main Attributes of the DataScroller Component*

Component Attribute Name	Component Attribute Explanation
for	A reference to a UIData component (such as <h:dataTable>)
fastStep	Indicates the value of the fast step
pageIndexVar	Provides the parameter name to access the actual page index in the request scope
pageCountVar	Provides the parameter name to access the actual page count in the request scope
rowsCountVar	Provides the parameter name to access the actual row count in the request scope
displayedRowsCountVar	Provides the parameter name to access the actual displayed row count in the request scope
firstRowIndexVar	Provides the parameter name to access the actual page first row index that is set in the request scope
lastRowIndexVar	Provides the parameter name to access the actual page last row index that is set in the request scope
paginator	Indicates whether to display page numbers
paginatorMaxPages	Indicates the maximum number of paginator pages
actionListener	An action-listener being executed when the DataScroller is clicked

The DataList Component

The Tomahawk DataList component can be rendered in different styles:

- `simple`: There is no separation between the elements that are rendered.
- `unordered`: `<ul>` and `<li>` tags are rendered as separators between the elements.
- `ordered`: `<ol>` and `<li>` tags are rendered as separators between the elements.
- `grid`: Elements will be rendered in a horizontal table.

Creating a Simple DataList

We'll start by looking at a simple data list, shown in Figure 2-6.

Simple DataList

Biology, Chemistry, English, Maths

Figure 2-6. *A simple DataList component*

For this example, we'll use a managed bean called `DataListBean`, shown in Listing 2-7, and we'll reuse the `Course` bean from the previous example.

Listing 2-7. *The DataList Managed Bean Class (DataListBean.java)*

```
import java.util.List;
import java.util.ArrayList;

public class DataListBean {
  private List list = new ArrayList();

  public DataListBean() {
    list.add(new Course("Biology", "C1", "1"));
    list.add(new Course("Chemistry", "C2", "2"));
    list.add(new Course("English", "C3", "3"));
    list.add(new Course("Maths", "C4", "4"));
  }

  public List getData() {
    return list;
  }
}
```

As shown in Listing 2-8, to implement a simple DataList, the `<t:dataList>` tag is used, setting the `layout` attribute value of the `<t:dataList>` to `simple`. In the `<t:dataList>` `value` attribute, the list of courses is passed. `count` is used as a parameter to represent the DataList row count, and index is used as a parameter that represents the DataList row index. In the DataList loop body, the names of the courses are displayed separated by commas.

Listing 2-8. *The Simple DataList Page (simpleDataList.jsp)*

```
<%@ taglib uri="http://java.sun.com/jsf/core" prefix="f"%>
<%@ taglib uri="http://java.sun.com/jsf/html" prefix="h"%>
<%@ taglib uri="http://myfaces.apache.org/tomahawk" prefix="t"%>
<html>
  <body>
    <f:view>
      <h1>Simple DataList</h1>
        <h:form>
          <t:dataList id="dataList" styleClass="standardList" var="course"
                      value="#{dataList.data}"
                      layout="simple"
                      rowCountVar="count"
                      rowIndexVar="index">
            <h:outputText value="#{course.name}" />
            <h:outputText value=", " rendered="#{index + 1 < count}" />
          </t:dataList>
        </h:form>
      </f:view>
  </body>
</html>
```

Creating an Unordered DataList

An unordered data list, shown in Figure 2-7, is just as easy to create.

UnOrdered DataList

- Biology
- Chemistry
- English
- Maths

Figure 2-7. *An unordered DataList*

As shown in Listing 2-9, to implement an unordered DataList, the <t:dataList> tag is used, setting the layout attribute value of the <t:dataList> to unorderedList. In the <t:dataList> value attribute, the list of courses is passed. In the DataList loop body, the names of the courses are displayed as an unordered list. We've used the same bean as before.

Listing 2-9. *The Unordered DataList Page (unOrderedDataList.jsp)*

```
<%@ taglib uri="http://java.sun.com/jsf/core" prefix="f"%>
<%@ taglib uri="http://java.sun.com/jsf/html" prefix="h"%>
<%@ taglib uri="http://myfaces.apache.org/tomahawk" prefix="t"%>
<html>
  <body>
    <f:view>
      <h1>Unordered DataList</h1>
      <h:form>
        <t:dataList id="dataList" styleClass="standardList" var="course"
                    value="#{dataList.data}"
                    layout="unorderedList" >
          <h:outputText value="#{course.name}" />
        </t:dataList>

      </h:form>
    </f:view>
  </body>
</html>
```

Creating an Ordered DataList

Creating an ordered DataList, shown in Figure 2-8, is a similar process.

Ordered DataList

1. Biology
2. Chemistry
3. English
4. Maths

Figure 2-8. *An ordered DataList*

As shown in Listing 2-10, to implement an ordered DataList, the `<t:dataList>` tag is used, setting the `layout` attribute value of the `<t:dataList>` to `orderedList`. In the `<t:dataList>` `value` attribute, the list of courses is passed. In the DataList loop body, the names of the courses are displayed as an ordered list.

Listing 2-10. *The Ordered DataList Page (orderedDataList.jsp)*

```
<%@ taglib uri="http://java.sun.com/jsf/core" prefix="f"%>
<%@ taglib uri="http://java.sun.com/jsf/html" prefix="h"%>
<%@ taglib uri="http://myfaces.apache.org/tomahawk" prefix="t"%>
<html>
  <body>
    <f:view>
      <h1>Ordered DataList</h1>
```

```
      <h:form>
        <t:dataList id="dataList" styleClass="standardList" var="course"
                    value="#{dataList.data}"
                    layout="orderedList">
          <h:outputText value="#{course.name}" />
        </t:dataList>
      </h:form>
    </f:view>
  </body>
</html>
```

Creating a Grid DataList

A grid DataList, shown in Figure 2-9, displays the elements in a horizontal table.

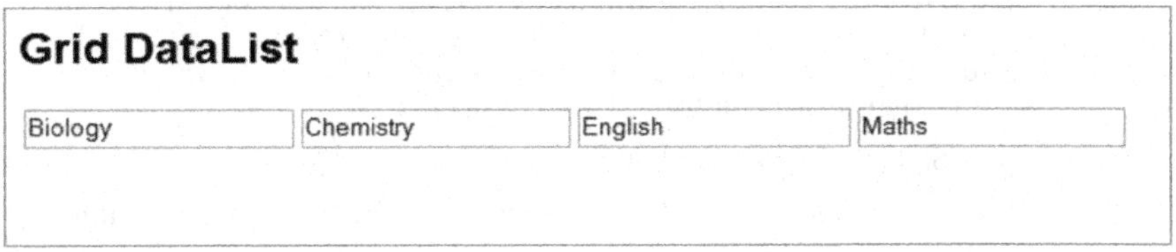

Grid DataList

Biology	Chemistry	English	Maths

Figure 2-9. *A grid DataList*

As shown in Listing 2-11, to implement a grid DataList, the `<t:dataList>` tag is used, setting the `layout` attribute value of the `<t:dataList>` to `grid`. In the `<t:dataList>` `value` attribute, the list of courses is passed. In the DataList loop body, the names of the courses are displayed as a horizontal table.

Listing 2-11. *The Grid DataList Page (gridDataList.jsp)*

```
<%@ taglib uri="http://java.sun.com/jsf/core" prefix="f"%>
<%@ taglib uri="http://java.sun.com/jsf/html" prefix="h"%>
<%@ taglib uri="http://myfaces.apache.org/tomahawk" prefix="t"%>
<html>
  <body>
    <f:view>
      <h1>Grid DataList</h1>
      <h:form>
        <t:dataList id="dataList" styleClass="standardList" var="course"
                    value="#{dataList.data}"
                    layout="grid">
          <h:inputText value="#{course.name}" />
        </t:dataList>
      </h:form>
    </f:view>
  </body>
</html>
```

The Main Attributes of the DataList Component

Table 2-5 shows the most important attributes of the DataList component.

Table 2-5. *Main Attributes of the DataList Component*

Component Attribute Name	Component Attribute Explanation
`value`	The content of the list.
`var`	The parameter name to access the current value in the request scope.
`rows`	Number of rows to display.
`first`	First element of the list to display.
`layout`	This can be `simple`, `unorderedList`, `orderedList`, or `grid`. `simple` indicates that for each dataRow all children are simply rendered, and the rowset is embedded in an HTML `<span>` tag. `unorderedList` indicates that the list is rendered as HTML unordered list (i.e., a bulleted list). `orderedList` indicates that the list is rendered as HTML ordered list. `grid` indicates that the list is rendered in a horizontal table. If the `layout` attribute is omitted, the component will use the simple layout without the HTML `<span>` tag.
`styleClass`	The CSS class used to style the list.
`itemStyleClass`	The CSS class used to style each element of the list (not applicable when `layout` is `simple`).
`rowIndexVar`	Provides the parameter name to access the current row index in the request scope.
`rowCountVar`	Provides the parameter name to access the current row count in the request scope.
`preserveDataModel`	Indicates whether the state for each row should be preserved before the data list is rendered again. The default is `false`.

The NewspaperTable Component

The NewspaperTable component is a data-bound component that can be used for displaying data entries in columns to optimize the screen display.

Using the NewspaperTable Component

Figure 2-10 shows an example NewspaperTable component that shows course details.

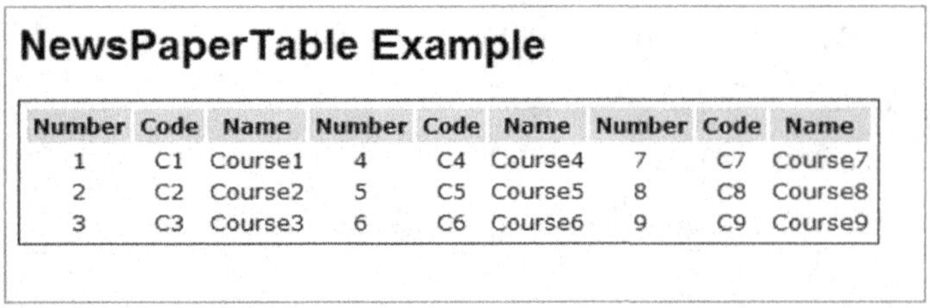

NewsPaperTable Example

Number	Code	Name	Number	Code	Name	Number	Code	Name
1	C1	Course1	4	C4	Course4	7	C7	Course7
2	C2	Course2	5	C5	Course5	8	C8	Course8
3	C3	Course3	6	C6	Course6	9	C9	Course9

Figure 2-10. *A NewspaperTable component*

The managed bean for this example is shown in Listing 2-12.

Listing 2-12. *The NewspaperTable Managed Bean Class (NewspaperTableBean.java)*

```
import java.util.List;
import java.util.ArrayList;

public class NewspaperTableBean {
  private List list = new ArrayList();

  public NewspaperTableBean() {
    for (int i = 1; i < 10; i++) {
      list.add(new Course("Course" + i, "C" + i, i + ""));
    }
  }

  public List getData() {
    return list;
  }
}
```

Implementing a NewspaperTable component is similar to implementing a DataTable component. The difference is in the `newspaperColumns` attribute, which indicates the number of columns used to lay out the content. Listing 2-13 shows the NewspaperTable example JSP page.

Listing 2-13. *The NewspaperTable Page (newspaperTable.jsp)*

```
<%@ taglib uri="http://java.sun.com/jsf/core" prefix="f"%>
<%@ taglib uri="http://java.sun.com/jsf/html" prefix="h"%>
<%@ taglib uri="http://myfaces.apache.org/tomahawk" prefix="t"%>
<html>
  <body>
    <f:view>
      <h:form>
        <t:newspaperTable id="dataTable" styleClass="standardTable"
                          headerClass="standardTable_Header"
          footerClass="standardTable_Header"
                          rowClasses="standardTable_Row1,standardTable_Row2"
                          columnClasses="standardTable_ColumnCentered"
                          var="course" value="#{newspaperTable.data}"
                          newspaperColumns="3">
          <h:column>
            <f:facet name="header">
              <h:outputText value="Number" />
            </f:facet>

            <h:outputText value="#{course.number}" />
          </h:column>
```

```
          <h:column>
            <f:facet name="header">
              <h:outputText value="Code" />
            </f:facet>

            <h:outputText value="#{course.code}" />
          </h:column>

          <h:column>
            <f:facet name="header">
              <h:outputText value="Name" />
            </f:facet>

            <h:outputText value="#{course.name}" />
          </h:column>
        </t:newspaperTable>
      </h:form>
    </f:view>
  </body>
</html>
```

The Main Attributes of the NewspaperTable Component

Table 2-6 shows the most important attributes of the NewspaperTable component.

Table 2-6. *Main Attributes of the NewspaperTable Component*

Component Attribute Name	Component Attribute Explanation
`newspaperColumns`	Indicates the number of columns to lay out the content. The default is `1`.
`newspaperOrientation`	Orientation of the columns in the newspaper table: `horizontal` or `vertical`. The default is `vertical`.

The JSCookMenu Component

The JSCookMenu component generates and displays a JavaScript-based menu similar to the menu bar of a desktop application. This component is useful for implementing sitewide navigation.

Using the JSCookMenu Component

Figure 2-11 shows the example JSCookMenu we are going to create. It will allow us to select the examples from this chapter.

Figure 2-11. *Our JSCookMenu component*

To implement a JSCookMenu component, we should use the `<t:jscookMenu>` tag indicating the theme, layout, and style sheet location of the JSCookMenu instance. To implement a JSCookMenu menu item, we should use the `<t:navigationMenuItem>` tag with the following attributes:

- `itemLabel`: The label of the menu item
- `action`: The action to be executed when the menu item is clicked
- `icon`: The menu item icon

Listing 2-14 shows the JSCookMenu example JSP page.

Listing 2-14. *The JSCookMenu Page (home.jsp)*

```
<%@ taglib uri="http://java.sun.com/jsf/core" prefix="f"%>
<%@ taglib uri="http://java.sun.com/jsf/html" prefix="h"%>
<%@ taglib uri="http://myfaces.apache.org/tomahawk" prefix="t"%>
<html>
  <body>
    <f:view>
      <h:form>
        <t:jscookMenu id="mainMenu" layout="vbr" theme="ThemeOffice"
                      styleLocation="css/jscookmenu">

          <t:navigationMenuItem id="nav_1" itemLabel="Calendar"
                                icon="images/component.gif">

            <t:navigationMenuItem id="nav_11"
                                  itemLabel="InLine Calendar Example"
                                  action="go_inLineCalendar"
                                  icon="images/myfaces.gif" />
```

```
            <t:navigationMenuItem id="nav_12"
                                  itemLabel="Input Calendar Example"
                                  action="go_inputCalendar"
                                  icon="images/myfaces.gif" />
          </t:navigationMenuItem>
        </t:jscookMenu>
      </h:form>
    </f:view>
  </body>
</html>
```

The Main Attributes of the JSCookMenu Component

Table 2-7 shows the most important attributes of the JSCookMenu component.

Table 2-7. *Main Attributes of JSCookMenu*

Component Attribute Name	Component Attribute Explanation
`layout`	Layout of the JSCookMenu component. One of the following values: `hbr`, `hbl`, `hur`, `hul`, `vbr`, `vbl`, `vur`, and `vul`. `h` means horizontal; `b` means lower; `u`, upper; `l`, left; and `r`, right).
`theme`	Theme of the component. One of the following values: `ThemeIE`, `ThemeMiniBlack`, `ThemeOffice`, and `ThemePanel`.
`styleLocation`	Location of the JSCookMenu CSS style sheet files.

The TabbedPane Component

The Tomahawk TabbedPane component organizes components in tabs. Selecting a tab shows the components on the given tab. Tab switching can be toggled from client- to server-side depending on your requirements.

Using the TabbedPane Component

Figure 2-12 shows the example tabbed pane we are going to create.

Figure 2-12. *A TabbedPane component*

Implementing a TabbedPane component is simple; it usually has the following form:

```
<t:panelTabbedPane ...>
  <t:panelTab ...>
    ...(anyComponents)...
  </t:panelTab>
</t:panelTabbedPane>
```

In this example, we are going to use the `calendar` and `course` managed beans we've already used. Listing 2-15 shows the server-side TabbedPane JSP example page.

Listing 2-15. *The Server-Side TabbedPane Page (ssTabbedPane.jsp)*

```
<%@ taglib uri="http://java.sun.com/jsf/core" prefix="f"%>
<%@ taglib uri="http://java.sun.com/jsf/html" prefix="h"%>
<%@ taglib uri="http://myfaces.apache.org/tomahawk" prefix="t"%>
<html>
  <body>
    <f:view>
      <h1>Server Side TabbedPane</h1>
      <h:form>
        <t:panelTabbedPane serverSideTabSwitch="true">

          <t:panelTab id="tab1" label="Calendar" rendered="true">
            <t:outputText id="birthDate" value="#{calendar.date}" />
            <br />

            <t:inputCalendar monthYearRowClass="yearMonthHeader"
                             weekRowClass="weekHeader"
                             currentDayCellClass="currentDayCell"
                             value="#{calendar.date}" />
          </t:panelTab>


          <t:panelTab id="tab2" label="Data List" rendered="true">
            <t:dataList id="dataList" styleClass="standardList" var="course"
                        value="#{dataList.data}" layout="simple" rowCountVar="count"
                        rowIndexVar="index">
              <h:outputText value="#{course.name}" />
              <h:outputText value=", " rendered="#{index + 1 < count}" />
            </t:dataList>
          </t:panelTab>

        </t:panelTabbedPane>
      </h:form>
    </f:view>
  </body>
</html>
```

The example uses two panel tabs. You can set the `serverSideTabSwitch` attribute to control whether the tabs' toggling is a server- or client-side. Setting the `serverSideTabSwitch` attribute to `true` will execute the tab switch on the server side.

The Main Attributes of the TabbedPane Component

Table 2-8 shows the most important attributes of the TabbedPane component.

Table 2-8. *Main Attributes of the TabbedPane Component*

Component Attribute Name	Component Attribute Explanation
`selectedIndex`	Index of the selected tab by default.
`serverSideTabSwitch`	Determines whether the tab switching is on server or client. The default is `false`.
`activeTabStyleClass`	The CSS class to be used for the active tab cell.
`inactiveTabStyleClass`	The CSS class to be used for the inactive tab cells.
`disabledTabStyleClass`	The CSS class to be used for the disabled tab cells.
`activeSubStyleClass`	The CSS class to be used for the active tab subcell.
`inactiveSubStyleClass`	The CSS class to be used for the inactive tab subcells.
`tabContentStyleClass`	The CSS class to be used for the active tab content cell.
`activePanelTabVar`	A Boolean variable that is set in request scope when rendering a `panelTab`. `true` means that the currently rendered `panelTab` is active.

The ValidateRegExpr Component

The Tomahawk ValidateRegExpr validator is used for validating user inputs using regular expressions.

Using the ValidateRegExpr Validator

As an example we will use ValidateRegExpr to validate a phone number. The phone number format is usually (xxx)xxx-xxxx, as shown in Figure 2-13.

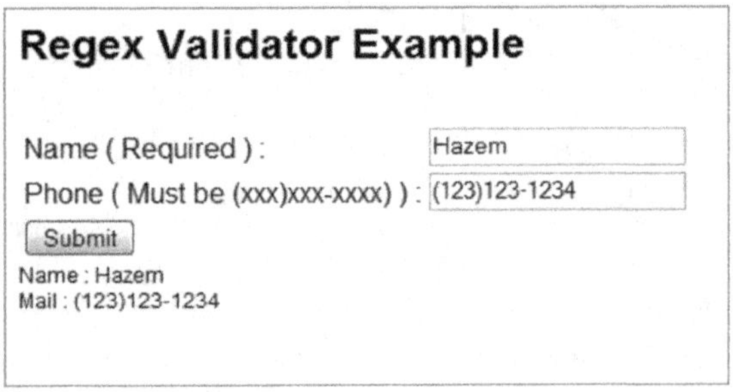

Figure 2-13. *A ValidateRegExpr validator*

The managed bean for this example is shown in Listing 2-16.

Listing 2-16. *The Person Managed Bean Class (Person.java)*

```
import java.io.Serializable;

public class Person implements Serializable {
  String name;
  String telephone;

  public String getTelephone() {
    return telephone;
  }
  public void setTelephone(String mail) {
    this.telephone = mail;
  }
  public String getName() {
    return name;
  }
  public void setName(String name) {
    this.name = name;
  }
}
```

In the example JSP page shown in Listing 2-17, the ValidateRegExpr validator is used for validating a regular expression that represents a U.S. phone number as follows:

```
<t:validateRegExpr pattern="\(\d{3}\)\d{3}-\d{4}" />
```

Providing the `pattern` attribute will make sure the validation is executed correctly.

Listing 2-17. *The ValidateRegExpr Example Page (validate.jsp)*

```
<%@ taglib uri="http://java.sun.com/jsf/core" prefix="f"%>
<%@ taglib uri="http://java.sun.com/jsf/html" prefix="h"%>
<%@ taglib uri="http://myfaces.apache.org/tomahawk" prefix="t"%>
<html>
  <body>
    <f:view>
      <h1>Regex Validator Example</h1>

      <t:saveState value="#{person}" />
      <h:form id="myForm">

        <t:outputLabel for="dialogInput"
                       value="Please enter your personal data :"
                       styleClass="dialogText"></t:outputLabel>
        <h:panelGrid id="dialogInput" columns="3" styleClass="dialogLayout">
```

```
          <h:outputText value="Name ( Required ) :" styleClass="dialogText" />
          <h:inputText id="txtName" value="#{person.name}" required="true" />
          <t:message id="nameError" for="txtName" styleClass="error" />

          <h:outputText value="Phone ( (xxx)xxx-xxxx) ) :"
                        styleClass="dialogText" />
          <h:inputText id="txtPhone" value="#{person.telephone}" required="true">
            <t:validateRegExpr pattern="\(\d{3}\)\d{3}-\d{4}" />
          </h:inputText>
          <t:message id="mailError" for="txtPhone" styleClass="error" />

          <h:commandButton value="Submit"/>

        </h:panelGrid>

        <br /><br />

        <t:outputLabel for="dialogResult" value="Your personal data :"
                       styleClass="dialogText"></t:outputLabel>
        <h:panelGrid id="dialogResult" columns="1" styleClass="dialogLayout">
          <t:outputText id="txtEnteredName" value="Name :  #{person.name}"
                        forceId="true" styleClass="dialogText" />

          <t:outputText id="txtEnteredPhone"
                        value="Phone :  #{person.telephone}" forceId="true"
                        styleClass="dialogText" />
        </h:panelGrid>

      </h:form>
    </f:view>
  </body>
</html>
```

Note A regular expression allows the programmer to rapidly manipulate data inputs based on an identified pattern or characteristic. For details on Java regular expressions, please check out *Java Regular Expressions: Taming the java.util.regex Engine* by Mehran Habibi (Apress, 2004).

The Main Attribute of the ValidateRegExpr Component

Table 2-9 shows the most important attribute of the ValidateRegExpr component.

Table 2-9. *Main Attribute of the ValidateRegExpr Component*

Component Attribute Name	Component Attribute Explanation
pattern	The regular expression, which is the base of the validation

The Tree2 Component

The Tomahawk Tree2 component presents information in a tree-like structure. Tree-like structures are good for displaying information organized in multilevel categories. Like the TabbedPane component, Tree2 supports both client- and server-side interactions.

Using the Tree2 Component

Figure 2-14 shows the Tree2 example we are going to create.

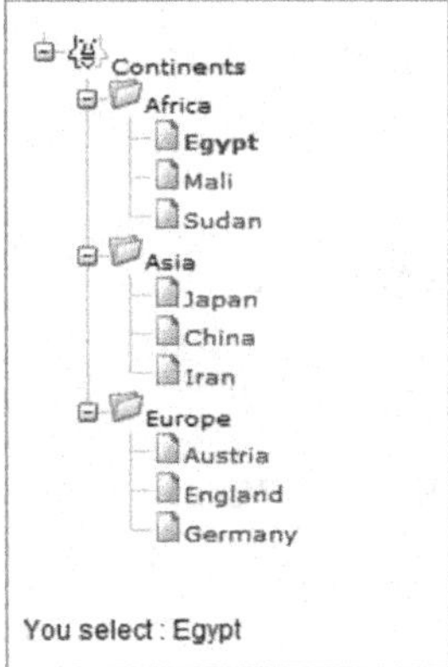

Figure 2-14. *A Tree2 component*

Listings 2-18 and 2-19 show how to implement a client-side interaction tree; for this, we use the `<t:tree2>` tag passing the `TreeModelBase` instance to its `value` attribute.

Listing 2-18. *The Tree2 Managed Bean Class (Tree2Bean.java)*

```
import org.apache.myfaces.custom.tree2.TreeNode;
import org.apache.myfaces.custom.tree2.TreeNodeBase;
import org.apache.myfaces.custom.tree2.TreeModelBase;

public class Tree2Bean {

  private TreeModelBase treeModelBase;

  public Tree2Bean() {
    // create base nodes.
    TreeNode continentNode =
      createNode(Tree2Constants.WORLD_FACET_NAME, "Continents", false);
    TreeNode africaNode =
      createNode(Tree2Constants.CONTINENT_FACET_NAME, "Africa", false);
    TreeNode asiaNode =
      createNode(Tree2Constants.CONTINENT_FACET_NAME, "Asia", false);
    TreeNode europeNode =
      createNode(Tree2Constants.CONTINENT_FACET_NAME, "Europe", false);
```

```
    // add continents.
    addNodeToTree(africaNode, continentNode);
    addNodeToTree(asiaNode, continentNode);
    addNodeToTree(europeNode, continentNode);

    // add asia countries.
    addNodeToTree(createNode(Tree2Constants.COUNTRY_FACET_NAME, "Japan", true),
                  asiaNode);
    addNodeToTree(createNode(Tree2Constants.COUNTRY_FACET_NAME, "China", true),
                  asiaNode);
    addNodeToTree(createNode(Tree2Constants.COUNTRY_FACET_NAME, "Iran", true),
                  asiaNode);

    // add africa countries
    addNodeToTree(createNode(Tree2Constants.COUNTRY_FACET_NAME, "Egypt", true),
                  africaNode);
    addNodeToTree(createNode(Tree2Constants.COUNTRY_FACET_NAME, "Mali", true),
                  africaNode);
    addNodeToTree(createNode(Tree2Constants.COUNTRY_FACET_NAME, "Sudan", true),
                  africaNode);

    // add europe countries
    addNodeToTree(createNode(Tree2Constants.COUNTRY_FACET_NAME, "Austria", true),
                  europeNode);
    addNodeToTree(createNode(Tree2Constants.COUNTRY_FACET_NAME, "England", true),
                  europeNode);
    addNodeToTree(createNode(Tree2Constants.COUNTRY_FACET_NAME, "Germany", true),
                  europeNode);

    // Update the treeModelBase
    treeModelBase = new TreeModelBase(continentNode);
  }

  /*
   * The addNodeToTree() static method is used for adding a tree node
   * (childNode) to a parent tree node (parentNode).
   */
  private static void addNodeToTree(TreeNode childNode, TreeNode parentNode) {
    parentNode.getChildren().add(childNode);
  }

  /*
   * This createNode() static method is used for creating a tree node.
   */
  private static TreeNode createNode(String facetName, String nodeText,
                                     boolean isLeaf) {
```

```
    /*
     * The TreeNodeBase constructor paramaters are :
     * 1. facetName : the Facet Name
     * 2. nodeText : the Node text
     * 3. isLeaf : Determines where the node is a leaf or not
     */
    return new TreeNodeBase(facetName, nodeText, isLeaf);
  }

  /*
   * The getData() method is used for returning the TreeModel that would be
   * used by the tree component value attribute.
   *
   * @return TreeModel
   */
  public TreeModelBase getData() {
    return treeModelBase;
  }
}
```

Listing 2-19. *The ClientSide Tree2 Page (tree2.jsp)*

```
<%@ taglib uri="http://java.sun.com/jsf/core" prefix="f"%>
<%@ taglib uri="http://java.sun.com/jsf/html" prefix="h"%>
<%@ taglib uri="http://myfaces.apache.org/tomahawk" prefix="t"%>
<html>
  <body>
    <f:view>
      <h1>Client Side Toggle Tree</h1>

      <h:form id="myForm">

        <t:tree2 id="clientTree" value="#{tree.data}" var="node"
                 varNodeToggler="t">

          <f:facet name="world">
            <h:panelGroup>
              <t:graphicImage value="images/myfaces.gif" border="0" />
              <h:outputText value="#{node.description}" styleClass="nodeFolder" />
            </h:panelGroup>
          </f:facet>

          <f:facet name="continent">
            <h:panelGroup>
              <f:facet name="expand">
                <t:graphicImage value="images/yellow-folder-open.png"
                                rendered="#{t.nodeExpanded}" border="0" />
              </f:facet>
```

```
            <f:facet name="collapse">
              <t:graphicImage value="images/yellow-folder-closed.png"
                              rendered="#{!t.nodeExpanded}" border="0" />
            </f:facet>

            <h:outputText value="#{node.description}"  styleClass="nodeFolder" />
          </h:panelGroup>
        </f:facet>

        <f:facet name="country">
          <h:panelGroup>
            <h:commandLink immediate="true"
                           styleClass="#{t.nodeSelected ?
                                        'documentSelected':'document'}"
                           actionListener="#{t.setNodeSelected}">
              <t:graphicImage value="images/document.png" border="0" />
              <h:outputText value="#{node.description}" />
              <f:param name="countryName"  value="#{node.description}" />
            </h:commandLink>
          </h:panelGroup>
        </f:facet>

      </t:tree2>

      <br/> <br />
      <t:outputText value="You selected : #{param.countryName}" />

    </h:form>
  </f:view>
 </body>
</html>
```

Note The `TreeModelBase` instance is actually a wrapper of a tree of `TreeNode` instances.

To create an instance of the `TreeNode` class, we provide the following information:

- `type`: The node type that should match the facet name indicated on the JSP page
- `description`: The node text
- `isLeaf`: Determines whether the node is a leaf

The example introduces three facets. A World facet representing the root node, a Continent facet representing the continent nodes, and a Country facet representing the country nodes.

In the Country facet, a `CommandLink` is used for passing the country name (node description) as a parameter when the node is clicked to display the selected country name.

Note To be able to implement a server-side tree, all that needs to be done is to set the `clientSideToggle` attribute to `false`. In a server-side toggled tree, only the visible part of the tree is sent to the client. This partial tree-state rendering method is more efficient than the `clientSideToggle=true` setting where the entire tree is returned to the client.

Creating a Lazy Loading Tree

A lazy loading tree is a server-side tree whose contents are loaded on demand. They are especially useful in scenarios when the tree has a large number of elements. Figure 2-15 shows the lazy loading Tree2 example.

Figure 2-15. *A lazy loading component*

To implement lazy loading on the Tree2 component, we should perform the following steps:

1. Set the `clientSideToggle` attribute to `false`.
2. Create lazy loading node classes that extend the `TreeNodeBase` class.
3. Make sure that every extending class overrides the `getChildren()` method of the `TreeNodeBase` class to load the child nodes dynamically.

To see the code for these steps, please check the following files in the `chapter2` directory available for download in the Source Code section of the Apress web site:

- Managed bean class: `Tree2LazyLoadingBean.java`
- JSP page file: `lazyLoadingTree2.jsp`

The Main Attributes of the Tree2 Component

Table 2-10 shows the most important attributes of the Tree2 component.

Table 2-10. *Main Attributes of the Tree2 Component*

Component Attribute Name	Component Attribute Explanation
`value`	Can accept a `TreeModel` instance that represents the tree data
`var`	A parameter that represents the tree node
`varNodeToggler`	A parameter that represents the tree node toggler
`ShowNav`	Shows the "plus" and "minus" navigation icons (defaults to `true`) and is ignored if `clientSideToggle` is `true`.
`ShowLines`	Shows the connecting lines (defaults to `true`)
`ShowRootNode`	Includes the root node when rendering the tree (defaults to `true`)
`PreserveToggle`	Preserves changes in client-side toggle information between requests (defaults to `true`)
`ClientSideToggle`	Determines if the node interaction should occur on the client or server side

The Schedule Component

The Schedule component allows you to render a schedule in a day, work week, week, or month view.

Using the Schedule Component

In this example, we'll create a Schedule as shown in Figure 2-16.

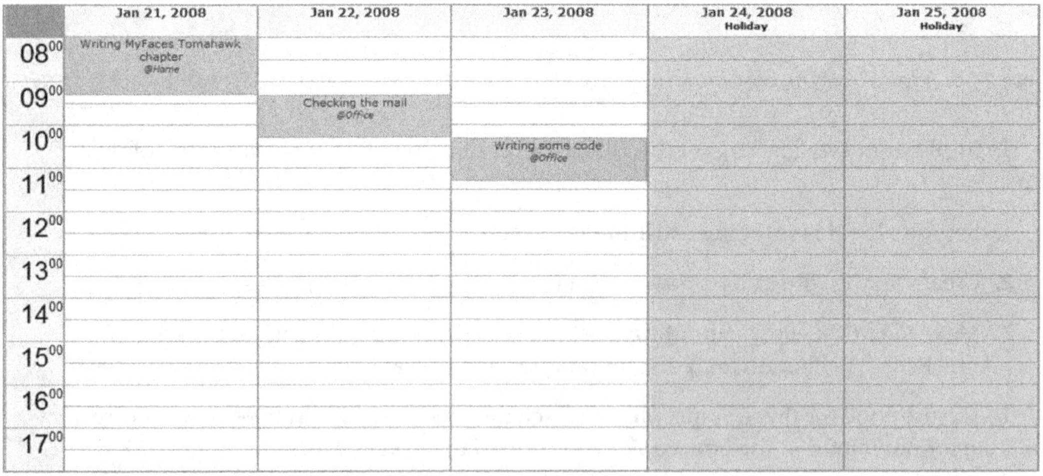

Figure 2-16. *A Schedule component*

Listing 2-20 shows the managed bean for this example.

Listing 2-20. *The Schedule Managed Bean Class (ScheduleBean.java)*

```
import java.util.Calendar;
import java.util.GregorianCalendar;

import org.apache.commons.lang.RandomStringUtils;

import org.apache.myfaces.custom.schedule.model.ScheduleModel;
import org.apache.myfaces.custom.schedule.model.SimpleScheduleModel;
import org.apache.myfaces.custom.schedule.model.DefaultScheduleEntry;

public class ScheduleBean {

  private ScheduleModel model;

  /*
   * Creating a SimpleScheduleModel object and
   * adding entries (Tasks + Holidays) to it.
   */
  public ScheduleBean() {
    Calendar calendar = GregorianCalendar.getInstance();

    // construct a SimpleScheduleModel object
    model = new SimpleScheduleModel();
    model.setMode(ScheduleModel.WORKWEEK);
    model.setSelectedDate(calendar.getTime());

    // making thursday, friday as holidays
    calendar.set(Calendar.DAY_OF_WEEK, Calendar.THURSDAY);
    ((SimpleScheduleModel) model).setHoliday(calendar.getTime(), "Holiday");

    calendar.set(Calendar.DAY_OF_WEEK, Calendar.FRIDAY);
    ((SimpleScheduleModel) model).setHoliday(calendar.getTime(), "Holiday");

    // adding entry1 (Writing Tomahawk chapter)from hour 9 to 11 a.m.
    DefaultScheduleEntry entry1 = createCalendarEntry(
      "Writing MyFaces Tomahawk chapter", "@Home",
      "Writing MyFaces Tomahawk chapter",
      calendar.get(Calendar.YEAR), calendar.get(Calendar.MONTH),
      Calendar.MONDAY, 9, 0, Calendar.AM, 2);
      model.addEntry(entry1);

    // adding entry2 (Checking mail) from hour 8 to 9 a.m.
    DefaultScheduleEntry entry2 = createCalendarEntry("Checking the mail",
      "@Office", "Checking the mail", calendar.get(Calendar.YEAR),
      calendar.get(Calendar.MONTH), Calendar.TUESDAY, 8, 0,
      Calendar.AM, 1);
    model.addEntry(entry2);
```

```
    // adding entry3 (Writing some code) from hour 1 to 2 p.m. and select.
    DefaultScheduleEntry entry3 = createCalendarEntry("Writing some code",
      "@Office", "Writing some code", calendar.get(Calendar.YEAR),
      calendar.get(Calendar.MONTH), Calendar.WEDNESDAY, 1, 0,
      Calendar.PM, 1);
    model.addEntry(entry3);
    model.setSelectedEntry(entry3);

    // update the model
    model.refresh();
  }

  /*
   * The addCalendarEntry() is used for creating a calendar entry.
   */
  private DefaultScheduleEntry createCalendarEntry(String title,
      String subtitle, String description, int year, int month,
      int dayOfWeek, int hour, int minute, int AM_PM, int durationInHours) {

    Calendar calendar = GregorianCalendar.getInstance();
    DefaultScheduleEntry scheduleEntry = new DefaultScheduleEntry();

    // set the entry id.
    scheduleEntry.setId(RandomStringUtils.randomNumeric(32));

    // set calendar day of the week.
    calendar.set(Calendar.DAY_OF_WEEK, dayOfWeek);

    // set the entry starting time.
    calendar.set(Calendar.HOUR, hour);
    calendar.set(Calendar.MINUTE, minute);
    calendar.set(Calendar.AM_PM, AM_PM);
    scheduleEntry.setStartTime(calendar.getTime());

    // set the entry ending time.
    calendar.add(Calendar.HOUR, durationInHours);
    scheduleEntry.setEndTime(calendar.getTime());

    // adding entry other information,
    scheduleEntry.setTitle(title);
    scheduleEntry.setSubtitle(subtitle);
    scheduleEntry.setDescription(description);

    return scheduleEntry;
  }
```

```
  public ScheduleModel getModel() {
    return model;
  }

  public void setModel(ScheduleModel model) {
    this.model = model;
  }
}
```

The example JSP page shown in Listing 2-21 creates a schedule; for this, we use the `<t:schedule>` tag passing a `ScheduleModel` instance to its `value` attribute.

Listing 2-21. *The Schedule Page (schedule.jsp)*

```
<%@ taglib uri="http://java.sun.com/jsf/core" prefix="f"%>
<%@ taglib uri="http://java.sun.com/jsf/html" prefix="h"%>
<%@ taglib uri="http://myfaces.apache.org/tomahawk" prefix="t"%>
<html>
  <body>
    <f:view>
      <h1>Schedule Example</h1>
      <h:form>
        <t:div style="position: absolute; left: 5px; top: 50px; right: 5px;">
          <t:schedule value="#{schedule.model}" id="mySchedule"
                      rendered="true" visibleEndHour="18" visibleStartHour="8"
                      workingEndHour="20" workingStartHour="8" readonly="false"
                      theme="default " tooltip="true"/>
        </t:div>
      </h:form>
    </f:view>
  </body>
</html>
```

`ScheduleModel` contains entries for the schedule. In the example, the `DefaultScheduleEntry` class is used for representing the `ScheduleModel` entry. It has the following main attributes:

- `id` represents the unique ID of the schedule entry.
- `startTime` represents the start time of the schedule entry.
- `endTime` represents the end time of the schedule entry.
- `title` represents the title of the schedule entry.
- `subtitle` represents the subtitle of the schedule entry.
- `description` represents the description of the schedule entry.

■ **Note** The previous example uses the `SimpleScheduleModel` as an implementation for the `ScheduleModel` interface. If you want to use something further up the class hierarchy to extend, you can use `SimpleScheduleModel`, which extends `AbstractScheduleModel`, which itself implements the `ScheduleModel` interface.

The Main Attributes of the Schedule Component

Table 2-11 shows the most important attributes of the Schedule component.

Table 2-11. *The Schedule Component's Main Attributes*

Component Attribute Name	Component Attribute Explanation
`value`	Accepts a `ScheduleModel` instance that represents the schedule data.
`visibleStartHour`	An integer value indicating the first hour of the day that should be visible in the schedule.
`visibleEndHour`	An integer value indicating the last hour of the day that should be visible in the schedule.
`workingStartHour`	An integer value indicating the start of the working day. Everything before this hour will be grayed out.
`workingEndHour`	An integer value indicating the end of the working day. Everything after this hour will be grayed out.
`readonly`	When a schedule is read-only, no entries can be selected.
`submitOnClick`	When this is `true` and the `readonly` property is set to `false`, clicking the schedule anywhere outside an entry box will submit the form, posting the date and the time of day that was clicked.
`mouseListener`	A method binding with parameter of type `ScheduleMouseEvent`. This allows a backing bean to listen for mouse click events on the schedule.
`tooltip`	Determines whether or not tooltips will be displayed for schedule entries.
`renderZeroLengthEntries`	Normally, when an entry has the same start and end time, the entry is not rendered in the detailed views. Setting this to `true` forces such entries to be rendered. The size of the entry box is then adapted to fit the text in it.
`expandToFitEntries`	By default, if an appointment exists outside the `visibleStartHour`/`visibleEndHour` limits, it does not appear in the day or work week modes. This setting checks for events outside the visible range and extends the visible range to display the events. If events only occur within the visible range, no adjustment is made.
`theme`	Name of the theme that should be used when rendering the schedule. Available themes are `default`, `outlookxp`, and `evolution`.
`headerDateFormat`	If we want to override the locale `dateFormat` for displaying the date in the header, we can specify the custom format here.
`compactWeekRowHeight`	The height in pixels of a row in the week view (defaults to `200`).
`compactMonthRowHeight`	The height in pixels of a row in the month view (defaults to `100`).

Component Attribute Name	Component Attribute Explanation
entryRenderer	A value binding to an instance of ScheduleEntryRenderer that is used to render entries on the schedule (defaults to DefaultScheduleEntryRenderer).
columnClass	The CSS class for columns in the detailed mode (defaults to column).
backgroundClass	The CSS class for the background of the detailed mode (defaults to background).
freeClass	The CSS class for nonworking hours in the detailed mode (defaults to free).
evenClass	The CSS class for even rows in the detailed mode (defaults to even).
unevenClass	The CSS class for uneven rows in the detailed mode (defaults to uneven).
gutterClass	The CSS class for the gutter on the left, containing hours of the day (defaults to gutter).
headerClass	The CSS class for the header, containing dates (defaults to header).
dateClass	The CSS class of the date in the header (defaults to date).
holidayClass	The CSS class of the holiday name in the header (defaults to holiday).
hoursClass	The CSS class of the hour in the gutter (defaults to hours).
minutesClass	The CSS class of the minutes in the gutter (defaults to minutes).
selectedEntryClass	The CSS class of the selected entry (defaults to entry-selected).
textClass	The CSS class of the contents of an entry in the detailed mode, when using DefaultScheduleEntryRenderer (defaults to text).
titleClass	The CSS class of the title of an entry in the detailed mode, when using the DefaultScheduleEntryRenderer (defaults to title).
subtitleClass	The CSS class of the subtitle of an entry in the detailed mode, when using the DefaultScheduleRenderer (defaults to subtitle).
entryClass	The CSS class of an entry (defaults to entry).
foregroundClass	The CSS class of the foreground table (defaults to foreground).
dayClass	The CSS class of a day in the compact mode (defaults to day).
inactiveDayClass	The CSS class of an inactive day in the compact mode (defaults to inactive-day).
contentClass	The CSS class of the entries of a day in the compact mode (defaults to content).
selectedClass	The CSS class of a selected entry in the compact mode (defaults to selected).
monthClass	The CSS class of a month in the compact mode (defaults to month).
weekClass	The CSS class of a week in the compact mode (defaults to week).

The SubForm Component

Although this component is still in the sandbox project (until Tomahawk 1.1.6), it is useful to know about as it provides a powerful feature: it allows you to execute model validation and update for only a part of the form page by defining the components inside the <s:subForm>

tag. Model validation and update for multiple subforms on the page can be configured using the `actionFor` attribute of the Tomahawk `CommandButton` or `CommandLink` components. Let's explore the SubForm component with the example in Listing 2-22.

Listing 2-22. *Using the SubForm Component*

```
<%@ taglib uri="http://java.sun.com/jsf/core" prefix="f"%>
<%@ taglib uri="http://java.sun.com/jsf/html" prefix="h"%>
<%@ taglib uri="http://myfaces.apache.org/tomahawk" prefix="t"%>
<%@ taglib uri="http://myfaces.apache.org/sandbox" prefix="s"%>
<html>
  <body>
    <f:view>
      <h:form id="myForm">
        <s:subForm id="personalForm">
          <t:outputLabel for="name" value="Name : " />
          <h:inputText id="name" value="#{person.name}" required="true"/>
          <t:outputLabel for="phone" value="Telephone number : " />
          <h:inputText id="phone" value="#{person.telephone}" required="true"/>
        </s:subForm>

        <s:subForm id="calendarForm">
          <t:outputLabel for="date" value="Preferred date : " />
          <h:inputText id="date" value="#{calendar.date}" required="true"/>
        </s:subForm>

        <s:subForm id="courseForm">
          <t:outputLabel for="course" value="Course : " />
          <h:inputText id="course" value="#{course.name}" required="true"/><br />
        </s:subForm>

        <t:commandButton value="Submit subForm"
                         actionFor="personalForm, calendarForm"/>
      </h:form>
    </f:view>
  </body>
</html>
```

The example uses a CommandButton component to execute a partial model validation and update for both the `personalForm` and the `calendarForm` subforms.

Putting It All Together

Now that we have shown you some of the popular components, we will show you how to put some of them together to create a simple application called Event Creator.

The Event Creator application allows users to create events for specific dates. They can also view their events in either workweek or month mode.

The application mainly uses a Tomahawk Calendar and Schedule and some basic JSF components. Figure 2-17 shows the final application.

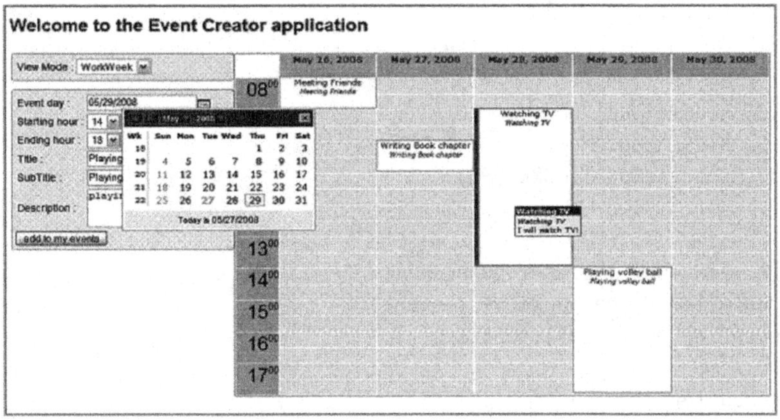

Figure 2-17. *The Event Creator application*

Listing 2-23 shows the managed bean for the application.

Listing 2-23. *The EventCreator Bean Class (EventCreatorBean.java)*

```
import java.util.Calendar;
import java.util.Date;

import java.io.Serializable;

import javax.faces.event.ValueChangeEvent;

import org.apache.commons.lang.RandomStringUtils;

import org.apache.myfaces.custom.schedule.model.ScheduleModel;
import org.apache.myfaces.custom.schedule.model.SimpleScheduleModel;
import org.apache.myfaces.custom.schedule.model.DefaultScheduleEntry;

public class EventCreatorBean implements Serializable {
  private ScheduleModel scheduleModel;
  private String description;
  private String title;
  private String subTitle;
  private String startingHour;
  private String endingHour;
  private Date date;
  private String scheduleViewMode;
```

```
/* initialize the schedule model */
public EventCreatorBean() {
  // initialize the world.
  startingHour = "8";
  endingHour = "9";

  // Construct a SimpleScheduleModel object
  scheduleModel = new SimpleScheduleModel();
  scheduleModel.setMode(ScheduleModel.WORKWEEK);
}

 /* Update the schedule view when the user changes it. */
public void updateScheduleView(ValueChangeEvent event) {
  scheduleViewMode = event.getNewValue().toString();

  if ("Month".equals(scheduleViewMode)) {
    scheduleModel.setMode(ScheduleModel.MONTH);
  } else {
    scheduleModel.setMode(ScheduleModel.WORKWEEK);
  }

  scheduleModel.refresh();
}

/* Add an entry to the schedule component. */
public String addToSchedule() {
  int AM_PM = Calendar.AM;
  int from = Integer.parseInt(startingHour);
  int to = Integer.parseInt(endingHour);
  Calendar calendar = Calendar.getInstance();

  /* initialize the calendar */
  calendar.setTime(date);

  /* set the selected calendar date in the scheduleModel */
  scheduleModel.setSelectedDate(calendar.getTime());

  /* adding entry information */
  DefaultScheduleEntry entry = new DefaultScheduleEntry();
  entry.setId(RandomStringUtils.randomNumeric(32));

  /* setting the starting date */
  if (from > 12) {
    from -= 12;
    AM_PM = Calendar.PM;
  }
```

```
    calendar.set(Calendar.HOUR, from);
    calendar.set(Calendar.MINUTE, 0);
    calendar.set(Calendar.AM_PM, AM_PM);
    entry.setStartTime(calendar.getTime());

    /* setting the ending date */
    if (to > 12) {
      to -= 12;
      AM_PM = Calendar.PM;
    }

    calendar.set(Calendar.HOUR, to);
    calendar.set(Calendar.MINUTE, 0);
    calendar.set(Calendar.AM_PM, AM_PM);
    entry.setEndTime(calendar.getTime());

    /* setting subtitle and description */
    entry.setTitle(title);
    entry.setSubtitle(subTitle);
    entry.setDescription(description);

    /* update the model */
    scheduleModel.addEntry(entry);
    scheduleModel.setSelectedEntry(entry);
    scheduleModel.refresh();

    return null;
  }

  public String getScheduleViewMode() {
    return scheduleViewMode;
  }

  public void setScheduleViewMode(String scheduleViewMode) {
    this.scheduleViewMode = scheduleViewMode;
  }

  public String getSubTitle() {
    return subTitle;
  }

  public void setSubTitle(String subTitle) {
    this.subTitle = subTitle;
  }
```

```
  public Date getDate() {
    return date;
  }

  public void setDate(Date date) {
    this.date = date;
  }

  public String getEndingHour() {
    return endingHour;
  }

  public void setEndingHour(String endingHour) {
    this.endingHour = endingHour;
  }

  public String getStartingHour() {
    return startingHour;
  }

  public void setStartingHour(String startingHour) {
    this.startingHour = startingHour;
  }

  public String getTitle() {
    return title;
  }

  public void setTitle(String title) {
    this.title = title;
  }

  public String getDescription() {
    return description;
  }

  public void setDescription(String description) {
    this.description = description;
  }

  public ScheduleModel getScheduleModel() {
    return scheduleModel;
  }
}
```

The `updateScheduleView()` method is used for updating the schedule view when the user changes it from workweek to month view, and vice versa. The other important method is `addToSchedule()`, which adds an entry to the schedule component, much as we did earlier in the chapter.

The application JSP page code is shown in Listing 2-24.

Listing 2-24. *The EventCreator Page (eventCreator.jsp)*

```
<%@ taglib uri="http://java.sun.com/jsf/core" prefix="f"%>
<%@ taglib uri="http://java.sun.com/jsf/html" prefix="h"%>
<%@ taglib uri="http://myfaces.apache.org/tomahawk" prefix="t"%>
<html>
  <body>
    <f:view>
      <t:saveState value="#{eventCreator}" />
      <h1>Welcome to the Event Creator application</h1>
      <h:form id="eventCreatorForm">

        <t:div styleClass="viewDialogLayout">
          <h:panelGrid id="eventModePanel" columns="2">
            <t:outputLabel for="viewMode" styleClass="dialogText"
                           value="View Mode : " />
            <t:selectOneMenu id="viewMode" forceId="true"
                  valueChangeListener="#{eventCreator.updateScheduleView}"
                  value="#{eventCreator.scheduleViewMode}" onchange="submit();">
              <f:selectItem itemLabel="WorkWeek" itemValue="WorkWeek"/>
              <f:selectItem itemLabel="Month" itemValue="Month"/>
            </t:selectOneMenu>
          </h:panelGrid>
        </t:div>

        <t:div styleClass="eventDialogLayout">
          <h:panelGrid id="eventCreatorPanel" columns="2">

            <t:outputLabel for="calendar" styleClass="dialogText"
                           value="Event day : " />
            <t:inputCalendar id="calendar" forceId="true"
                             monthYearRowClass="yearMonthHeader"
                             weekRowClass="weekHeader"
                             currentDayCellClass="currentDayCell"
                             value="#{eventCreator.date}"
                             renderAsPopup="true"
                             popupLeft="true"
                             popupDateFormat="MM/dd/yyyy"
                             renderPopupButtonAsImage="true">
            </t:inputCalendar>
```

```
<t:outputLabel for="startFrom" styleClass="dialogText"
               value="Starting hour : " />
<t:selectOneMenu id="startFrom" forceId="true"
                value="#{eventCreator.startingHour}">
  <f:selectItem itemLabel="8" itemValue="8"/>
  <f:selectItem itemLabel="9" itemValue="9"/>
  <f:selectItem itemLabel="10" itemValue="10"/>
  <f:selectItem itemLabel="11" itemValue="11"/>
  <f:selectItem itemLabel="12" itemValue="12"/>
  <f:selectItem itemLabel="13" itemValue="13"/>
  <f:selectItem itemLabel="14" itemValue="14"/>
  <f:selectItem itemLabel="15" itemValue="15"/>
  <f:selectItem itemLabel="16" itemValue="16"/>
  <f:selectItem itemLabel="17" itemValue="17"/>
  <f:selectItem itemLabel="18" itemValue="18"/>
</t:selectOneMenu>

<t:outputLabel for="endAt" styleClass="dialogText"
               value="Ending hour : " />
<t:selectOneMenu id="endAt" forceId="true"
                value="#{eventCreator.endingHour}">
  <f:selectItem itemLabel="8" itemValue="8"/>
  <f:selectItem itemLabel="9" itemValue="9"/>
  <f:selectItem itemLabel="10" itemValue="10"/>
  <f:selectItem itemLabel="11" itemValue="11"/>
  <f:selectItem itemLabel="12" itemValue="12"/>
  <f:selectItem itemLabel="13" itemValue="13"/>
  <f:selectItem itemLabel="14" itemValue="14"/>
  <f:selectItem itemLabel="15" itemValue="15"/>
  <f:selectItem itemLabel="16" itemValue="16"/>
  <f:selectItem itemLabel="17" itemValue="17"/>
  <f:selectItem itemLabel="18" itemValue="18"/>
</t:selectOneMenu>

<t:outputLabel for="eventTitle" styleClass="dialogText"
               value="Title : " />
<t:inputText id="eventTitle" forceId="true"
             value="#{eventCreator.title}"
             required="true"></t:inputText>

<t:outputLabel for="eventSubTitle" styleClass="dialogText"
               value="SubTitle : " />
<t:inputText id="eventSubTitle" forceId="true"
             value="#{eventCreator.subTitle}"
             required="true"></t:inputText>
```

```
            <t:outputLabel for="eventDesc" styleClass="dialogText"
                           value="Description : "/>
            <t:inputTextarea id="eventDesc" forceId="true"
                             value="#{eventCreator.description}"
                             cols="15" required="true"></t:inputTextarea>

          </h:panelGrid>

          <h:commandButton value="add to my events"
                           onclick="if (!validate()) return false"
                           action="#{eventCreator.addToSchedule}"></h:commandButton>
        </t:div>

        <t:div styleClass="scheduleDialog">
          <t:schedule value="#{eventCreator.scheduleModel}" id="mySchedule"
                      rendered="true" visibleEndHour="18" visibleStartHour="8"
                      workingEndHour="20" workingStartHour="8" readonly="false"
                      theme="default" tooltip="true"/>
        </t:div>
      </h:form>
    </f:view>
  </body>
</html>
```

The application JSP page code utilizes some of the components we detailed earlier in the chapter. It uses the `<t:schedule>` and `<t:calendar>` components and some of basic components like `<t:div>` (which is used for rendering an HTML `div` around its children), `<t:inputText>` (which is used for rendering an HTML `input` element), `<t:outputLabel>` (which is used for rendering an HTML `label` element), `<t:inputTextarea>` (which is used for rendering an HTML `textArea` element), and `<t:selectOneMenu>` (which is used for rendering an HTML drop-down menu).

Summary

In this chapter, you learned about the Tomahawk project: what components it offers, how to set it up inside your JSF applications, how to use some of its popular components, and finally how to use its components together for building a useful application.

CHAPTER 3

Facelets

When JavaServer Faces (JSF) was devised, the intention was to reuse JSP as the main technology to create pages, as it was already a standard in the web community. The idea was to simplify the adoption of JSF by using a familiar tag language that already had a high adoption rate within the Java community.

Unfortunately, JSP and JSF don't naturally complement each other. JSP is used to create static or dynamic web content but not to create component trees. Its elements are processed in a page from top to bottom with the basic objective of creating a response to a request. JSF, however, has a more complex life cycle, and component generation and rendering happen in clearly separated phases.

Facelets fills the gap between JSP and JSF. It is a view technology focused on building component trees and interweaving content with the complex JSF life cycle. Facelets replaces JSP with a very straightforward API that is a reflection of its simple principles, and it incorporates numerous developer-friendly features, which we will describe in this chapter.

The Gap Between JSP and JSF

JSP and JSF both write output to the response, but they do so differently: the JSP container creates output as soon as it finds JSP content, whereas JSF components dictate their own rendering. This difference can cause some problems when using JSP and JSF together, as the following code snippet illustrates:

```
<h:outputText value="I am first" />
I am second
```

In this snippet, we mix a JSF tag, `h:outputText`, with free text (analyzed directly by the JSP container) just after it. As we expect, we get this output in the rendered page:

```
I am first
I am second
```

However, we can encapsulate our previous snippet in a panel (`h:panelGroup`) like so:

```
<h:panelGroup>
      <h:outputText value="I am first"/>
      I am second
</h:panelGroup>
```

If we do, the output is reversed:

```
I am second
I am first
```

We would naturally expect the second snippet to produce output like the first one. However, the JSP container adds the "I am second" text as soon as it encounters it, whereas the `h:panelGroup`, which is a component that renders its own children, won't produce the "I am first" output until the closing tag is reached.

Why Use Facelets?

There are multiple reasons to use Facelets instead of JSP to create JSF pages. First, Facelets does not depend on a web container, so you can use JSF 1.2 without having to use Java Enterprise Edition 5 (JEE5) or a container that already has JSP 2.1. Facelets can also work with any implementation and version of JSF, requiring no special render kits.

Also, as described in the previous section, interweaving JSP and JSF can cause difficulties. In addition, JavaServer Pages Standard Tag Library (JSTL) cannot be used with JSF. Facelets provides a solution for this incompatibility while also providing a compilation process that is quicker than JSP compilation, because Java bytecode is not actually generated and compiled behind the scenes when you first visit your page.

In addition, Facelets provides templating, so you can reuse your code extensively to simplify the development and maintenance of large-scale applications.

It also allows the creation of lightweight components, which are quite trivial to develop compared to the pure JSF components. For example, you don't need to create tags for the UI components (the Appendix is a reference for the Facelets UI components).

Then too, Facelets has Unified Expression Language (EL) support, including support for EL functions and compile-time EL validation. The Unified EL takes the features of the JSP EL and adds a few additional capabilities such as deferred expression evaluation, JSTL iteration tags, and method invocation within an expression definition. Facelets also provides precise error reporting, showing detailed information about the line where the exception occurs.

It is possible to use the `jsfc` attribute (which is the equivalent to the `jwcid` concept in Tapestry) to provide integration with existing HTML editors. In the following example, `jsfc` is used to tell the compiler to build a text field component (`h:inputText`) instead of just outputting the `input` tag:

```
<input id="myId" type="text"
jsfc="h:inputText"
value="#{bean.foo}"/>
```

Creating an Application with Facelets

In this section, we are going to create from scratch a very simple application that uses Facelets. You will learn how to configure Facelets and get acquainted with some of the basic ideas behind the framework.

Facelets, like JSF, is based on standards and does not depend on any particular operating system or product.

Downloading Facelets

The Facelets project is hosted at Java.net (`http://facelets.dev.java.net/`). There, you can choose the download option that best meets your needs. You can go with the release binary with the sample applications bundled, or you can compile it from source.

The bundle includes the Facelets JAR at the root level (`jsf-facelets.jar`), and the dependencies can be found in the `lib` folder. Later, we will explain which dependencies Facelets needs.

A few demonstrations are also included; these can be used to start testing the framework. The WAR files for these demonstrations can be found at the root level and their sources in the `demo` folder. Some of the demonstrations follow:

- *starterkit*: A blank Facelets application that can be used when starting an empty Facelets project
- *numberguess*: The traditional demonstration of JSF, where the user needs to guess a number, migrated to Facelets
- *hangman*: Demonstration of a migration from Tapestry to JSF and Facelets
- *portlet*: A small Facelets and MyFaces portlet example that supports the edit and help modes

CVS

You can also check out the source code using Concurrent Versions System (CVS) if you are a member of Java.net. To do this, execute the following commands, replacing `USERNAME` with your Java.net login name:

```
cvs -d :pserver:USERNAME@cvs.dev.java.net:/cvs login
cvs -d :pserver:USERNAME@cvs.dev.java.net:/cvs \
    checkout facelets
```

You can find more information on how to check out Facelets from CVS at `http://facelets.dev.java.net/servlets/ProjectSource`.

Maven

The Facelets artifact can be found in the Maven Central Repository (`http://www.ibiblio.org/maven2/`) and in the Java.net Maven Repository (`https://maven-repository.dev.java.net/repository/`). You can include the artifact in your project by adding the following dependency to your Project Object Model (POM):

```
<dependency>
    <groupId>com.sun.facelets</groupId>
    <artifactId>jsf-facelets</artifactId>
    <version>1.1.13</version>
</dependency>
```

Version 1.1.13 is the current one at the time of this writing. You should use a newer version if one exists.

Adding Dependencies

Facelets can work with any implementation and version of JSF. It also uses the recent EL API, and it can work with any version or implementation of this API as well. Table 3-1 summarizes the dependencies of Facelets.

Table 3-1. *Facelets Dependencies*

Project	Build*	Included**	Description
Apache MyFaces	No	No	Implements JSF 1.1 and JSF 1.2
JavaServer Faces RI	No	No	The Reference Implementations of JSF 1.1 and JSF 1.2 available for use with your application
JavaServer Faces API	Yes	Yes	JSF 1.2 API that works with the new EL specification (Optionally, MyFaces Core API could be used.)
EL API	Yes	Yes	The API for the EL 1.0 specification
EL RI	No	Yes	The Reference Implementation that is used by Facelets for handling EL
Servlet API	Yes	Yes	The Servlet API
XML SAX	Yes	No	The Simple API for XML (This dependency should not be an issue for most deployments, as it is a standard part of web containers and Java Runtime Environments [JREs].)

** Required at build time for building the Facelets project*

*** Libraries included in the Facelets distribution, required by Facelets at runtime*

Creating a Project Structure

Ensuring that your web application has the correct list of libraries included can be one of the trickiest parts when starting a project. Missing libraries or incompatibilities between library versions can lead to obscure exceptions and increase your frustration. The diversity of web containers, each of them with its own libraries and particularities, makes this task even more complex.

If we were to set up a project that uses Facelets and MyFaces, a common directory structure would look like this:

```
$PROJECT
+- /WEB-INF
   +- /lib
      +- /commons-beanutils.jar
      +- /commons-collections.jar
      +- /commons-digester.jar
      +- /commons-logging.jar
      +- /el-api
      +- /el-impl
      +- /jsf-facelets.jar
      +- /myfaces-api.jar
      +- /myfaces-impl.jar
```

```
   +- /web.xml
   +- /faces-config.xml
+- /[xhtml documents]
```

The EL libraries (el-api and el-impl) need to be excluded if the container is JSP 2.1 compliant. JSP 2.1 already contains an EL implementation, and you would have a conflict when starting the application.

If you are using the Reference Implementation (RI), replace `myfaces-api.jar` and `myfaces-impl.jar` with `jsf-ri.jar` and `jsf-api.jar`.

■ **Note** If you're using Maven, you do not need to worry about the dependencies, as Maven will get them for you. You need to declare the JSF implementation in your POM file, though.

Configuring the Web Descriptor (web.xml)

To enable Facelets in your application, you need to configure the `web.xml` file—you need to include the context parameter `javax.faces.DEFAULT_SUFFIX`, which defines the suffix of the documents for your views. By convention, the default extension for pages built using Facelets is `*.xhtml`. The modifications for `web.xml` follow:

```
<web-app>
  <!-- Use Documents Saved as *.xhtml -->
  <context-param>
    <param-name>javax.faces.DEFAULT_SUFFIX</param-name>
    <param-value>.xhtml</param-value>
  </context-param>
</web-app>
```

Optionally, you can specify other parameters in the web descriptor to further configure the behavior of Facelets. Table 3-2 summarizes the available parameters.

Table 3-2. *web.xml Initialization Parameters*

Parameter	Description
`facelets.BUFFER_SIZE`	Defines the buffer size to set on the response when the `ResponseWriter` is generated. By default, this value equals `-1`, which means that no buffer size will be assigned to the response. To ensure that a page is rendered when an error is generated, this value could be increased so the rendered output is not sent to the client before the debug response is generated.
`facelets.DECORATORS`	List of classes, separated by a semicolon (;), that implement `com.sun.facelets.tag.TagDecorator` and have a no-argument constructor. These decorators will be loaded when the first request hits the `FaceletViewHandler` for page compilation.

Continued

Table 3-2. *Continued*

Parameter	Description
facelets.DEVELOPMENT	If this attribute is true, the FaceletViewHandler will print out debug information when an error occurs during rendering. The default is false.
facelets.LIBRARIES	List of paths to the Facelets tag libraries delimited by a semicolon (;). The paths must be relative to your application's root. These libraries will be loaded when the first request hits the FaceletViewHandler for page compilation.
facelets.REFRESH_PERIOD	This is the period, in seconds, in which the compiler is checking for changes after a page is requested. Lower values are useful during development, as you can edit your page in a running application, and the page will be compiled. Very low values should be avoided in production, as the constant compilation will degrade the overall performance. If you don't want the page to be checked for changes, set this parameter to -1. The default is 2.
facelets.RESOURCE_RESOLVER	Used to provide a custom ResourceResolver so other ways of resolving resources can be implemented. The default is com.sun.facelets.impl.DefaultResourceResolver.
facelets.SKIP_COMMENTS	When true, the compiler skips the comments in the page, and nothing within the comments is rendered in the view. When it is false, although the tags won't be compiled, the EL expressions will be parsed as if they were inline. The default is true.

Faces Descriptor (faces-config.xml)

Facelets replaces the default JSF ViewHandler with its own implementation represented by the class com.sun.facelets.FaceletViewHandler. To do this, it takes advantage of JSF's composite nature. To configure our web application to use the Facelets handler instead of the default JSF ViewHandler, we need to specify the <view-handler> element in the faces-config.xml file:

```
<faces-config>
  <application>
    <view-handler>
      com.sun.facelets.FaceletViewHandler
    </view-handler>
  </application>
</faces-config>
```

Creating JSF Views

Now that we have configured the web application, let's create some JSF view documents using Facelets, as a simple example of what Facelets is capable of doing. For more detailed information and the Facelets tag reference, see the Appendix.

The Happy Birds Directory Example

Let's imagine we need to create a simple directory of birds—the Happy Birds Directory—that consists of pages containing information about different birds, with navigation provided by a table of contents. To do this, we decide to create one page per bird, and as a prototype, we'll create the pages for the parrot and the eagle.

As all pages have a similar layout (content and navigation box), we can create a template and define the different areas. Implementing a page for a bird will be a matter of implementing the specific content for that bird.

So, we can create a project structure like the following:

```
$PROJECT
+- /WEB-INF
   +- /lib [with dependencies]
   +- /web.xml
   +- /faces-config.xml
+- template.xhtml
+- index.xhtml
+- parrot.xhtml
+- eagle.xhtml
+- menu.xhtml
```

In WEB-INF, we have the lib folder with dependencies, the web.xml file configured as explained in the previous section, and the faces-config.xml file.

We create five documents (with the extension *.xhtml). One of them is the template (template.xhtml) used by three of the other pages (index.xhtml, parrot.xhtml, and eagle.xhtml). The last page is the menu (menu.xhtml), which we are going to use to navigate through the application.

The Template

In the template, we define the basic layout of the page with the Facelets UI tag ui:insert, which we can use to define areas in the page that can be overwritten.

To enable the Facelets tags, we use the http://java.sun.com/jsf/facelets namespace. By convention, we define ui as the prefix for the UI Facelets library tags. We declare the namespaces for all the tags we are using in a document. If an invalid namespace is provided, Facelets will report an error during compilation.

The code for the template is shown in Listing 3-1.

Listing 3-1. *template.xhtml*

```
<!DOCTYPE html PUBLIC "-//W3C//DTD
XHTML 1.0 Transitional//EN"
"http://www.w3.org/TR/xhtml1/DTD/ ➥
xhtml1-transitional.dtd">
<html xmlns="http://www.w3.org/1999/xhtml"
      xmlns:ui="http://java.sun.com/jsf/facelets"
      xmlns:f="http://java.sun.com/jsf/core"
      xmlns:h="http://java.sun.com/jsf/html">
<head>
    <title>The Happy Birds Directory</title>
```

```
    <style type="text/css">
        <!--
        .box {
            float: right;
            width: 50%;
            border: black dotted 1px;
            padding: 5px
        }
        -->
    </style>
</head>
<body>
    <h:form>

        <h1>The Happy Birds Directory</h1>

        <div class="box">
            <ui:insert name="navigation"/>
        </div>

        <ui:insert name="main">
            Welcome to the nest!
        </ui:insert>

    </h:form>

</body>
</html>
```

This simple template contains a floating div element that we use to render the content table, followed by a main section that describes our birds. The most important elements on this page are the two ui:insert tags, named navigation and main. So, in the template, we declare the navigation area inside the div element and an open main section. In the construction of the other three pages, you will see how we can override these two areas.

We can define default content for the areas just by nesting this content in the ui:insert tag. For example, if we don't override the main area, the phrase "Welcome to the nest!" will be shown.

The Home Page

The home page, which is the page that greets the user, is index.xhtml. The code for the home page is shown in Listing 3-2.

Listing 3-2. *index.xhtml*

```
<!DOCTYPE html
        PUBLIC "-//W3C//DTD XHTML ➥
1.0 Transitional//EN"
        "http://www.w3.org/TR/xhtml1/DTD/➥
xhtml1-transitional.dtd">
<html xmlns="http://www.w3.org/1999/xhtml"
      xmlns:ui="http://java.sun.com/jsf/facelets"
      xmlns:h="http://java.sun.com/jsf/html">
<body>

This and everything before will be ignored

    <ui:composition template="template.xhtml">

        <ui:define name="navigation">
            <ui:include src="menu.xhtml"/>
        </ui:define>

    </ui:composition>

    This and everything after will be ignored

</body>
</html>
```

Here, we are using three new Facelets tags: `ui:composition`, `ui:define`, and `ui:include`.

We use the `ui:composition` tag's `template` attribute to reference the template we want to use for the page (in our case, the `template.xhtml` document). Everything inside the `ui:composition` tag will be evaluated by Facelets when compiling the document. All elements outside the `ui:composition` tag will be ignored.

Tip Some JSF editor tools are not ready to work with Facelets yet. In this case, the `ui:composition` tag can be handy. We can use it to define elements that these tools might expect outside the `ui:composition` tag, as they will not be processed by Facelets to create the view, but they will be used by the tool to validate the page.

We use the `ui:define` tag to define the content that will go in the areas declared in the template. The `name` attribute of the `ui:define` tag must match the one of the `ui:insert` tag in the template. For the `index.xhtml` view, we only defined the `navigation` area and will use the default `main` area.

In the navigation area, the `ui:include` tag allows us to include the content from another document, in our case, `menu.xhtml`.

The Navigation Menu

As in the home page, we include a menu in the page. The menu is defined in Listing 3-3.

Listing 3-3. *menu.xhtml*

```
<!DOCTYPE html
        PUBLIC "-//W3C//DTD XHTML 1.0 Transitional//EN"
        "http://www.w3.org/TR/xhtml1/DTD/ ➥
xhtml1-transitional.dtd">
<html xmlns="http://www.w3.org/1999/xhtml"
      xmlns:ui="http://java.sun.com/jsf/facelets"
      xmlns:h="http://java.sun.com/jsf/html">
<body>
This and everything before will be ignored
    <ui:composition>

        <h3>Contents table</h3>
        <hr/>

        <h:panelGrid columns="1">

           <h:commandLink value="Home" action="home" />
           <h:commandLink value="Parrot"
                          action="parrot" />
           <h:commandLink value="Eagle"
                          action="eagle" />

        </h:panelGrid>

    </ui:composition>
This and everything after will be ignored
</body>
</html>
```

Again, we use the `ui:composition` tags, and everything outside the tags will be removed when the menu is included in a page. This page uses just a few link elements (`h:commandLink`) with `action` attributes defined to trigger the navigation in our application.

We have defined these rules in the `faces-config.xml` file shown in Listing 3-4.

Listing 3-4. *faces-config.xml*

```
<!DOCTYPE faces-config PUBLIC
  "-//Sun Microsystems, Inc.//DTD ➥
JavaServer Faces Config 1.0//EN"
  "http://java.sun.com/dtd/web-facesconfig_1_1.dtd" >

<faces-config>
```

```
    <application>
        <view-handler>com.sun.facelets.FaceletViewHandler ➥
</view-handler>
    </application>

    <navigation-rule>
        <navigation-case>
            <from-outcome>home</from-outcome>
            <to-view-id>/index.xhtml</to-view-id>
        </navigation-case>
    </navigation-rule>
    <navigation-rule>
        <navigation-case>
            <from-outcome>parrot</from-outcome>
            <to-view-id>/parrot.xhtml</to-view-id>
        </navigation-case>
    </navigation-rule>
    <navigation-rule>
        <navigation-case>
            <from-outcome>eagle</from-outcome>
            <to-view-id>/eagle.xhtml</to-view-id>
        </navigation-case>
    </navigation-rule>
</faces-config>
```

As you can see from the navigation declaration, each link will take the user to one of the pages.

The Bird Pages

The other two pages (`parrot.xhtml` and `eagle.xhtml`) are just sample pages showing information for a couple of birds. They are almost identical to the index page, in the sense that they use the template and specify which content to show in the main and navigation parts. The parrot's page is in Listing 3-5.

Listing 3-5. *parrot.xhtml*

```
<!DOCTYPE html
        PUBLIC "-//W3C//DTD XHTML 1.0 ➥
Transitional//EN"
        "http://www.w3.org/TR/xhtml1/DTD/ ➥
xhtml1-transitional.dtd">
<html xmlns="http://www.w3.org/1999/xhtml"
      xmlns:ui="http://java.sun.com/jsf/facelets"
      xmlns:h="http://java.sun.com/jsf/html">
<body>
This and everything before will be ignored
    <ui:composition template="template.xhtml">
```

```
        <ui:define name="navigation">
            <ui:include src="menu.xhtml"/>
        </ui:define>

        <ui:define name="main">

            <h1>Parrot</h1>

            <p>
                Parrots are interesting birds...
            </p>

        </ui:define>
    </ui:composition>

This and everything after will be ignored

</body>
</html>
```

This time, we put a description of the parrot in the main area by using the `ui:define` tag and matching its name with the one in the `ui:insert` tag of the template. The navigation area just includes the menu, as on the index page.

And, we have a similar page for the eagle in Listing 3-6.

Listing 3-6. *eagle.xhtml*

```
<!DOCTYPE html
        PUBLIC "-//W3C//DTD XHTML 1.0 Transitional//EN"
        "http://www.w3.org/TR/xhtml1/DTD/ ➥
xhtml1-transitional.dtd">
<html xmlns="http://www.w3.org/1999/xhtml"
      xmlns:ui="http://java.sun.com/jsf/facelets"
      xmlns:h="http://java.sun.com/jsf/html">
<body>
This and everything before will be ignored
    <ui:composition template="template.xhtml">

        <ui:define name="navigation">
            <ui:include src="menu.xhtml"/>

            <p>An eagle flying high...</p>
        </ui:define>

        <ui:define name="main">
```

```
            <h1>Eagle</h1>

            <p>
                Eagles are bigger than parrots.
            </p>

        </ui:define>
    </ui:composition>

This and everything after will be ignored

</body>
</html>
```

This page is almost identical to the parrot one, except for implementing the eagle-specific content. We could add more pages to describe different birds and just implement different information for each bird without having to alter the layout.

Of course, this simple version of the Happy Birds Directory could also be implemented using a database and some managed beans, but we wanted to illustrate the most important capabilities of the templating in Facelets.

Migrating an Existing Application from JSP to Facelets

Migrating an existing application that uses JSP for its views to Facelets is pretty straightforward:

1. Include the Facelets JAR and its dependencies.
2. Change the page declaration of your pages from

   ```
   <%@ taglib uri=http://java.sun.com/jsf/html
              prefix="h"%>
   <%@ taglib uri=http://java.sun.com/jsf/core
              prefix="f"%>
   ```

   to

   ```
   <html xmlns="http://www.w3.org/1999/xhtml"
         xmlns:h="http://java.sun.com/jsf/html"
         xmlns:f="http://java.sun.com/jsf/core">
   ```

3. Verify and validate your documents, so they are XHTML compliant.

Now you can forget about some of the headaches you had when using JSP with JSF. With that dealt with, it is time to examine the Unified EL support in Facelets.

Unified Expression Language

The Unified EL was successfully created in an attempt to align the ELs used in JSP 2.0 and JSF 1.1. The Unified EL allowed expressions to be evaluated in a deferred manner, instead of immediately as in the original EL. In JSF, immediate evaluation would be OK the first time a page is rendered, but on postback, that page must be evaluated in the different phases of the cycle and not only in the rendering. JSF needs to convert the values resulting from the expressions, validate them, bind them to server-side components, use them to process events, and so on.

There are other differences between the two ELs. The classic JSP EL can use functions, which are calls to static methods that can be defined in the top-level domain (TLD). However, support for functions didn't go into the JSF EL, because functions cannot be used to dynamically invoke methods on objects.

Also, each of the EL versions uses different syntax for its expressions. JSP EL uses ${...}, and JSF EL uses #{...}.

Because of these differences, the JSF and JSP versions of the EL are not compatible and cannot be mixed in a page. The next piece of code would render an unexpected response when using JSF 1.1 and JSP 2.0:

```
<c:forEach var="bird" items="${directoryBean.birds}">
<h:inputText id="birdName" value="#{bird.name}" />
 </c:forEach>
```

In this example, as `c:forEach` is only evaluated during rendering of the page, the `bird` variable is not available during the other phases of the JSF life cycle. Therefore, the value of the `h:inputText` component will never be updated in the model. Moreover, the previous example would throw an exception when duplicate IDs are found, as JSF would try to create a new `h:inputText` component, with the same ID, for each iteration.

The ELs defined by JSF 1.1 and JSP 2.0 have been integrated into the new Unified EL. Thanks to the Unified EL, JSTL tags such as the iteration tags can now be used intuitively with JSF components.

Facelets uses the new Unified EL. It supports the use of ${...} and #{...} syntax and makes no distinction between the two. Therefore, you can use either one, depending on your particular taste.

Inline Text

With Facelets, you can insert an EL expression anywhere in the page, so the expression can appear in line with text without using a component to output the value referenced by the expression. For instance, the following code will be correctly evaluated when rendering the document:

```
<p>The Happy Birds Directory
   contains #{directoryBean.totalCount} birds.
</p>
```

Tag Libraries

Several tag libraries are already included in the Facelets binaries:

Templating library: This contains the tags using for templating, which was shown in the previous example and will be explained in more detail in the Appendix.

JSF libraries: The two tag libraries for the JavaServer Faces Specification are supported by default by Facelets. They contain all the necessary information to allow you to use JSF tags in your documents the same way you would do in JSP.

JSTL: Facelets provides partial support for JSTL tags. While the Function library is fully supported, the Core library's tags are only partially so. The Core tags supported by Facelets are `c:if`, `c:forEach`, `c:catch`, and `c:set`.

■ **Note** In the current JSTL implementation, all EL variables used in the implemented JSTL tags are backed by the new EL API. Their scope is limited to the current `FaceletContext` and no others. Hence, those variables exist only for the purpose of creating the component tree and do not work to assign variables in other scopes. The reason behind this is that the EL expressions are actually bound to `FaceletContext` and not the evaluated `Object`.

Other Tag Libraries

Other component libraries, such as MyFaces Trinidad, already support Facelets out of the box, as they include the Facelets tag library file in the `/META-INF` folder of the JAR.

However, at the time of this writing, the MyFaces Tomahawk library and its sandbox are not included in that library. When we want to use Tomahawk, we will need to specifically import the taglib file into our application, as shown in the next section. The MyFaces wiki pages contain the most up-to-date information on how to use Tomahawk with Facelets; see `http://wiki.apache.org/myfaces/Use_Facelets_with_Tomahawk`.

Creating a Tag Library

If you want to use other libraries in your Facelets application, you will need to create the tag library file yourself and register it in your `web.xml` file. In this XML document, you need to specify the namespace for the tags and define every tag.

For example, to illustrate how to register the tags, we can use the limited tag library implementation for Tomahawk shown in Listing 3-7.

Listing 3-7. *tomahawk-partial.taglib.xml*

```
<!DOCTYPE facelet-taglib PUBLIC
  "-//Sun Microsystems, Inc.//DTD Facelet ➥
Taglib 1.0//EN"
  "http://java.sun.com/dtd/facelet-taglib_1_0.dtd">
```

```
<facelet-taglib>
 <namespace>http://myfaces.apache.org/tomahawk
</namespace>

<tag>
        <tag-name>inputCalendar</tag-name>
        <component>
            <component-type>
               org.apache.myfaces.HtmlInputCalendar
            </component-type>
            <renderer-type>org.apache.myfaces.Calendar
            </renderer-type>
        </component>
 </tag>
<tag>
        <tag-name>saveState</tag-name>
        <component>
            <component-type>
               org.apache.myfaces.SaveState
        </component-type>
        </component>
 </tag>
<facelet-taglib>
```

This library would only be supporting the `t:inputCalendar` and `t:saveState` components. Of course, this implementation of the Tomahawk library would be very limited, but you can see the MyFaces wiki pages for a more comprehensive implementation. Every Facelets taglib must contain the namespace for the tags followed by the listing of tags (and functions, as you will see later).

Facelets uses a simple document type definition (DTD) to describe the library files:

```
<!ELEMENT facelet-taglib (libraryclass| ➥
(namespace,(tag|function)+))>
<!ATTLIST facelet-taglib xmlns
CDATA #FIXED
"http://java.sun.com/JSF/Facelet">
<!ELEMENT namespace (#PCDATA)>
<!ELEMENT library-class (#PCDATA)>
<!ELEMENT tag (tag-name,(handler- ➥
class|component|converter ➥
|validator|source))>
<!ELEMENT tag-name (#PCDATA)>
<!ELEMENT handler-class (#PCDATA)>
<!ELEMENT component (component-type, ➥
renderer-type?,handler-class?)>
<!ELEMENT component-type (#PCDATA)>
<!ELEMENT renderer-type (#PCDATA)>
```

```
<!ELEMENT converter (converter-id, handler-class?)>
<!ELEMENT converter-id (#PCDATA)>
<!ELEMENT validator (validator-id, handler-class?)>
<!ELEMENT validator-id (#PCDATA)>
<!ELEMENT source (#PCDATA)>
<!ELEMENT function (function-name, ➥
function-class,function-signature)>
<!ELEMENT function-name (#PCDATA)>
<!ELEMENT function-class (#PCDATA)>
<!ELEMENT function-signature (#PCDATA)>
```

Here, we can use the `library-class` element to delegate the definition of the library. This class must implement `com.sun.facelets.tag.TagLibrary`, which is useful when you want to maintain your library from Java.

Tip The abstract class `com.sun.facelets.tag.AbstractTagLibrary` inside Facelets is a basic implementation of `com.sun.facelets.tag.TagLibrary`. You might want to extend this class, as it contains convenient methods to register the elements of the library.

If you are not using the `library-class` element, you must specify a namespace. You will use this namespace in your documents as explained in the beginning of this section. In the rest of the document, you will find the tags and functions.

Remember to register the tag library in the web descriptor file (`web.xml`), if the tag library was not already included in a JAR. Add the library under the parameter `facelets.LIBRARIES`, and separate multiple libraries with semicolons.

Functions

In the tag libraries, you can declare functions, which are invocations of Java static methods. For example, you could have Listing 3-8 in the taglib file.

Listing 3-8. *bird-functions.taglib.xml*

```
<!DOCTYPE facelet-taglib PUBLIC
  "-//Sun Microsystems, Inc.//DTD
Facelet Taglib 1.0//EN"
  "http://java.sun.com/dtd/facelet-taglib_1_0.dtd">

<facelet-taglib>
 <namespace>http://myfaces.apress.com/birds</namespace>
```

```
<function>
        <function-name>isBirdAbleToSpeak</function-name>
        <function-class>
            com.apress.myfaces.BirdFunctions
        </function-class>
        <function-signature>java.lang.String canSpeak(java.lang.String)
</function-signature>
 </function>
</facelet-taglib>
```

In this library, we have defined a single function (though we can define as many as we want) that calls the method with the signature `String canSpeak(String)` from the `BirdFunctions` class. The `BirdFunctions` class is show in Listing 3-9.

Listing 3-9. *BirdFunctions.java*

```
package com.apress.myfaces;

public class BirdFunctions {

    public static String canSpeak(String birdName) {
        if (birdName.equals("parrot")) {
            return "YES";
        }
        return "If you try hard enough, who knows!";
     }
}
```

Functions are part of the EL specification, so we could use the previous function in our JSF views, like in the following snippet:

```
<!DOCTYPE html PUBLIC "-//W3C//DTD
        XHTML 1.0 Transitional//EN"
        "http://www.w3.org/TR/xhtml1/DTD/ ➥
         xhtml1-transitional.dtd">
<html xmlns="http://www.w3.org/1999/xhtml"
      xmlns:b="http://myfaces.apress.com/birds">
<body>
     Parrots can speak:
#{b:isBirdAbleToSpeak('parrot')} <br/>
     Eagles can speak: #{b:isBirdAbleToSpeak('eagle')}
</body></html>
```

And this simple page, which includes two uses of our function, would render

```
Parrots can speak: YES
Eagles can speak: If you try hard enough, who knows!
```

Now that we've seen the Facelets tag libraries, let's look at another useful feature: the `jsfc` attribute.

The jsfc Attribute

Like the Apache Tapestry framework, Facelets provides a way to convert an XML tag into another at compile time via the jsfc attribute. This attribute can be used to create tags for rendering by visual tools and convert them to another. A typical jsfc example follows:

```
<!DOCTYPE html PUBLIC "-//W3C//DTD ➥
XHTML 1.0 Transitional//EN" "http://www.w3.org/TR/xhtml1/DTD/ ➥
xhtml1-transitional.dtd">
<html xmlns="http://www.w3.org/1999/xhtml"
      xmlns:h="http://java.sun.com/jsf/html">

<body>
  <input type="text" jsfc="h:inputText"                    value="#{bird.name}" />
</body>
</html>
```

Compiling this code will convert the input tag into an h:inputText component so we can use its JSF features.

Although using jsfc is more limiting than using the JSF components, it can help when writing pages. Many designers are used to writing pages using visual tools that generate HTML; with the jsfc attribute, they can continue using these tools. By simply decorating the HTML with the jsfc attribute, they can take advantage of JSF simultaneously as well. When using jsfc, the same rules for namespaces and naming apply to the jsfc attribute value.

Facelets Templating and Template Clients

Using templates helps you to meet some of the major goals of developing web applications in the following ways:

- Increase the core's reusability, thus reducing the development and maintenance costs of an application.
- Achieve a common look and feel, as all pages using a specific template will look similar.
- Separate the content from its display and layout, as the relationship Extensible Stylesheet Language (XLST) does for Extensible Markup Language (XML).

Facelets templates can be created from JSF components and HTML tags. Templates can be interwoven thanks to the fact that they are compiled during the render phase.

In Facelets, we distinguish between templates and template clients. The latter use the templates to create variations of the same pattern.

A template defines areas where content can be replaced. Which content is used in those areas is defined by the clients. The template defines the areas using the ui:insert tag, and the clients use the templates with ui:component, ui:composition, ui:fragment, or ui:decorate tags.

Templating in Facelets is not limited to one level. It is possible to have multilevel templating, as a client for one template can be a template for other client templates. Hence, Facelets's powerful templating support allows you to create complex composite applications.

Creating Composition Components

One of the greatest features of Facelets is the ability to create lightweight composition components. You have seen how to use the Facelets templating tags, and now, we will show you how easy it is to create custom and reusable components using those tags. In this section, you will also see how to register those components in a custom taglib, which you can use in any of your Facelets applications.

Facelets provides a simple and fast way to create reusable components using tag source files, which will define the components and fragments that will compose our new component. As you will see in the next sections, creating a component is a fairly simple operation that involves two basic steps:

1. Create the tag source file, which will contain the XHTML code that defines your component.
2. Register the tag in your custom tag library, so it can be used in your Facelets applications.

And finally, you should reuse your component as much as possible. Let's look now at a few examples of custom component creation.

Creating the Custom inputTextLabeled Component

The first demonstration component we are going to create is a combined `h:outputLabel` and `h:inputText` component, which we are going to call `inputTextLabeled`. As combining this functionality is really common in our applications, writing such a component will help us reuse code and simplify our pages.

We want the component to be used like this in the JSF documents:

```
<custom:inputTextLabeled
     label="Name"
     value="#{bird.name}" />
```

We are going to use the `custom` namespace for the components we create in these examples.

Creating the Tag Source File

The first step in creating the component is creating of the tag file. To have a clear organization of the files in our project, we will create a file named `InputTextLabeled.xhtml` under `/WEB-INF/facelets/components`:

```
$PROJECT
+- /WEB-INF
   +- /web.xml
   +- /faces-config
   +- /facelets
```

```
        +- /mycustom.taglib.xml
        +- /components
            +- /InputTextLabeled.xhtml
            +- [other tag files]
+- /[xhtml documents]
```

Listing 3-10 shows the code contained in the source file.

Listing 3-10. *InputTextLabeled.xhtml*

```
<!DOCTYPE html PUBLIC "-//W3C//DTD ➥
XHTML 1.0 Transitional//EN"
        "http://www.w3.org/TR/xhtml1/DTD/ ➥
xhtml1-transitional.dtd">
<html xmlns="http://www.w3.org/1999/xhtml"
      xmlns:ui="http://java.sun.com/jsf/facelets"
      xmlns:h="http://java.sun.com/jsf/html">
<ui:component>
    <h:outputLabel value="#{label}: ">
        <h:inputText value="#{value}"/>
    </h:outputLabel>
</ui:component>

</html>
```

The implementation is really simple. We have created an h:outputLabel component with a nested h:inputText, which is one of the ways to use these two components together (instead of nesting the components, you could use an id in the h:inputText and make the for attribute of the h:outputLabel refer to that id).

The source file shows the use of two EL expressions for the value attributes of the h:outputLabel and h:inputText components. The value of the EL expressions matches the name of the attributes of the custom tag, so we use it on our page like so:

```
<custom:inputTextLabeled
    label="Name"
    value="#{bird.name}" />
```

The label attribute in the custom:inputTextLabeled component will be used as the value of the h:outputLabel, and the value attribute will be used as the value of the h:inputText.

Registering the Tag in the Tag Library

Now that we have our tag file, let's register it in a custom tag library. First, we will need to create the tag library file, which we are going to put in the /WEB-INF/facelets folder. We will arbitrarily call it mycustom.taglib.xml; see Listing 3-11.

Listing 3-11. *mycustom.taglib.xml*

```
<!DOCTYPE facelet-taglib PUBLIC
        "-//Sun Microsystems, Inc.//DTD ➥
Facelet Taglib 1.0//EN"
        "http://java.sun.com/dtd/ ➥
facelet-taglib_1_0.dtd">

<facelet-taglib>
    <namespace>http://myfaces.apress.com/custom ➥
</namespace>

    <tag>
        <tag-name>inputTextLabelled</tag-name>
        <source>components/InputTextLabeled.xhtml
</source>
    </tag>

</facelet-taglib>
```

We have decided to call the tag library namespace `http://myfaces.apress.com/custom`, and we will need to declare this namespace in any pages where we are using the custom component.

After the namespace definition, we can find the tag element that defines our brand new tag. The `tag-name` element refers to the name we want to give to the tag, which in our case is `inputTextLabeled`. The `source` element contains the relative path to the tag file.

The next step is to tell Facelets that we want to use this library in our pages. To do so, we need to declare the library file in the `facelets.LIBRARIES` context parameter in the `web.xml` file shown in Listing 3-12.

Listing 3-12. *web.xml*

```
<context-param>
        <param-name>facelets.LIBRARIES</param-name>
        <param-value>
/WEB-INF/facelets/mycustom.taglib.xml
</param-value>
    </context-param>
...
```

And now we are ready to use the tag in our pages! As you can see, creating a new composite component with a tag and registering it is a fairly simple process.

Using the Tag

To use the tag, we declare the namespace in the top of the page and use the component. For instance, we could have a simple form to create new birds:

```
<!DOCTYPE html
        PUBLIC "-//W3C//DTD XHTML 1.0 Transitional//EN"
        "http://www.w3.org/TR/xhtml1/DTD/ ➥
xhtml1-transitional.dtd">
<html xmlns="http://www.w3.org/1999/xhtml"
      xmlns:ui="http://java.sun.com/jsf/facelets"
      xmlns:f="http://java.sun.com/jsf/core"
      xmlns:h="http://java.sun.com/jsf/html"
      xmlns:custom="http://myfaces.apress.com/custom">
<body>

<f:view>
    <h:form>
        <h:panelGrid columns="1">
          <custom:inputTextLabeled ➥
label="Name" value="#{bird.name}"/>
          <custom:inputTextLabeled ➥
label="Order" value="#{bird.order}"/>
          <custom:inputTextLabeled ➥
label="Family" value="#{bird.family}"/>
           <h:commandButton ➥
value="Add Bird" ➥ actionListener="#{birdDirectory.addBird}"/>
        </h:panelGrid>
    </h:form>
</f:view>
</body>
</html>
```

Creating the simpleColumn Custom Component

The custom tag we are going to create now is `custom:simpleColumn`, which will simplify the creation of columns in a data table. It will define the header of the column and what to show in each cell, and we will use it like this:

```
<h:dataTable …>
    <custom:simpleColumn ➥
headerText="Name" ➥
cellText="#{item.name}"/> ➥
    …
</h:dataTable>
```

Creating the Tag Source File

In this case, the source file for the tag is very simple too; see Listing 3-13. We create it in `WEB-INF/facelets/components`, with the rest of our custom components.

Listing 3-13. *SimpleColumn.xhtml*

```
<!DOCTYPE html PUBLIC "-//W3C//DTD ➥
XHTML 1.0 Transitional//EN"
        "http://www.w3.org/TR/xhtml1/DTD/ ➥
xhtml1-transitional.dtd">
<html xmlns="http://www.w3.org/1999/xhtml"
      xmlns:ui="http://java.sun.com/jsf/facelets"
      xmlns:f="http://java.sun.com/jsf/core"
      xmlns:h="http://java.sun.com/jsf/html">

<ui:composition>
    <h:column>
        <f:facet name="header">
            <h:outputText value="#{headerText}"/>
        </f:facet>
        <h:outputText value="#{cellText}"/>
    </h:column>
</ui:composition>

</html>
```

This case is very similar to the implementation used for `custom:inputTextLabeled`. However, we are using `ui:composition` here instead of `ui:component`, so no component instance will be added to the JSF tree. Here too, we are using a couple of EL expressions (`headerText` and `cellText`) that must match the attributes of the custom tag.

Registering the Tag in the Tag Library

Again, we need to register the custom tag in our `mycustom.taglib.xml` file, shown in Listing 3-14.

Listing 3-14. *Updated mycustom.taglib.xml*

```
<facelet-taglib>
    ...
    <tag>
        <tag-name>simpleColumn</tag-name>
        <source>components/SimpleColumn.xhtml</source>
    </tag>
    ...
</facelet-taglib>
```

The library should be already declared in the `facelets.LIBRARIES` context parameter in the `web.xml` file, because we did so for the previous custom tag.

Note It is possible to register more than one library in the `facelets.LIBRARIES` context parameter by using a semicolon (;) to separate the libraries.

Using the Tag

We could use our custom tag to replace any existing `h:column` in our applications, as shown in Listing 3-15.

Listing 3-15. *simplecolumn-example.xhtml*

```
<!DOCTYPE html
        PUBLIC "-//W3C//DTD XHTML 1.0 Transitional//EN"
        "http://www.w3.org/TR/xhtml1/DTD/ ➥
xhtml1-transitional.dtd">
<html xmlns="http://www.w3.org/1999/xhtml"
      xmlns:ui="http://java.sun.com/jsf/facelets"
      xmlns:f="http://java.sun.com/jsf/core"
      xmlns:h="http://java.sun.com/jsf/html"
      xmlns:custom="http://myfaces.apress.com/custom">
<body>

        <h:dataTable var="item" ➥
value="#{birdDirectory.allBirds}">
            <custom:simpleColumn ➥
headerText="Name"
cellText="#{item.name}"/> ➥
         <custom:simpleColumn headerText="Order"
cellText="#{item.order}"/>
         <custom:simpleColumn headerText="Family"
cellText="#{item.family}"/>
        </h:dataTable>

</body>
</html>
```

The resulting page will look simpler and cleaner, and by reusing code (we don't have to declare the header facet all the time and so on), maintenance is simplified.

Creating the scrollableDataTable Custom Component

Now it's time to start creating some cooler composition components. The one we are going to create now will be a composition of a `h:dataTable` component and Tomahawk's `t:dataScroller`, so using the custom tag will produce tables with scrolling capabilities. To create such a table, we will only need to write this piece of code in our pages:

```
<custom:scrollableDataTable id="table1" value="#{birdDirectory.allBirds}">
...
</custom:scrollableDataTable>
```

Creating the Tag Source File

In the tag file, we are going to use one `h:dataTable` and two `t:dataScroller` components, one to create navigation between table pages and the other to show contextual information about the rows shown to the user.

Note In this example, we are using the MyFaces Tomahawk library of components. As we mentioned earlier, Facelets does not include support for Tomahawk out of the box, and at the time of this writing, Tomahawk does not include a default tag library file in its JAR file. Therefore, we must create such a tag library or download an existing tag library for Tomahawk, which is an easier option. A useful place to check on Facelets support for Tomahawk is in the MyFaces wiki pages (`http://wiki.apache.org/myfaces/Use_Facelets_with_Tomahawk`).

In our `WEB-INF/facelets` folder, we include the `tomahawk.taglib.xml` file, which, at least for this example's purposes, should include the tag for `t:dataScroller`; see Listing 3-16.

Listing 3-16. *tomahawk.taglib.xml*

```
<!DOCTYPE facelet-taglib PUBLIC
  "-//Sun Microsystems, Inc.//DTD ➥
Facelet Taglib 1.0//EN"
  "http://java.sun.com/dtd/facelet-taglib_1_0.dtd">

<facelet-taglib>
    <namespace>http://myfaces.apache.org/tomahawk
</namespace>

   ...
    <tag>
        <tag-name>dataScroller</tag-name>
        <component>
            <component-type>
org.apache.myfaces.HtmlDataScroller</component-type>
            <renderer-type>
org.apache.myfaces.DataScroller</renderer-type>
        </component>
    </tag>
   ...

</facelet-taglib>
```

Now, we are ready to use the `dataScroller` in our tag files. As we have done with the previous custom tags, we create the source file under `WEB-INF/facelets/components`, and this time, we name it `ScrollableDataTable.xhtml`; see Listing 3-17.

Listing 3-17. *ScrollableDataTable.xhtml*

```
<!DOCTYPE html PUBLIC "-//W3C//DTD ➥
XHTML 1.0 Transitional//EN"
        "http://www.w3.org/TR/xhtml1/DTD/ ➥
xhtml1-transitional.dtd">
<html xmlns="http://www.w3.org/1999/xhtml"
      xmlns:ui="http://java.sun.com/jsf/facelets"
      xmlns:f="http://java.sun.com/jsf/core"
      xmlns:h="http://java.sun.com/jsf/html"
      xmlns:t="http://myfaces.apache.org/tomahawk">

<ui:component>

    <h:dataTable id="#{id}" var="item" ➥
value="#{value}" rows="10">
         <ui:insert/>
     </h:dataTable>

           <h:panelGrid columns="1">

               <t:dataScroller
                      for="#{id}"
                      fastStep="10"
                      pageCountVar="pageCount"
                      pageIndexVar="pageIndex"
                      paginator="true"
                      paginatorMaxPages="9"
                 paginatorActiveColumnStyle="font-weight:bold;"
                      immediate="true">
               </t:dataScroller>

               <t:dataScroller
                   for="#{id}"
                   rowsCountVar="rowsCount"
                   displayedRowsCountVar="rowCountVar"
                   firstRowIndexVar="firstRowIndex"
                   lastRowIndexVar="lastRowIndex"
                   pageCountVar="pageCount"
                   immediate="true"
                   pageIndexVar="pageIndex">
```

```
            <h:outputFormat
value="Total {0}. ➥
Displaying {1} rows, from {2} to {3}. ➥
Page {4}/{5}">
                    <f:param value="#{rowsCount}" />
                    <f:param
                       value="#{rowCountVar}" />
                    <f:param
                       value="#{firstRowIndex}" />
                    <f:param
                       value="#{lastRowIndex}" />
                          <f:param value="#{pageindex}" />
                          <f:param value="#{pagecount}" />
                      </h:outputFormat>
                  </t:dataScroller>

            </h:panelGrid>
    </ui:component>

</html>
```

The h:dataTable component used contains only a nested ui:insert component. Hence, whatever we put as nested content for our custom tag will appear as a child of h:dataTable, so we can insert the columns as we would do normally.

Next, we have the two dataScroller components. Both have the for attribute pointing to the id of the dataTable, which is defined by an EL expression. We will need to provide an id attribute in our custom tag. We could have decided to hard-code the id in the source tag, but in that case, we would only be able to use one custom:scrollableDataTable per page.

Note that we cannot use an EL expression for the var attribute of the dataTable. In the previous example, the value for the var attribute value is item (it could have been foobar or any other arbitrary name). This means that whenever we use the variable item in any expression inside the table, we will be referring to each element from the collection or data model passed to the table in the value attribute.

Registering the Tag in the Tag Library

We add the custom tag to the mycustom.taglib.xml; see Listing 3-18.

Listing 3-18. *mycustom.taglib.xml for the scrollableDataTable Custom Component*

```
<facelet-taglib>
    ...
    <tag>
        <tag-name>scrollableDataTable</tag-name>
        <source>components/ScrollableDataTable.xhtml
        </source>
    </tag>
     ...
</facelet-taglib>
```

Using the Tag

Now, we can start using our new fancy composite component by inserting the tag where we desire.

Listing 3-19 shows a small example where we use the composite component explained in the previous section. The custom scrollable table is used to show some of our familiar birds.

Listing 3-19. *scrollabledatatable-example.xhtml*

```
<!DOCTYPE html
        PUBLIC "-//W3C//DTD XHTML 1.0 Transitional//EN"
        "http://www.w3.org/TR/xhtml1/DTD/ ➥
xhtml1-transitional.dtd">
<html xmlns="http://www.w3.org/1999/xhtml"
      xmlns:ui="http://java.sun.com/jsf/facelets"
      xmlns:h="http://java.sun.com/jsf/html"
      xmlns:custom="http://myfaces.apress.com/custom">
<body>
    <h:form>

        <custom:scrollableDataTable
                 id="table1"
                 value="#{birdDirectory.allBirds}">
           <custom:simpleColumn
                 headerText="Name"
                 cellText="#{item.name}"/>
           <custom:simpleColumn
                 headerText="Order"
                 cellText="#{item.order}"/>
            <custom:simpleColumn
                 headerText="Family"
                 cellText="#{item.family}"/>
               <h:column>
                   <h:outputText value="Empty column"/>
               </h:column>
        </custom:scrollableDataTable>

    </h:form>
</body>
</html>
```

As you can see, like in the standard `h:dataTable`, we can nest columns (be they `h:columns` or our custom columns). The rendered result will be completely different than the `h:dataTable` component's results though, as our custom `dataTable` will be paged and will have scrolling capabilities.

Creating the editableColumn Custom Component

When creating a tag, we can use other custom tags in our code. This is the case for the tag we are going to create now, `custom:editableColumn`, which render cells that can be edited:

```
<h:dataTable ...>
    <custom:editableColumn
        headerText="Name"
        cellText="#{item.name}"
        editMode="true"/>
    ...
</h:dataTable>
```

Creating the Tag Source File

The tag file is similar to that of `custom:simpleColumn`, as both contain columns with simple headers. Depending on the value of the `editMode` attribute, which must be a Boolean value, an `h:outputText` or a `custom:inputTextLabeled` component will be shown. The tag source file is shown in Listing 3-20.

Listing 3-20. *EditableColumn.xhtml*

```
<!DOCTYPE html PUBLIC "-//W3C//DTD ➥
XHTML 1.0 Transitional//EN"
        "http://www.w3.org/TR/xhtml1/DTD/ ➥
xhtml1-transitional.dtd">
<html xmlns="http://www.w3.org/1999/xhtml"
      xmlns:ui="http://java.sun.com/jsf/facelets"
      xmlns:f="http://java.sun.com/jsf/core"
      xmlns:h="http://java.sun.com/jsf/html"
      xmlns:custom="http://myfaces.apress.com/custom">

<ui:composition>
    <h:column>
        <f:facet name="header">
            <h:outputText value="#{headerText}"/>
        </f:facet>
        <h:outputText value="#{cellText}"
                      rendered="#{!editMode}"/>

        <h:panelGroup rendered="#{editMode}">
           <custom:inputTextLabeled
             label="#{headerText}" value="#{cellText}"/>
        </h:panelGroup>

    </h:column>
</ui:composition>

</html>
```

Registering the Tag in the Tag Library

We add the custom tag to the `mycustom.taglib.xml` file; see Listing 3-21.

Listing 3-21. *mycustom.taglib.xml with the editableColumn Tag*

```
<facelet-taglib>
    ...
    <tag>
        <tag-name>editableColumn</tag-name>
        <source>components/EditableColumn.xhtml</source>
    </tag>
    ...
</facelet-taglib>
```

Using the Tag

We could use the `editableColumn` tag in our `scrollableDataTable` component to allow for editing of the content in the table. For instance, we could have buttons to toggle between normal and edit mode as shown in Listing 3-22.

Listing 3-22. *editablecolumn-example.xhtml*

```
<!DOCTYPE html
        PUBLIC "-//W3C//DTD XHTML 1.0 Transitional//EN"
        "http://www.w3.org/TR/xhtml1/DTD/ ➥
xhtml1-transitional.dtd">
<html xmlns="http://www.w3.org/1999/xhtml"
      xmlns:ui="http://java.sun.com/jsf/facelets"
      xmlns:h="http://java.sun.com/jsf/html"
      xmlns:custom="http://myfaces.apress.com/custom">
<head>
    <title>custom:simpleColumn</title>
</head>
<body>
    <h:form>

        <custom:scrollableDataTable
          id="table2" value="#{birdDirectory.allBirds}">
            <custom:simpleColumn
                headerText="Name"
                cellText="#{item.name}"/>
            <custom:editableColumn
                headerText="Order"
                cellText="#{item.order}"
                editMode="#{userBean.editMode}"/>
```

```
            <custom:editableColumn
                headerText="Family"
                cellText="#{item.family}"
                editMode="#{userBean.editMode}"/>
        </custom:scrollableDataTable>

        <h:commandButton value="Edit Mode"
         actionListener="#{userBean.switchToEditMode}"
         rendered="#{!userBean.editMode}"/>
        <h:commandButton value="Normal Mode"
         actionListener="#{userBean.switchToNormalMode}"
         rendered="#{userBean.editMode}"/>
    </h:form>
</body>
</html>
```

Cool, isn't it? And simple.

Reusing the Custom Tag Library

For our custom tags, we have directly created the necessary files under `WEB-INF/facelets`, so our nice composite components can be used in only one application. Of course, we can create a tag library that can be used in many applications.

To do that, we could bundle everything in a JAR file that could have the following structure:

```
$JAR_PROJECT
+- /META-INF
   +- /mycustom.taglib.xml
+- /tags
   +- InputTextLabeled.xhtml
   +- SimpleColumn.xhtml
   +- [other tag files]
```

In the `/META-INF/mycustom.taglib.xml` file, we would be registering the tags, as shown in Listing 3-23.

Listing 3-23. *Registering Tags in mycustom.taglib.xml*

```
<!DOCTYPE facelet-taglib PUBLIC
        "-//Sun Microsystems, Inc.//DTD ➥
Facelet Taglib 1.0//EN"
        "http://java.sun.com/dtd/ ➥
facelet-taglib_1_0.dtd">

<facelet-taglib>
    <namespace>http://myfaces.apress.com/custom
     </namespace>
```

```
    <tag>
        <tag-name>inputTextLabeled</tag-name>
        <source>/tags/InputTextLabeled.xhtml
</source>
    </tag>
    <tag>
        <tag-name>scrollableDataTable</tag-name>
        <source>/tags/ScrollableDataTable.xhtml</source>
    </tag>
    ...

</facelet-taglib>
```

And you are ready to use your custom tag library in any application, as Facelets will automatically search for tag library definitions in the META-INF folder of the JAR files.

Extending Facelets

Like JSF, Facelets was designed with extensibility in mind. It has a simple and open architecture focused only on the creation of the component tree and interweaving of content. As Facelets only extends one part of JSF, it can be used with any other framework built on top of JSF.

Facelets Architecture

Facelets extends the ViewHandler class with the FaceletViewHandler class to tweak the rendering behavior and the strategy for saving and restoring the view state. Facelets view creation follows the process outlined in this section.

First, the FaceletViewHandler creates a new UIViewRoot when there is a request for a new JSF page. The default behavior of JSF 1.1 (not 1.2) is to invoke the restore of the view in the first request, but FaceletViewHandler skips this step and goes directly to render the view if using JSF 1.1.

If Facelets is not supposed to handle the request, the rendering will be delegated to the parent ViewHandler class.

Before rendering the view, a Facelets instance is created by the FaceletFactory class that is used to populate the UIComponent elements of the view. To do this, UIViewRoot is applied to the Facelets instance:

```
FacesContext faces = FacesContext.getCurrentInstance();
FaceletFactory factory = FaceletFactory.getInstance();
Facelet facelet = factory.getFacelet("/main.xhtml");
facelet.apply(faces, faces.getViewRoot());
```

Next, UIViewRoot is rendered to the response, and the page is shown to the user. The essential information (e.g., form data) from the state of the tree is saved for subsequent requests. Inline text and other transient components are not stored.

When a subsequent request comes to the JSF application, the view is restored with the state information saved from the previous request. This view is then passed through the JSF life cycle, which will end, depending on the action that was fired, in the creation of a new view or a rerendering of the same view (if there were validation errors).

If the view is rerendered, the Facelets class is used to complement the restoring of the view with the unsaved inline text and transient components.

`UIViewRoot` is then asked by the view handler to render itself to the response.

This process is repeated again when a new request comes.

The Facelets class's (`com.sun.facelets.Facelet`) only mission is to populate the component tree. It can be accessed at the same time by several threads, and it is compiled into memory so it can be effectively shared by all the requests. Only one `com.sun.facelets.Facelet` instance exists per XML or XHTML resource.

■ **Note** Optimized tree generation is one of the major advantages of Facelets over JSP. The purpose of JSP is to render output by generating a class that contains a long list of `out.println()` methods. In JSF, JSP is used to create the component tree by encapsulating the rendered output into components along with the JSF ones. As we are interested in building the tree, Facelets is more optimal than JSP, as it was designed particularly for this purpose.

Once the Facelets instance is applied to the `UIViewRoot`, the component tree is populated. The logic to populate the tree is delegated to an internal tree of participants, implementations of `FaceletHandler` (`com.sun.facelets.FaceletHandler`) created by the Facelets compiler. They participate in the tree creation by receiving `UIComponent` elements and processing them accordingly.

The `FaceletHandler` interface is very simple and only contains a method to apply some behavior when the `UIComponent` object is passed:

```
public void apply(FaceletContext ctx,
                  UIComponent parent)
        throws IOException, FacesException,
               FaceletException, ELException;
```

You will see in the next section how a `FaceletHandler` can be used to define the behavior of the tags and components that are part of the Facelets framework.

Custom Tag Development

`TagHandler` is an essential element in the Facelets framework. Facelets builds a stateless tree of `TagHandler` components shared by all request to coordinate the building of the `UIComponent` objects. The `TagHandler` components have the logic to decide whether the body of a tag should be added to the component tree.

Note A `TagHandler` component is effective for all events other than postbacks. On postback, the tree is not rebuilt.

The attributes of a tag are defined in the `TagHandler` component and not in a separate XML or `*.tld` file like for JSP.

As an example, let's create a `TagHandler` component that calculates a random number and puts it into the context so it can be reused in the page. The code for `RandomGeneratorTagHandler` could be something like this:

```
public class RandomGeneratorTagHandler extends TagHandler
{
    private TagAttribute min;
    private TagAttribute max;
    private TagAttribute var;

    public RandomGeneratorTagHandler ➥
          (TagConfig tagConfig)
    {
        super(tagConfig);

        // min attribute
        this.min = getAttribute("min");

        // max attribute
        this.max = getAttribute("max");

        // var attribute
        this.var = getRequiredAttribute("var");
    }

    public void apply(FaceletContext faceletContext,
                      UIComponent parent)
                throws IOException, FacesException,
                       FaceletException, ELException
    {
            int minValue = Integer.MIN_VALUE;
            if (this.min != null)
            {
                minValue = min.getInt(faceletContext);
            }
```

```
            int maxValue = Integer.MAX_VALUE;
            if (this.max != null)
            {
                maxValue = max.getInt(faceletContext);
            }

            int randomNum =
              new Random().nextInt(maxValue)+ minValue;

            faceletContext.setAttribute
             (var.getValue(faceletContext), randomNum);
            this.nextHandler.apply(faceletContext,
             parent);
        }
    }
```

As the previous snippet shows, our class extends the foundation abstract class `TagHandler` and implements its abstract method, `apply(FaceletContext,UIComponent)`. In the constructor, we have defined the three possible variables that this handler is going to accept:

- `min`: An optional attribute that defines the minimum random number. By default, the value is `Integer.MIN_VALUE`.
- `max`: An optional attribute that defines the maximum random number. By default, the value is `Integer.MAX_VALUE`.
- `var`: A required attribute that contains the name of the variable to be set with the `random` attribute. In our page, we will use this variable name when using this attribute.

We use the method `getAttribute()` or `getRequiredAttribute()` to get the appropriate attribute from the list of attributes passed to the tag in a JSF page. The `getRequiredAttribute()` method checks if the attribute has been used and throws an exception if it has not.

In the `apply(FaceletContext,UIComponent)` method, we implement the behavior of the tag. We check if the `min` and `max` attributes are `null`, initializing them to the minimum and maximum values if that is the case. Next, we generate the random value and set it to `FaceletContext`, so it can be used by other tags in the page. Finally, we invoke the `apply` method for the subsequent Facelets handler to continue generating the tree for the children of the tag.

Once we have implemented the tag handler, we register it in the tag library. We need to use the `handler-class` element to point to the tag handler we have created, as shown in Listing 3-24.

Listing 3-24. *mycustom.taglib.xml Using handler-class*

```
<facelet-taglib>
 <namespace>http://myfaces.apress.com/custom
</namespace>
...
    <tag>
        <tag-name>random</tag-name>
         <handler-class>
            com.apress.myfaces.RandomGeneratorTagHandler
         </handler-class>
    </tag>
...
</facelet-taglib>
```

In our view document, we would use the tag like in this snippet:

```
<custom:random var="randomValue" min="0" max="10">
        <h:outputText
            value="Random number: #{randomValue}"/>
 </custom:random>
```

The preceding snippet would output something like this:

```
Random number: 6
```

Using Metatags

In some cases, tag attributes need to be set in a special way. For instance, a specialized component with an attribute must be evaluated to a method with a specific signature. Facelets provides the class `com.sun.facelets.tag.MetaTagHandler`, which we can extend to use its automatic wiring capabilities for setting these special attributes. This class, which itself extends `TagHandler`, uses a few objects to coordinate the wiring:

- `MetaData`: This defines how to wire dynamic or literal state into the passed `Object`.
- `MetaDataTarget`: This determines how and which `MetaData` will be wired in `MetaRule`.
- `MetaRule`: This defines the rule for `MetaData` on the passed `MetaDataTarget`.
- `MetaRuleset`: This mutable set of rules will be used in automatically wiring state to a particular object instance. Rules assigned to this object will be composed into a single `MetaData` instance.

The `MetaDataHandler` declares two methods, which can be extended: `setAttributes(FaceletContext,Object)` and `createMetaRuleset(Class)`. The first method will be invoked by the subclasses according to the set of rules (`MetaRuleset`) created by the second method.

As you have seen in previous sections, if we create a custom tag handler, we will need to register it by using the `handler-class` element in the tag library.

The Facelets API provides three implementations of the MetaTagHandler that can be customized to automatically wire the attributes in components, converters, or validators. We are going to see these in the following sections.

Custom ComponentHandlers

Wiring in components can be customized by extending the com.sun.facelets.tag.jsf.ComponentHandler class. One of the implementations already provided by Facelets is HtmlComponentHandler:

```
public class HtmlComponentHandler extends ComponentHandler {
     public HtmlComponentHandler
              (ComponentConfig config)
     {
         super(config);
     }

     protected MetaRuleset
              createMetaRuleset(Class type) {
         return super.createMetaRuleset(type)
                    .alias("class", "styleClass");
     }
}
```

In HtmlComponentHandler, the createMetaRuleset method is overridden to wire the class attribute to the styleClass bean property. If we want to enable the automatic wiring for an existing component, we need to register the handler in the taglib, associating it with the component:

```
<facelet-taglib>
<namespace>
   http://myfaces.apress.com/custom
</namespace>
...
    <tag>
        <tag-name>anotherTag</tag-name>
        <component>
          <component-type>
             com.apresss.myfaces.SomeComponent
          </component-type>
          <renderer-type>
             com.apresss.myfaces.SomeComponentRenderer
          </rendere-type>
```

```
        <handler-class>
          com.apresss.myfaces.HtmlComponentHandler
        </handler-class>
      </component>
    </tag>
...
</facelet-taglib>
```

Once we've compiled the preceding code, when using the `anotherTag` in our page, the attribute `class` would be wired to the attribute `styleClass` of `SomeComponent`.

Let's now look at a more complex example not provided by Facelets: the component handler needed by the Tomahawk's `inputSuggestAjax` component (at the time of this writing, this handler is in the sandbox). The following example shows how to make it work properly in Facelets:

```
public class InputSuggestAjaxComponentHandler
                           extends HtmlComponentHandler
{
    private TagAttribute maxSuggestedItems;

   public InputSuggestAjaxComponentHandler ➥
             (ComponentConfig tagConfig) {
      super(tagConfig);

       maxSuggestedItems =
               getAttribute("maxSuggestedItems");
   }

   protected MetaRuleset createMetaRuleset(Class type)
    {
        MetaRuleset metaRuleset =
            super.createMetaRuleset(type);
        Class[] paramList =
            (maxSuggestedItems != null) ?
              new Class[]{String.class, Integer.class} :
                new Class[]{String.class};
        MetaRule metaRule =
              new MethodRule("suggestedItemsMethod",
                             List.class, paramList);

        metaRuleset.addRule(metaRule);

        return metaRuleset;
    }
}
```

The inputSuggestAjax tag contains the suggestedItemsMethod attribute, which accepts an EL method expression. The expression must evaluate to a method in a backing bean, which is the method that provides suggestions to the component based on a prefix (whatever the user has already introduced in the field rendered by the component). Optionally, the method invoked can contain a second parameter, corresponding to the value of the maxSuggestedItems attribute, to limit the amount of suggestions returned by the method.

To do the wiring, in the component tag handler, we override the createMetaRuleSet method to return a set with a MetaRule for the method we want to invoke. We use the MetaRule's extension MethodRule, where we define the name of the attribute, the type returned, and an array of parameter types. As the method we need to invoke has two variations, depending on the presence of the maxSuggestedItems attribute, the size of the array of parameter types is variable.

Finally, we need to register the tag, as shown in Listing 3-25.

Listing 3-25. *tomahawk-sandbox.taglib.xml*

```
...
<tag>
        <tag-name>inputSuggestAjax</tag-name>
        <component>
            <component-type>
               org.apache.myfaces.InputSuggestAjax
            </component-type>
            <renderer-type>
               org.apache.myfaces.InputSuggestAjax
            </renderer-type>
            <handler-class>
     com.apress.myfaces.InputSuggestAjaxComponentHandler
            </handler-class>
      </component>
    </tag>
...
```

Custom ConvertHandlers

As MetaTagHandler can wire attributes on any instance of Object, not just UIComponents like in the previous example, we can use it to implement custom validators by extending com.sun.facelets.tag.jsf.ConvertHandler. For example, we can find the class com.sun.facelets.tag.jsf.core.ConvertNumberHandler in the API:

```
public final class ConvertNumberHandler
                           extends ConvertHandler
{

    private final TagAttribute locale;
```

```
    public ConvertNumberHandler(TagConfig config)
    {
        super(config);
        this.locale = this.getAttribute("locale");
    }

    /**
     * Returns a new NumberConverter
     */
    protected Converter createConverter
                        (FaceletContext ctx)
                  throws FacesException, ELException,
                         FaceletException
    {
        return ctx.getFacesContext().getApplication()
         .createConverter(NumberConverter.CONVERTER_ID);
    }

    protected void setAttributes
                   (FaceletContext ctx, Object obj)
    {
        super.setAttributes(ctx, obj);
        NumberConverter c = (NumberConverter) obj;
        if (this.locale != null) {
            c.setLocale(ComponentSupport.getLocale(ctx,
                        this.locale));
        }
    }

    protected MetaRuleset createMetaRuleset
                            Class type)
    {
        return super.createMetaRuleset(type)
                   .ignore("locale");
    }
}
```

This example implements custom wiring for the `locale` attribute in the `setAttributes(Faceletscontext,Object)` method. As we are taking care of the handling of the locale, we can tell the `createMetaRuleset(Class)` method to ignore that attribute. The other properties of the `NumberConverter` will be treated normally.

Custom ValidateHandlers

We can wire validators too, by extending `com.sun.facelets.tag.jsf.ValidateHandler`. There is a default implementation in the Facelets API, which is `com.sun.facelets.tag.jsf.core.ValidateDelegateHandler`:

```
public final class ValidateDelegateHandler
                            extends ValidateHandler
{

  private final TagAttribute validatorId;

  public ValidateDelegateHandler(TagConfig config)
  {
      super(config);
      this.validatorId =
          this.getRequiredAttribute("validatorId");
  }

  /**
   * Uses the specified "validatorId"
   * to get a new Validator instance from the
   * Application.
   *
   */
  protected Validator createValidator
                        (FaceletContext ctx)
  {
      return ctx.getFacesContext()
                .getApplication()
                .createValidator(
                    this.validatorId.getValue(ctx));
  }

  protected MetaRuleset
            createMetaRuleset(Class type)
  {
      return super.createMetaRuleset(type).ignoreAll();
  }
}
```

As we are doing all the attribute mapping ourselves, we can call the `ignoreAll()` method for the `MetaRuleset`.

Custom Resource Resolvers

It is possible to modify the behavior of Facelets when resolving URL resources. Let's have a look at this case:

```
<ui:include source="/myFavoritecode.xhtml"/>
```

By default, Facelets will try to get the URL `myFavoriteCode.xtml` by resolving the resource from the file system. But, like many other parts in Facelets, the resource resolver could be extended, for instance, to fetch the resources from the classpath as well. This would allow you to use in your pages or components, templates, or source files that can be found in other JARs.

This could be possible by extending the `com.sun.facelets.impl.DefaultResourceResolver` class, like in the following implementation:

```
public class SourceJarResolver
       extends DefaultResourceResolver
{
    public SourceJarResolver() {
        super();
    }

    public URL resolveUrl(String path)
    {
        // delegate the default URL resolution
        // to the superclass
        URL url = super.resolveUrl(path);

        // if no URL is found, try to
        // get the resource from the classpath
        if (url == null)
        {
            // remove the starting forward slash
            // if found
            if (path.startsWith("/"))
            {
                path = path.substring(1);
            }

            // get the resource from the classpath
            url = Thread.currentThread()
                        .getContextClassLoader()
                        .getResource(path);
        }
        return url;
    }

    public String toString()
    {
        return "SourceJarResolver";
    }
}
```

In this custom resource resolver, we first try the default resolution by delegating to the superclass, and if no resource is found, we try to get the resource from the classpath.

To use this custom resolver, you would need to register it in the web.xml file:

```
<context-param>
   <param-name>facelets.RESOURCE_RESOLVER</param-name>
   <paramvalue>
      com.apress.myfaces.SourceJarResolver
   </param-value>
</context-param>
```

Extending the ViewHandler

The Facelets ViewHandler (com.sun.facelets.FaceletViewHandler) class can be extended as well. It also has many protected methods that can be overridden, so you can tweak the initialization, compiler selection, response writer, response encoding, view rendering, and more.

To extend ViewHandler, we need to provide the view handler class in the faces-config.xml file:

```
<faces-config>
    <application>
        <view-handler>
           com.sun.facelets.MyExtendedFaceletViewHandler
        </view-handler>
    </application>
...
</faces-config>
```

Summary

In this chapter, you learned about Facelets. You now know what Facelets is and how to extend it. You saw how it neatly bridges the gap between JSP and JSF and how it can be useful in templating and in easily creating JSF components, as well as its support for Unified Expression Language. You learned also how to migrate an existing JSF application that uses JSP for its view to Facelets.

CHAPTER 4

The Trinidad Project

Apache Trinidad is a subproject of MyFaces donated by Oracle to the Apache Software Foundation (ASF). The project was formerly known as Oracle ADF Faces and renamed "Trinidad" after a long voting process. Although Trinidad contains a wide range of components, it is more than a component library: it also contains many goodies that solve common development challenges and add capabilities by expanding JSF.

These goodies include pageFlowScope, a dialog framework, client-side conversion and validation, skinning, partial page rendering, and more. This chapter begins with Trinidad's core, goes through its extensions, covers some of the advanced components, and ends with configuration tips.

Trinidad Setup

Setting up an application for using Trinidad can be done with the following steps:

1. Download the latest MyFaces Trinidad binary distribution from `http://myfaces.apache.org/trinidad/download.html`.
2. Extract the downloaded zip file.
3. Copy `lib/trinidad-api-1.x.x.jar` and `lib/trinidad-impl-1.x.x` to the `WEB-INF/lib` folder of the web application.
4. Set up the Trinidad filter and resource servlet in `web.xml`; see Listing 4-1.
5. Set up the Trinidad render kit in `faces-config.xml`; see Listing 4-2.
6. Add the Trinidad tag library declarations to JSP files.

   For JSP documents, use this declaration:

   ```
   <jsp:root version="2.0" xmlns:tr="http://myfaces.apache.org/trinidad" >
   ```

   For JSP pages, use this one:

   ```
   <%@ taglib uri="http://myfaces.apache.org/trinidad" prefix="tr" %>
   ```

You can read more about tuning and configuring Trinidad applications in the "Tuning and Configuration" section.

Tip If you are starting a Trinidad application from scratch, you can download the example distribution, which contains a blank Trinidad application (`trinidad-blank-1.x.x.war`) with all of the setup steps already configured.

Listing 4-1. *Trinidad Filter and Resource Servlet in web.xml*

```
<web-app>
    ...
    <filter>
        <filter-name>trinidad</filter-name>
        <filter-class>
            org.apache.myfaces.trinidad.webapp.TrinidadFilter
        </filter-class>
    </filter>

    <filter-mapping>
        <filter-name>trinidad</filter-name>
        <servlet-name>Faces Servlet</servlet-name>
    </filter-mapping>

    <servlet>
        <servlet-name>Faces Servlet</servlet-name>
        <servlet-class>
            javax.faces.webapp.FacesServlet
        </servlet-class>
    </servlet>

    <servlet>
        <servlet-name>resources</servlet-name>
        <servlet-class>
            org.apache.myfaces.trinidad.webapp.ResourceServlet
        </servlet-class>
    </servlet>

    <servlet-mapping>
        <servlet-name>Faces Servlet</servlet-name>
        <url-pattern>/faces/*</url-pattern>
    </servlet-mapping>

    <servlet-mapping>
        <servlet-name>resources</servlet-name>
        <url-pattern>/adf/*</url-pattern>
    </servlet-mapping>
    ...
</web-app>
```

Listing 4-2. *Trinidad Render Kit in faces-config.xml*

```
<faces-config>
  <application>
    <default-render-kit-id>
      org.apache.myfaces.trinidad.core
    </default-render-kit-id>
  </application>
  ...
</faces-config>
```

Why Use Trinidad?

Many JSF frameworks and component libraries are available and provide numerous different features. The main drawbacks of using several libraries together are the compatibility issues between each library and the amount of time you need for the evaluation process to decide which ones to use. Using Trinidad gives you several solutions packaged together that will meet many possible requirements; here are a few of its features:

- Hundreds of components that are well implemented, well tested, and well documented
- Built-in AJAX support with partial page rendering
- Dialog framework
- Client-side conversion and validation
- Skinning
- Workflow support with pageFlowScope (described below in the pageFlowScope section)
- Optimized state saving and good performance

With these features, you will probably not need any other third-party frameworks or component libraries.

Extended JSF Capabilities

As previously mentioned, Trinidad is not just a set of components. It also provides extended capabilities to solve some of the many development challenges faced by JSF programmers. Table 4-1 summarizes the most notable features provided by Trinidad.

Table 4-1. *Trinidad Features*

Feature	Description
`RequestContext`	Context class, similar to `FacesContext`, for programmatically executing and managing Trinidad features and components.
pageFlowScope	Bean scope that is between request and session scope. Solves the problem of short conversations between the client and server side that falls into neither request nor session scope.
Partial Page Rendering (PPR)	Provides Ajax support for the Trinidad components.
Dialog Framework	Framework for working with dialog windows known from desktop GUI programming.
Client-side conversion and validation	Equivalent to the conversion and validation performed by JSF, but executed on the client side, rather than the server side.
Skinning	This feature offers the ability to control the outward appearance of components, similar to the Pluggable Look and Feel (PLAF) API used for Swing GUI development. More about this feature in the "Skinning" section.

RequestContext

`RequestContext` is a context class providing access to information about the application as well as each request made by the client. Although there is no relation between `RequestContext` and `FacesContext`, the usage is the same; just like `FacesContext`, `RequestContext` is placed in `ThreadLocal` and retrieved via `RequestContext.getCurrentInstance()`. In short, `RequestContext` is the bridge that ties your application with Trinidad. Throughout this chapter, you'll encounter several uses of this class.

■ **Note** Placing objects in `ThreadLocal` simply means that each thread will manage its own copy of the object. Therefore, for each thread there is only one active `RequestContext` object, which can be retrieved using `getCurrentInstance()`.

pageFlowScope

Whether you are developing a web-based or desktop application, workflows (also known as conversations or wizards) are common requirements. Workflows are primarily based on passing data between pages. Because of the stateless nature of HTTP, for a web application, managing the state of a workflow is not a simple task. You can overcome this problem by using Request- and Session-scoped beans, but doing so requires extra code for starting and stopping the workflow. Table 4-2 summarizes the problems with managed bean scopes.

Table 4-2. *Problems with the Managed Bean Scopes in Core JSF*

Scope	Problem
Request	When used to pass some data from one page to another, although it's possible to display the data passed in the second page, the data gets lost in a consecutive postback. An example of this is where one selects a row from a `DataTable` and executes an action like display, update, or delete. Another major drawback is the inability to bookmark, since the URL is not rewritten. In order to rewrite the URL, a redirect is needed instead of a forward by using `<redirect>`. The major issue here is that the data in Request scope gets lost when redirecting, since a new request is made.
Session	The idea behind the session scope is to open temporary storage that will keep data for individual users throughout their sessions. That way, the data being kept is ready to be used in a later request by the same user. Although this idea seems nice at first glance, it has its drawbacks. First of all, a user cannot execute different instances of the same workflow in different windows simultaneously, because the session is shared for all the requests by the same user and changes made to one workflow affect the other.

Trinidad introduces a new scope, pageFlowScope, that aims to provide an elegant way to manage workflows without the drawbacks of the approaches described in Table 4-2. pageFlowScope is somewhere in between the request and session scope; the data is only saved per workflow and is then disposed of afterwards. Redirects and simultaneous executions are also available with pageFlowScope along with the conversation data. To illustrate the use of pageFlowScope, we have created the customer registration example.

Customer Registration pageFlowScope Example

Suppose you have a simple class called `Customer` (with the basic fields `firstName`, `lastName`, `age`, `phone`, and `email`) that you would like to populate in a three-step workflow (see Figure 4-1). The first two steps will be used for gathering customer details, and the third is a confirmation of the collected information.

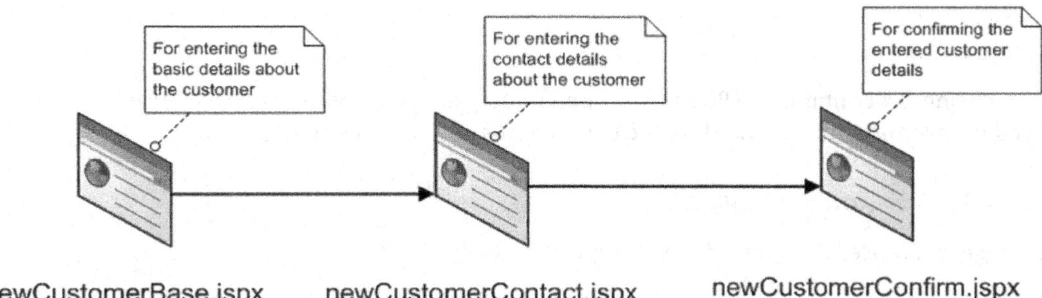

Figure 4-1. *Three-step customer registration workflow*

The page in Listing 4-3 contains three input fields for obtaining the first name, last name, and age of the customer. When the Next button is clicked, the `setActionListener` is triggered. The action listener copies the customer object from the `newCustomerBase` bean (shown in Listing 4-4) to the `pageFlowScope`.

Listing 4-3. *newCustomerBase.jspx*

```
<?xml version="1.0" encoding="UTF-8"?>
<jsp:root xmlns:jsp="http://java.sun.com/JSP/Page" version="2.0"
          xmlns:h="http://java.sun.com/jsf/html"
          xmlns:f="http://java.sun.com/jsf/core"
          xmlns:tr="http://myfaces.apache.org/trinidad" >
  <jsp:directive.page contentType="text/html;charset=utf-8"/>
  <f:view>
    <h:form id="newCustomer">
    <h:message for="newCustomer" style="color: green;" />
    <h:panelGrid columns="2">
      <tr:outputLabel for="firstName" value="First Name" />
      <tr:inputText id="firstName"
                    value="#{newCustomerBase.customer.firstName}" />

      <tr:outputLabel for="lastName" value="Last Name" />
      <tr:inputText id="lastName"
                    value="#{newCustomerBase.customer.lastName}" />

      <tr:outputLabel for="age" value="Age" />
      <tr:inputText id="age"
                    value="#{newCustomerBase.customer.age}" />
    </h:panelGrid>

    <tr:commandButton text="Next" action="next">
      <tr:setActionListener from="#{newCustomerBase.customer}"
                            to="#{pageFlowScope.customer}" />
      </tr:commandButton>
    </h:form>
  </f:view>
</jsp:root>
```

Listing 4-4 contains the Request-scoped managed bean `NewCustomerBase`. The bean is used for instantiating and holding the basic details of a new customer.

Listing 4-4. *NewCustomerContact.java*

```
package com.apress.myfaces.trinidad.jsf;

import com.apress.myfaces.trinidad.domain.Customer;

public class NewCustomerBase {

  private Customer customer = new Customer();

  public NewCustomerBase() {
  }
```

```
  public Customer getCustomer() {
    return customer;
  }

  public void setCustomer(Customer customer) {
    this.customer = customer;
  }
}
```

The page in Listing 4-5 contains two input fields for obtaining the phone and e-mail address of the customer. Unlike Listing 4-3, the input fields are bound directly to the customer object in the pageFlowScope.

Listing 4-5. *newCustomerContact.jspx*

```
<?xml version="1.0" encoding="UTF-8"?>
<jsp:root xmlns:jsp="http://java.sun.com/JSP/Page" version="2.0"
          xmlns:h="http://java.sun.com/jsf/html"
          xmlns:f="http://java.sun.com/jsf/core"
          xmlns:tr="http://myfaces.apache.org/trinidad" >
  <jsp:directive.page contentType="text/html;charset=utf-8"/>
  <f:view>
    <h:form>
      <h:panelGrid columns="2">
        <tr:outputLabel for="phone" value="Cell Phone" />
        <tr:inputText id="phone"
                      value="#{pageFlowScope.customer.phone}" />

        <tr:outputLabel for="email" value="Email" />
        <tr:inputText id="email"
                      value="#{pageFlowScope.customer.email}" />
      </h:panelGrid>

      <tr:commandButton text="Next" action="next" />
    </h:form>
  </f:view>
</jsp:root>
```

Listing 4-6 contains the confirmation page where the details collected about the new customer are presented.

Listing 4-6. *newCustomerConfirm.jspx*

```
<?xml version="1.0" encoding="UTF-8"?>
<jsp:root xmlns:jsp="http://java.sun.com/JSP/Page" version="2.0"
          xmlns:h="http://java.sun.com/jsf/html"
          xmlns:f="http://java.sun.com/jsf/core"
          xmlns:tr="http://myfaces.apache.org/trinidad" >
```

```
  <jsp:directive.page contentType="text/html;charset=utf-8"/>
  <f:view>
    <h:form>
      <h:panelGrid columns="2">
        <tr:outputLabel for="firstName" value="First Name" />
        <tr:outputText id="firstName"
                       value="#{pageFlowScope.customer.firstName}" />

        <tr:outputLabel for="lastName" value="Last Name" />
        <tr:outputText id="lastName"
                       value="#{pageFlowScope.customer.lastName}" />

        <tr:outputLabel for="age" value="Age" />
        <tr:outputText id="age"
                       value="#{pageFlowScope.customer.age}" />

        <tr:outputLabel for="phone" value="Phone" />
        <tr:outputText id="phone"
                       value="#{pageFlowScope.customer.phone}" />

        <tr:outputLabel for="email"value="Email" />
        <tr:outputText id="email"
                       value="#{pageFlowScope.customer.email}" />
      </h:panelGrid>

      <tr:commandButton text="Save" action="#{newCustomerConfirm.save}" />
    </h:form>
  </f:view>
</jsp:root>
```

When the Save button is clicked, the details are saved, and the user is returned to the first page; see Listing 4-7.

Listing 4-7. *NewCustomerConfirm.java*

```
package com.apress.myfaces.trinidad.jsf;

import java.util.Map;
import javax.faces.application.FacesMessage;
import javax.faces.context.FacesContext;
import org.apache.myfaces.trinidad.context.RequestContext;

public class NewCustomerConfirm {

  public NewCustomerConfirm() {
  }
```

```
  public String save() {
    RequestContext requestContext = RequestContext.getCurrentInstance();
    Map pageFlowScope = requestContext.getPageFlowScope();
    pageFlowScope.remove("customer");

    FacesMessage msg = new FacesMessage("Customer saved");
    FacesContext facesContext = FacesContext.getCurrentInstance();
    facesContext.addMessage("newCustomer", msg);

    return "start";
  }
}
```

Finally, the managed beans are declared, and the pages are linked in Listing 4-8.

Listing 4-8. *faces-config.xml*

```
<?xml version="1.0" encoding="UTF-8"?>
<!DOCTYPE faces-config PUBLIC
    "-//Sun Microsystems, Inc.//DTD JavaServer Faces Config 1.0//EN"
    "http://java.sun.com/dtd/web-facesconfig_1_0.dtd" >
<faces-config>

  <application>
    <default-render-kit-id>
      org.apache.myfaces.trinidad.core
    </default-render-kit-id>
  </application>

  <managed-bean>
    <managed-bean-name>newCustomerBase</managed-bean-name>
    <managed-bean-class>
      com.apress.myfaces.trinidad.jsf.NewCustomerBase
    </managed-bean-class>
    <managed-bean-scope>request</managed-bean-scope>
  </managed-bean>
  <managed-bean>
    <managed-bean-name>newCustomerConfirm</managed-bean-name>
    <managed-bean-class>
      com.apress.myfaces.trinidad.jsf.NewCustomerConfirm
    </managed-bean-class>
    <managed-bean-scope>request</managed-bean-scope>
  </managed-bean>
```

```
  <navigation-rule>
    <from-view-id>/newCustomerBase.jspx</from-view-id>
    <navigation-case>
      <from-outcome>next</from-outcome>
      <to-view-id>/newCustomerContact.jspx</to-view-id>
    </navigation-case>
  </navigation-rule>
  <navigation-rule>
    <from-view-id>/newCustomerContact.jspx</from-view-id>
    <navigation-case>
      <from-outcome>next</from-outcome>
      <to-view-id>/newCustomerConfirm.jspx</to-view-id>
    </navigation-case>
  </navigation-rule>
  <navigation-rule>
    <from-view-id>/newCustomerConfirm.jspx</from-view-id>
    <navigation-case>
      <from-outcome>start</from-outcome>
      <to-view-id>/newCustomerBase.jspx</to-view-id>
    </navigation-case>
  </navigation-rule>
</faces-config>
```

Programmatic Access to pageFlowScope

pageFlowScope is a java.util.Map implementation and can be accessed using the RequestContext; see Listing 4-9.

Listing 4-9. *Obtaining PageFlowScope Programmically*

```
RequestContext requestContext = RequestContext.getCurrentInstance();

// Obtain pageFlowScope
Map pageFlowScope = requestContext.getPageFlowScope();

// Add object to pageFlowScope
pageFlowScope.put("customer", this.customer);

// Get object from pageFlowScope
Object myObject = pageFlowScope.get("objectName");

// Remove all objects from pageFlowScope
pageFlowScope.clean()
```

■ Note Unlike built-in scope variables, like `sessionScope` and `requestScope`, beans located in `pageFlowScope` cannot be accessed directly by using the bean's name at the beginning of the EL expression. So instead of `#{bean}`, you can use `#{pageFlowScope.bean}`. Similarly, `pageFlowScope` is not a valid parameter for `<managed-bean-scope>`.

MyFaces Orchestra's Alternative

Similar to `pageFlowScope`, MyFaces Orchestra (`http://myfaces.apache.org/orchestra/`) also provides a workflow scope named `conversation` with additional support for persistence contexts. You can read more about Conversation scope and Orchestra in Chapter 5.

Partial Page Rendering (PPR)

As Ajax gets more attention in web development, the complexity of developing Ajaxified applications becomes apparent. To implement a simple use case like a form submission with Ajax (see Figure 4-2), a lot of JavaScript code is needed on the client side to make the request, parse the response, and finally update the page status with DOM utilities. On the server side, the response needs to be prepared in a way that the client can interpret. Another risk is browser compatibility; writing JavaScript code that is compatible with every browser is not a guaranteed task.

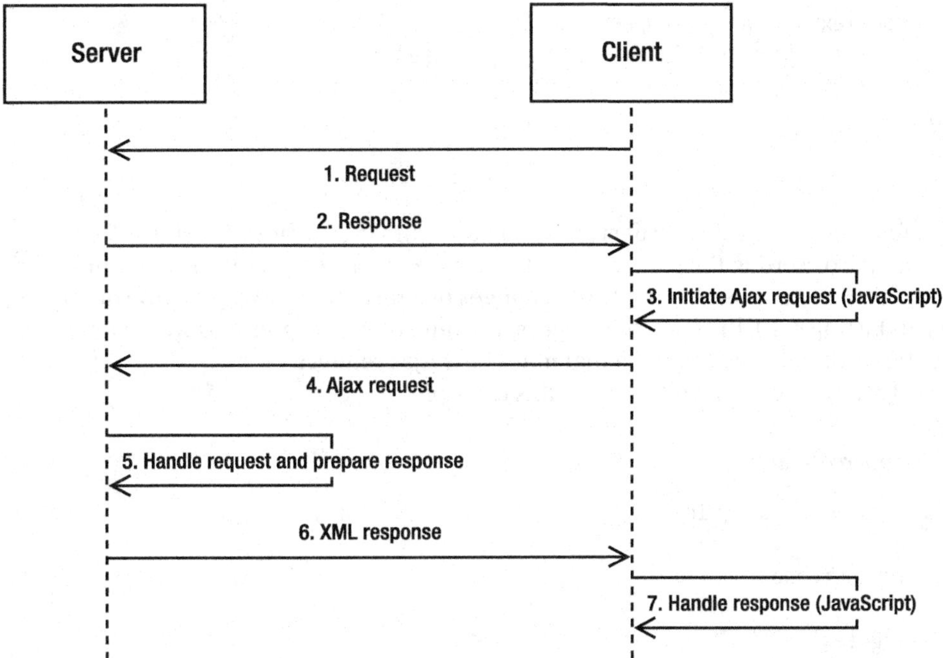

Figure 4-2. *Sequence diagram of a simple use case using Ajax*

Trinidad Partial Page Rendering (PPR) provides a solution that does all the hard work. From a developer's perspective, no JavaScript is necessary, and on the server side, there is no need to create the response manually. Behind the scenes, Trinidad generates all the required JavaScript code to make the request and handle the response. Listing 4-10 shows a simple example of converting a string to uppercase using PPR.

Listing 4-10. *toUppercase.jspx*

```
<?xml version="1.0" encoding="UTF-8"?>
<jsp:root xmlns:jsp="http://java.sun.com/JSP/Page" version="2.0"
          xmlns:h="http://java.sun.com/jsf/html"
          xmlns:f="http://java.sun.com/jsf/core"
          xmlns:tr="http://myfaces.apache.org/trinidad" >
  <jsp:directive.page contentType="text/html;charset=utf-8"/>
  <f:view>
    <h:form>
      <h:panelGrid columns="3">
        <tr:inputText value="#{toUppercase.text}" />

        <tr:commandButton id="btnToUppercase"
                          partialSubmit="true"
                          text="To Uppercase >>"
                          action="#{toUppercase.click}" />

        <tr:inputText value="#{toUppercase.text}"
                      partialTriggers="btnToUppercase" />
      </h:panelGrid>
    </h:form>
  </f:view>
</jsp:root>
```

PPR is enabled by two attributes: `partialSubmit` and `partialTriggers`. The form data is submitted with Ajax by setting the `partialSubmit` attribute of `commandButton` to `true`. The `partialTriggers` attribute is used to apply the changes of a response and repaint the defined components. In Listing 4-10, the `partialTriggers` attribute of the second `inputText` component is set to the ID of the `commandButton` that makes the Ajax request.

Listing 4-11 shows the managed bean for this example.

Listing 4-11. *ToUppercase.java*

```
package com.apress.myfaces.trinidad.jsf;

public class ToUppercase {

  private String text = "";

  public ToUppercase() {
  }
```

```
  public String getText() {
    return text;
  }

  public void setText(String text) {
    this.text = text;
  }

  public String click() {
    text = text.toUpperCase();
    return null;
  }
}
```

Notifying the Users

Ajax-enabled applications might not be trivial for end users who are only familiar with the regular request and response architecture that loads entire pages. While an Ajax request is being processed, the user cannot see any change on the page. A mechanism to notify the user about the progress is necessary, as the user might think nothing is happening and repeat clicking the buttons, which results in sending the same request more than once. Trinidad's `statusIndicator` component displays a progress icon while the application is processing Ajax requests. As you may expect the progress icon can be customized using the facets `busy` and `ready`; see Listing 4-12.

Listing 4-12. *Using the Status Indicator Component*

```
<!-- Standard status indicator -->
<tr:statusIndicator partialTriggers="componentId" />

<!-- Customised status indicator -->
<tr:statusIndicator partialTriggers="componentId">
  <f:facet name="ready">
    <tr:outputText value="I am ready for your request" />
  </f:facet>
  <f:facet name="busy">
    <tr:outputText value="Please hold, I am processing your request" />
  </f:facet>
</tr:statusIndicator>
```

autoSubmit

All Trinidad input components support the `autoSubmit` attribute, which makes Ajax requests when the value of the input component changes and loses focus. In the example in Listing 4-13, `autoSubmit` is used for checking the strength of a password.

Listing 4-13. *passwordStrength.jspx*

```
<?xml version="1.0" encoding="UTF-8"?>
<jsp:root xmlns:jsp="http://java.sun.com/JSP/Page" version="2.0"
          xmlns:h="http://java.sun.com/jsf/html"
          xmlns:f="http://java.sun.com/jsf/core"
          xmlns:tr="http://myfaces.apache.org/trinidad" >
  <jsp:directive.page contentType="text/html;charset=utf-8"/>
  <f:view>
    <h:form>
      <h:panelGrid columns="3">
        <tr:outputLabel for="newPassword" value="Enter password:" />
        <tr:inputText id="newPassword"
                      value="#{passwordStrength.password}"
                      autoSubmit="true"
                      secret="true" />
        <tr:messages partialTriggers="newPassword"  />
      </h:panelGrid>
    </h:form>
  </f:view>
</jsp:root>
```

Whenever text is entered and the field loses focus, an Ajax request is made to the backing bean, shown in Listing 4-14, setting the value and checking the strength of the password.

Listing 4-14. *PasswordStrength.java*

```
package com.apress.myfaces.trinidad.jsf;

import javax.faces.application.FacesMessage;
import javax.faces.context.FacesContext;

public class PasswordStrength {

  private static final int MINIMUM_PASSWORD_LENGTH = 6;

  private String password = "";

  public PasswordStrength() {
  }

  public String getPassword() {
    return password;
  }
```

```
  public void setPassword(String password) {
    this.password = password;
    checkStrength();
  }

  public void checkStrength() {
    if (this.password != null) {
      FacesMessage msg = new FacesMessage();
      if (this.password.length() < MINIMUM_PASSWORD_LENGTH) {
        msg.setSeverity(FacesMessage.SEVERITY_WARN);
        msg.setSummary("Password is too short");
      } else {
        msg.setSeverity(FacesMessage.SEVERITY_INFO);
        msg.setSummary("Password is good");
      }
      FacesContext.getCurrentInstance().addMessage("password", msg);
    }
  }
}
```

Polling

Trinidad comes with a polling component, similar to the `statusIndicator` component, that can execute a listener at a given interval after which other components can rerender. A newsflash in a newspaper application is a great example for polling where a certain part of the page is updated regularly without having to refresh the page. Listing 4-15 shows the polling component used in this way. Note the double colons (`::`) in the `newsTable` component's `partialTriggers` attribute. This tells the component (in this case `newsTable`) to search its parent component (the `news` form) for the trigger (the `newsPoll` poll). We have to do this here because the `newsTable` itself is a containing component.

Listing 4-15. *polling.jspx*

```
<?xml version="1.0" encoding="UTF-8"?>
<jsp:root xmlns:jsp="http://java.sun.com/JSP/Page" version="2.0"
          xmlns:h="http://java.sun.com/jsf/html"
          xmlns:f="http://java.sun.com/jsf/core"
          xmlns:tr="http://myfaces.apache.org/trinidad" >
  <jsp:directive.page contentType="text/html;charset=utf-8"/>
  <f:view>
    <h:form id="news">
      <tr:poll id="newsPoll"
               pollListener="#{polling.onCheckNews}"
               interval="10000" />
      <tr:messages partialTriggers="newsPoll"  />
      <tr:statusIndicator partialTriggers="newsPoll" />
```

```
      <tr:table id="newsTable" rows="10"
                partialTriggers="::newsPoll"
                value="#{polling.news}"
                var="news">
        <tr:column headerText="Title">
          <tr:outputText value="#{news.title}" />
        </tr:column>
        <tr:column headerText="Description">
          <tr:outputText value="#{news.description.value}"
                         escape="false" />
        </tr:column>
      </tr:table>
    </h:form>
  </f:view>
</jsp:root>
```

The backing bean in Listing 4-16 uses the Rome RSS API (`http://rome.dev.java.net`) to fetch news from an external newsfeed.

Listing 4-16. *Polling.java*

```
package com.apress.myfaces.trinidad.jsf;

import com.sun.syndication.feed.synd.SyndFeed;
import com.sun.syndication.io.SyndFeedInput;
import com.sun.syndication.io.XmlReader;

import java.net.URL;

import javax.faces.application.FacesMessage;
import javax.faces.context.FacesContext;
import javax.faces.model.DataModel;
import javax.faces.model.ListDataModel;

import org.apache.myfaces.trinidad.event.PollEvent;

public class Polling {

  private static final String FEED_URL = "http://www.apress.com/resource/" +
                                         "feed/newbook";

  private DataModel news = new ListDataModel();

  public Polling() {
  }
```

```
  public void onCheckNews(PollEvent event) {
    try {
      URL url = new URL(FEED_URL);
      SyndFeedInput input = new SyndFeedInput();
      SyndFeed feed = input.build(new XmlReader(url));
      this.news = new ListDataModel(feed.getEntries());
    } catch (Exception ex) {
      FacesMessage msg = new FacesMessage();
      msg.setSeverity(FacesMessage.SEVERITY_ERROR);
      msg.setSummary(ex.getMessage());
      FacesContext.getCurrentInstance().addMessage("news", msg);
    }
  }

  public DataModel getNews() {
    return news;
  }

  public void setNews(DataModel news) {
    this.news = news;
  }
}
```

Programmatic PPR

PPR can also be implemented programmatically without explicitly setting `partialTriggers` on components. There may be cases where the partial update of the component depends on a case that may be checked on the server side or it is not certain which component needs to be rerendered. Programmatic access to PPR can be done easily via the `addPartialTarget` method on `RequestContext`, as shown in Listing 4-17.

Listing 4-17. *Adding a Partial Target Programmatically.*

```
RequestContext rc = RequestContext.getCurrentInstance();
rc.addPartialTarget(componentInstance);
```

Since a page may contain regular requests along with partial requests, the `RequestContext.isPartialRequest(FacesContext)` method can be used to determine the type of request. Note that using `addPartialTarget` would be ignored in a regular request, since the whole page is refreshed.

Adding PPR to Custom Components

Writing Ajax-enabled custom components is not a trivial task considering the amount of JavaScript rendering and maintenance required. However, the Trinidad PPR API lets you add Ajax support to your custom components in a simple way. If your component is the target of

PPR, it can support partialTriggers with the help of the addPartialTriggerListeners() method. Just add the partialTriggers attribute to your component and add the list of triggers to RequestContext as shown in Listing 4-18.

Listing 4-18. *Support for partialTriggers in a Custom Component*

```
public void decode(FacesContext context) {
  // Support for the partialTriggers attribute
  Object partialTriggers = getAttributes().get("partialTriggers");

  // Add triggers to RequestContext
  RequestContext ctx = RequestContext.getCurrentInstance();
  ctx.addPartialTriggerListeners(this, (String[]) triggers);

  // Custom decoding
  ...
}
```

On the other hand, your custom component might fire events and be the source of the PPR like a commandButton. In this case, override the broadcast() method and add PPR functionality as shown in Listing 4-19.

Listing 4-19. *Support for Firing Partial Update Notifications*

```
public void broadcast(FacesEvent event) throws AbortProcessingException {
  super.broadcast(event);

  // Notify Trinidad that your component has executed an event
  RequestContext.getCurrentInstance().partialUpdateNotify(this);
}
```

PPR JavaScript API

Although Trinidad PPR does all the hard work and abstracts you from any client-side scripting, a JavaScript API is provided. Let's take a look at some of its features now.

PPR Request

The basic form of sending a PPR request can be done by getting an instance of TrPage and using the sendPartialFormPost method; see Listing 4-20.

Listing 4-20. *Executing a PPR Request from JavaScript*

```
TrPage.getInstance().sendPartialFormPost(document.getElementById('myform'));
```

By referencing the HTML form instance, the method gathers all the input from the form fields and makes a POST request that starts the JSF life cycle for the current view. You can also add optional parameters and request headers; see Listing 4-21.

Listing 4-21. *Executing a PPR Request from JavaScript*

```
TrPage.getInstance().sendPartialFormPost(
    document.getElementById('myform'),
    {param1: "value1", param2: "value2"},
    {header1: "headerValue1", header2: "headerValue2"});
```

File Upload

sendPartialFormPost also supports multipart and IFRAME requests along with standard Ajax requests. The good news for page authors is that there is no need to change the code in these cases; the PPR API is smart enough to identify the type of the request by looking at the non-empty form fields with type="file".

Ajax Request

A PPR request is bound to the JSF life cycle. To take the full control of the Ajax request and do non-JSF requests, the RequestQueue class can be used instead. Listing 4-22 provides an example of making a non-JSF Ajax request, and Table 4-3 lists the possible request parameters.

Listing 4-22. *Making a Non-JSF Ajax Request*

```
var queue = TrPage.getInstance().getRequestQueue();
queue.sendRequest(context,callback,url,headers,content);
```

Table 4-3. *Non-JSF Ajax Request Parameters*

Parameter	Description
context	Argument object that can be used in the callback method. null is allowed.
callback	JavaScript method to be called to handle the Ajax response.
url	URL of the request.
headers	Optional HTTP header parameters for the request.
content	Optional content of the Ajax POST request.

The example in Listing 4-23 sends a parameter called id to the server side to be processed by a servlet; later, the callback functions alerts the servlet response text.

Listing 4-23. *Sending a Parameter to the Server and Receiving the Response*

```
function oncomplete(event) {
  alert(event.getResponseText());
}

function sendAjaxRequest() {
  var queue = TrPage.getInstance().getRequestQueue();
  queue.sendRequest(null, oncomplete,"trinidadbox/pprwall.ppr?id=2");
}
```

An instance of `TrXMLRequestEvent` object is passed to the callback method allowing access to the servlet response. Table 4-4 illustrates the methods of the `TrXMLRequestEvent` object.

Table 4-4. *Methods of the TrXMLRequestEvent Object*

Method	Description
`getStatus()`	Returns the status of the request and has the possible values `STATUS_QUEUED`, `STATUS_SEND_BEFORE`, `STATUS_SEND_AFTER`, and `STATUS_COMPLETE`
`getResponseXML()`	Returns the XML version of the response
`getResponseText()`	Returns the text version of the response
`getResponseStatusCode()`	Returns the HTTP status code
`getResponseHeader()`	Returns the HTTP header
`getResponseContentType()`	Returns the content type of the response

Monitoring Requests

Although the `statusIndicator` component provides basic support for monitoring Ajax requests, the Trinidad API also makes it possible to plug in custom callback functions to be notified while waiting for the server response. There are two types of listeners that can be implemented, as described in Table 4-5.

Table 4-5. *Types of Client-Side Ajax Listeners*

Listener	Description	Example
`stateChangeListener`	The listener is declared using the client-side `RequestQueue`. The call-back method implementing the listener must take a state parameter, which is either `TrRequestQueue.STATE_READY` or `TrRequestQueue.STATE_BUSY`.	`TrPage.getInstance().getRequestQueue().addStateChangeListener(customCallback);`
`domReplaceListener`	Used to listen for replace events in case the DOM is changed as a result of the Ajax response. Old and new DOM elements are passed as parameters consecutively.	`TrPage.getInstance().addStateChangeListener(customCallback);`

Dialog Framework

Collecting data from different pages and navigation back to a master page is a common requirement in a web application. In Trinidad, this is referred to as a dialog. Trinidad simplifies the effort needed to manage dialogs and handles the communication between the dialog pages. Dialogs can be displayed in either a separate pop-up window or the original window. You can configure the display using the `useWindow` attribute on the component opening the dialog.

Shipping Address Dialog Example

In this example, we will show you how to allow the users to add shipping addresses to their profiles. This could be part of an online shopping application where the users will decide where they want to ship the order in their shopping cart. The example consists of a domain class, `Address` (see Listing 4-24), a JSP page for selecting the shipping address (see Listings 4-25 and 4-26), and a JSP page for the dialog of creating a new shipping address (see Listings 4-27 and 4-28). Each of the JSP pages will have a corresponding backing bean. Figure 4-3 illustrates the flow of the example.

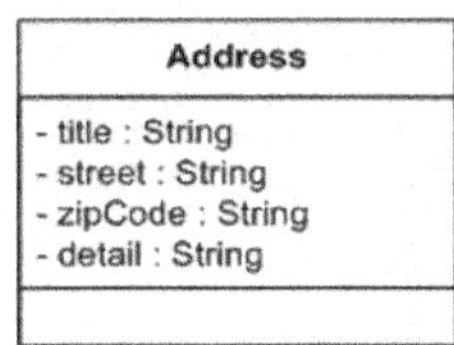

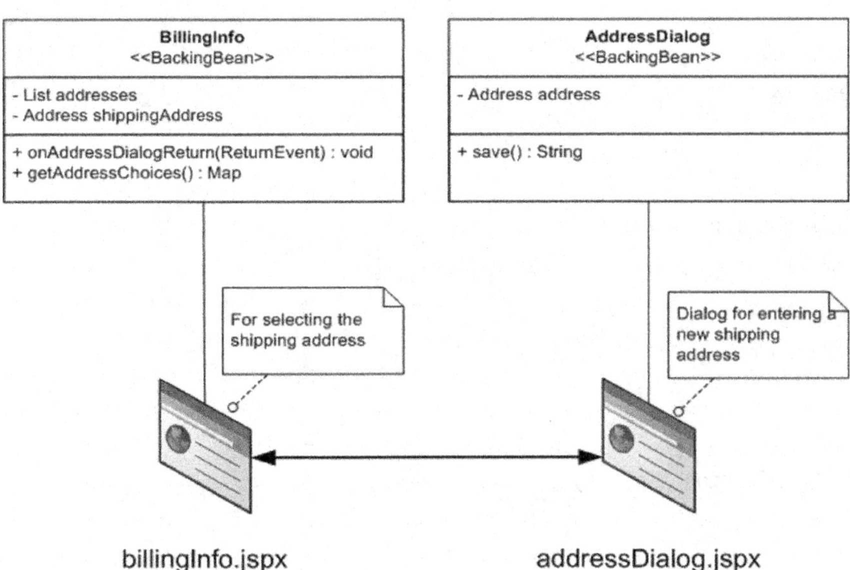

Figure 4-3. *The flow of the shipping address example*

Listing 4-24. *Address.java*

```
package com.apress.myfaces.trinidad.domain;

public class Address {

  private String title = "";
  private String street = "";
  private String zipCode = "";
  private String detail = "";
```

```
  public Address() {
  }

  public String getDetail() {
    return detail;
  }

  public void setDetail(String detail) {
    this.detail = detail;
  }

  public String getStreet() {
    return street;
  }

  public void setStreet(String street) {
    this.street = street;
  }

  public String getTitle() {
    return title;
  }

  public void setTitle(String title) {
    this.title = title;
  }

  public String getZipCode() {
    return zipCode;
  }

  public void setZipCode(String zipCode) {
    this.zipCode = zipCode;
  }
}
```

Launching a dialog needs two elements: a `Command` component (see Listing 4-25) and a navigation rule in `faces-config.xml` (see Listing 4-29). Dialog navigations are similar to regular JSF navigations except they are prefixed `dialog:` indicating the target is a dialog.

Listing 4-25. *billingInfo.jspx*

```
<?xml version="1.0" encoding="UTF-8"?>
<jsp:root xmlns:jsp="http://java.sun.com/JSP/Page" version="2.0"
          xmlns:h="http://java.sun.com/jsf/html"
          xmlns:f="http://java.sun.com/jsf/core"
          xmlns:tr="http://myfaces.apache.org/trinidad" >
  <jsp:directive.page contentType="text/html;charset=utf-8"/>
  <f:view>
    <tr:document>
      <tr:form>
        <tr:selectOneChoice id="addressSelection"
                            value="#{billingInfo.shipmentAddress}"
                            partialTriggers="btn_address">
          <f:selectItems value="#{billingInfo.addressChoices}" />
        </tr:selectOneChoice>
        <tr:commandButton id="btn_address"
                          text="New Address"
                          action="dialog:newAddress"
                          partialSubmit="true"
                          useWindow="true"
                          windowWidth="300"
                          windowHeight="400"
                          returnListener="#{billingInfo.onAddressDialogReturn}"/>
      </tr:form>
    </tr:document>
  </f:view>
</jsp:root>
```

The action of the New Address button is set to `dialog:newAddress`, and `useWindow` is `true`, which means clicking the button will open a pop-up window containing the address dialog. The added address is passed to the `returnFromDialog(Object)` method of the `RequestContext` and obtained on the master page through the specified return listener.

Listing 4-26 is the managed bean for this JSP page, which also contains the return listener.

Listing 4-26. *BillingInfo.java*

```
package com.apress.myfaces.trinidad.jsf;

import com.apress.myfaces.trinidad.domain.Address;

import java.util.ArrayList;
import java.util.HashMap;
import java.util.List;
import java.util.Map;

import org.apache.myfaces.trinidad.event.ReturnEvent;
```

```
public class BillingInfo {

  private List<Address> addresses;

  private Address shipmentAddress;

  public BillingInfo() {
  }

  public void onAddressDialogReturn(ReturnEvent returnEvent) {
    if (returnEvent.getReturnValue() != null) {
      getAddresses().add((Address) returnEvent.getReturnValue());
    }
  }

  public List<Address> getAddresses() {
    if (addresses == null) {
      addresses = new ArrayList<Address>();
    }
    return addresses;
  }

  public void setAddresses(List<Address> addresses) {
    this.addresses = addresses;
  }

  public Address getShipmentAddress() {
    return shipmentAddress;
  }

  public void setShipmentAddress(Address shipmentAddress) {
    this.shipmentAddress = shipmentAddress;
  }

  public Map getAddressChoices() {
    Map<String, Address> map = new HashMap<String, Address>();
    for (Address address : getAddresses()) {
      map.put(address.getTitle(), address);
    }

    return map;
  }
}
```

A return listener takes `ReturnEvent` as a parameter, and the returned dialog value can be accessed using the `getReturnValue()` method. In our case, the listener gets the returned address from the dialog and adds it to the address list. Finally, PPR is used to rerender the address selection drop-down with the newly added address without refreshing the whole page.

Listing 4-27 shows the address dialog.

Listing 4-27. *addressDialog.jspx*

```
<?xml version="1.0" encoding="UTF-8"?>
<jsp:root xmlns:jsp="http://java.sun.com/JSP/Page" version="2.0"
          xmlns:h="http://java.sun.com/jsf/html"
          xmlns:f="http://java.sun.com/jsf/core"
          xmlns:tr="http://myfaces.apache.org/trinidad" >
  <jsp:directive.page contentType="text/html;charset=utf-8"/>
  <f:view>
    <tr:document>
      <tr:form>
        <tr:panelFormLayout>
          <tr:inputText label="Title"
                        value="#{addressDialog.address.title}" />
          <tr:inputText label="Street"
                        value="#{addressDialog.address.street}" />

          <tr:inputText label="Zip Code"
                        value="#{addressDialog.address.zipCode}" />

          <tr:inputText label="Detail"
                        value="#{addressDialog.address.detail}" />
        </tr:panelFormLayout>

        <tr:commandButton text="Submit"
                          action="#{addressDialog.save}" />
        <tr:commandButton text="Cancel"
                          action="#{addressDialog.cancel}" />
                          immediate="true" />
      </tr:form>
    </tr:document>

  </f:view>
</jsp:root>
```

The dialog uses the `addressDialog` managed bean, which is shown in Listing 4-28.

Listing 4-28. *AddressDialog.java*

```
package com.apress.myfaces.trinidad.jsf;

import com.apress.myfaces.trinidad.domain.Address;
import org.apache.myfaces.trinidad.context.RequestContext;

public class AddressDialog {

  private Address address = new Address();

  public AddressDialog() {
  }

  public Address getAddress() {
    return address;
  }

  public void setAddress(Address address) {
    this.address = address;
  }

  public String save() {
    RequestContext ctx = RequestContext.getCurrentInstance();
    ctx.returnFromDialog(address, null);
    return null;
  }

  Public String cancel() {
    RequestContext ctx = RequestContext.getCurrentInstance();
    ctx.returnFromDialog(null, null);
    return null;
  }
}
```

The part that makes the difference is the code executed in the `save()` method. Using `returnFromDialog(Object, Map)`, we specify the object that will be returned to the master page from the dialog, in this case, the address instance. The final stage is to configure the example, as shown in Listing 4-29. Here we set the navigation rule for the `addressDialog` dialog.

Listing 4-29. *faces-config.xml*

```
<?xml version="1.0" encoding="UTF-8"?>
<!DOCTYPE faces-config PUBLIC
    "-//Sun Microsystems, Inc.//DTD JavaServer Faces Config 1.0//EN"
    "http://java.sun.com/dtd/web-facesconfig_1_0.dtd" >
```

```
<faces-config>
  <application>
    <default-render-kit-id>
      org.apache.myfaces.trinidad.core
    </default-render-kit-id>
  </application>
  <managed-bean>
    <managed-bean-name>addressDialog</managed-bean-name>
    <managed-bean-class>
      com.apress.myfaces.trinidad.jsf.AddressDialog
    </managed-bean-class>
    <managed-bean-scope>request</managed-bean-scope>
  </managed-bean>
  <managed-bean>
    <managed-bean-name>billingInfo</managed-bean-name>
    <managed-bean-class>
      com.apress.myfaces.trinidad.jsf.BillingInfo
    </managed-bean-class>
    <managed-bean-scope>session</managed-bean-scope>
  </managed-bean>
  <navigation-rule>
    <from-view-id>/*</from-view-id>
    <navigation-case>
      <from-outcome>dialog:newAddress</from-outcome>
      <to-view-id>/addressDialog.jspx</to-view-id>
    </navigation-case>
  </navigation-rule>
</faces-config>
```

Passing Data to the Dialog

The `addressDialog` is handy for creating new shipping addresses, but what happens if the user wants to edit an existing address? In this situation, the selected address needs to be passed to the dialog to enable editing. You can achieve this by specifying a `launchListener`; see Listing 4-30.

Listing 4-30. *Specifying a Launch Listener*

```
<tr:commandButton id="btn_address"
                  text="New / Edit Address"
                  action="dialog:newAddress"
                  partialSubmit="true"
                  useWindow="true"
                  windowWidth="300"
                  windowHeight="400"
                  returnListener="#{billingInfo.onAddressDialogReturn}"
                  launchListener="#{billingInfo.onAddressDialogLaunch}"/>
```

The launchListener method takes a LaunchEvent, which can be used to pass data into the pageFlowScope for retrieval in the dialog; see Listings 4-31 and 4-32.

Listing 4-31. *Implementation of the launchListener*

```
public void onAddressDialogLaunch(LaunchEvent launchEvent) {
  if (this.shipmentAddress != null) {
    launchEvent.getDialogParameters().put("address", shipmentAddress);
  } else {
    // Address was not selected for editing
    launchEvent.getDialogParameters().put("address", new Address());
  }
}
```

Listing 4-32. *Obtaining Dialog Parameters*

```
public AddressDialog() {
  RequestContext ctx = RequestContext.getCurrentInstance();
  Map pageFlowScope = ctx.getPageFlowScope();
  this.address = (Address) pageFlowScope.get("address");
}
```

It is also possible to obtain dialog parameters directly using EL: #{pageFlowScope.address.title}

Simplified Dialogs

Enabling dialogs requires a Command component with several attributes configured, like useWindow, partialTriggers, returnListener, and optionally launchListener. Trinidad comes up with a handy inputListOfValues component encapsulating these mechanics by taking care of launching and transferring data, thereby simplifying dialog usage for common cases (see Listing 4-33).

Listing 4-33. *Simplified Dialog*

```
<tr:inputListOfValues label="Input Value"
                      action="dialog:inputValue" value="#{launchingBean.value}"
                      windowWidth="300"
                      windowHeight="200" />
```

Using this component, a dialog shows up; the returned value is implicitly set to the value property of launchingBean; and the field is updated with PPR. Notice that partialSubmit and useWindow are not necessary anymore, since the underlying mechanics are handled by the component.

Programmatic Dialog Management

You can also launch dialogs programmatically using the `launchDialog` method of the `RequestContext`. This can sometimes be necessary if the opening of the dialog depends on the state of the application.

`launchDialog` takes five parameters as specified in Table 4-6.

Table 4-6. *Parameters of the launchDialog Method*

Parameter	Type	Description
`root`	`UIViewRoot`	`ViewRoot` instance of the dialog page.
`component`	`UIComponent`	Source component used to open the dialog.
`dialogParameters`	`Map`	`Map` containing parameters to pass to the dialog.
`useWindow`	`Boolean`	Should the dialog be opened in a separate window?
`windowProperties`	`Map`	`Map` containing window properties such as `height` and `width`.

The example in Listings 4-34 and 4-35 shows how to use `launchDialog` to launch a customized error page in case of an exception while executing an action.

Listing 4-34. *Launching a Dialog Programmatically*

```
public String doSubmit() {
  try {
      //logic to execute
  } catch(Exception exception) {
      launchErrorDialog(exception);
  }
  return null;
}

private void launchErrorDialog(Exception exception) {
  FacesContext ctx = FacesContext.getCurrentInstance();
  ViewHandler viewHandler = ctx.getApplication().getViewHandler();

  UIViewRoot errorDialog = viewHandler.createView(ctx, "/error.jspx");

  Map windowProperties = new HashMap();
  windowProperties.put("width", new Integer(300));
  windowProperties.put("height", new Integer(200));

  Map dialogParameters = new HashMap();
  dialogParameters.put("exception", exception);
```

```
    RequestContext requestContext = RequestContext.getCurrentInstance();
    requestContext.launchDialog(dialog, null,dialogParameters, true,
                                windowProperties);
}
```

Listing 4-35. *error.jspx*

```
<?xml version="1.0" encoding="iso-8859-1" standalone="yes" ?>
<jsp:root xmlns:jsp="http://java.sun.com/JSP/Page" version="2.0"
          xmlns:f="http://java.sun.com/jsf/core"
          xmlns:tr="http://myfaces.apache.org/trinidad">
  <jsp:directive.page contentType="text/html;charset=utf-8" />
  <f:view>
    <tr:document title="ERROR">
      <tr:form>
        <tr:outputText value="Exception: #{pageFlowScope.exception.class}" />
        <tr:outputText value="#{pageFlowScope.exception.message}" />
      </tr:form>
    </tr:document>
  </f:view>
</jsp:root>
```

Client-Side Conversion and Validation

Client-side validation is a common technique in web applications to execute simple checks like required fields, number formats, value comparison, and length validation. Developers may favor running form validations on the client side rather than the server side to improve performance and to avoid server round-trips. Submitted form values are passed through the conversion process before being validated on the server side, so we need client-side converters as well as validation. Although JSF 2.0 will have this feature, JSF 1.x does not provide client-side validation or conversion. Trinidad brings the validation phase of the JSF life cycle to the client and handles the conversion and validation with JavaScript instead of Java. Just like their server-side counterparts, client converters implement the `getAsString` and `getAsObject` methods, and client validators implement the `validate` method. In addition, the extendable API enables developers to write their own client-side converters and validators.

Configuration

Inline client-side validation is turned on by default. It is also possible to use JavaScript alerts instead of inline texts or disable them altogether. The configuration is handled in Trinidad's configuration file, `trinidad-config.xml`, with the `<client-validation>` tag that accepts three values; see Table 4-7. We'll examine `trinidad-config.xml` in detail later in the chapter.

Table 4-7. *Client-Side Validation Values*

Value	Description
`Inline`	Error messages are displayed as inline text.
`Alert`	Error messages are displayed as JavaScript alert boxes.
`Disabled`	Disable client-side conversion and validation.

In the validation phase of the JSF life cycle, submitted values of a component are converted first and then validated. This is exactly the same on the client side. In order to perform conversion on the client side, the converter class needs to implement the `org.apache.myfaces.trinidad.convert.ClientConverter` interface. The main purpose of the interface is to specify the client-side conversion script. We will illustrate the usage of client-side validation and conversion in the following example, where we will create a validator and converter for e-mail addresses.

E-mail Conversion and Validation Example

The e-mail convertor is responsible for converting an e-mail address into an `Email` object, which keeps the username and hostname separate in different properties. When creating client-side convertors and validators you need to create the client-side equivalent of the convertor and validator, as well as classes used in the conversion. For this example, therefore, we will need three client-side scripts: one to represent the `Email` class, another to represent the convertor, and a third to represent the validator (see Figure 4-4).

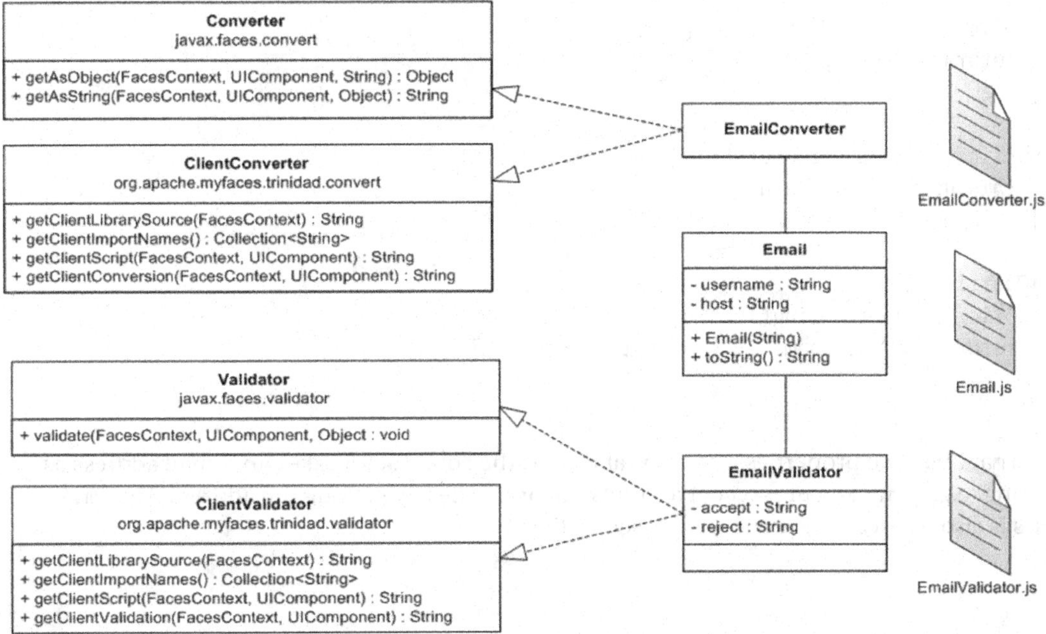

Figure 4-4. *Classes and JavaScript libraries required for the e-mail conversation and validation example*

Listing 4-36 shows the Email Java class.

Listing 4-36. *Email.java*

```
package com.apress.myfaces.trinidad.domain;

public class Email {

  private String username = "";

  private String host = "";

  public Email(String address) {
    this.username = address.split("@")[0];
    this.host = address.split("@")[1];
  }

  public String getHost() {
    return host;
  }

  public void setHost(String host) {
    this.host = host;
  }

  public String getUsername() {
    return username;
  }

  public void setUsername(String username) {
    this.username = username;
  }

  @Override
  public String toString() {
    return this.username + "@" + this.host;
  }
}
```

Email has two properties: username and host; the constructor takes an e-mail address as a string (e.g., myfaces@apress.com) and sets the properties by parsing the address. The Email class is also needed on the client side; see Listing 4-37.

Listing 4-37. *Email.js*

```
Email = function(value) {
    this.username = value.split('@')[0];

    this.host = value.split('@')[1];

    Email.prototype.toString = function(){
        return username + "@" + host;
    }
}
```

Listing 4-38 shows the `EmailConverter` Java class.

Listing 4-38. *EmailConverter.java*

```
package com.apress.myfaces.trinidad.jsf.clientside;

import com.apress.myfaces.trinidad.domain.Email;

import java.util.Collection;

import javax.faces.component.UIComponent;
import javax.faces.context.ExternalContext;
import javax.faces.context.FacesContext;
import javax.faces.convert.Converter;
import javax.faces.convert.ConverterException;

import org.apache.myfaces.trinidad.convert.ClientConverter;

public class EmailConverter implements Converter, ClientConverter {

  public Object getAsObject(FacesContext context,
      UIComponent component,
      String submittedValue) throws ConverterException {
    if (submittedValue != null) {
      if (submittedValue.length() > 0) {
        return new Email(submittedValue);
      }
    }
    return null;
  }
```

```
  public String getAsString(FacesContext context,
      UIComponent component,
      Object value) throws ConverterException {
    if (value != null) {
      return value.toString();
    }
    return null;
  }

  public String getClientConversion(FacesContext context,
      UIComponent component) {
    return "new EmailConverter()";
  }

  public Collection<String> getClientImportNames() {
    return null;
  }

  public String getClientLibrarySource(FacesContext ctx) {
    ExternalContext externalContext = ctx.getExternalContext();
    String path = externalContext.getRequestContextPath();
    return path + "/EmailConverter.js";
  }

  public String getClientScript(FacesContext context,
      UIComponent component) {
    return null;
  }
}
```

In Listing 4-38, `getAsObject` and `getAsString` are regular conversion methods. The important point to notice is that `EmailConverter` implements the `ClientConverter` four methods:

- `getClientConversion` returns the constructor initialization script. If your converter has parameters, this is the perfect place to supply them.
- `getClientImportNames` is used to import built-in Trinidad scripts upon which the converter may depend. In this case, there are none.
- `getClientLibrarySource` returns the JavaScript file containing the conversion script.
- `getClientScript` returns the JavaScript conversion script directly rather than referring to an external script.

The client-side script for `EmailConverter` is similar to its server counterpart; see Listing 4-39.

Listing 4-39. *EmailConverter.js*

```
EmailConverter = function() {}

EmailConverter.prototype = new TrConverter();

EmailConverter.prototype.getAsString = function(value, label){
    return value.username + "@" + value.host;
}

EmailConverter.prototype.getAsObject = function(value, label) {
    if(value != null) {
        if(value.length > 0) {
            var emailExp = /^.+@.+\..{2,3}$/

            if(emailExp.test(value)) {
                return new Email(value);
            }
            else {
                var facesMessage = new TrFacesMessage("Conversion Error",
                "Not a valid email",
                TrFacesMessage.SEVERITY_ERROR);
                throw new TrConverterException(facesMessage);
            }
        }
    }
    return null;
}
```

In Listing 4-39, we use a regular expression in `getAsObject` to check whether the input fits the textual pattern of an e-mail address. If the submitted value cannot be converted to an `Email` instance, a client-side `TrConverterException` is thrown with a `FacesMessage`.

Validation takes place after the conversion process, and similar to the conversion implementation, a validator needs to implement `ClientValidator` and provide a client-side validation script. `EmailValidator` checks if an e-mail address can be accepted based on allowed hostnames stored in the attributes `accept` and `reject`; see Listing 4-40.

Listing 4-40. *EmailValidator.java*

```
package com.apress.myfaces.trinidad.jsf.clientside;

import com.apress.myfaces.trinidad.domain.Email;

import java.util.Collection;
```

```
import javax.faces.application.FacesMessage;
import javax.faces.component.UIComponent;
import javax.faces.context.ExternalContext;
import javax.faces.context.FacesContext;
import javax.faces.validator.Validator;
import javax.faces.validator.ValidatorException;

import org.apache.myfaces.trinidad.validator.ClientValidator;

public class EmailValidator implements Validator, ClientValidator {

  private String accept;

  private String reject;

  public void validate(FacesContext context,
      UIComponent component,
      Object value) throws ValidatorException {
    if (value != null) {
      Email email = (Email) value;
      FacesMessage facesMessage = new FacesMessage();
      facesMessage.setSeverity(FacesMessage.SEVERITY_ERROR);
      facesMessage.setSummary("Validation Error");
      facesMessage.setDetail("Email is not valid");

      if (accept != null && email.getHost().indexOf(accept) == -1) {
        throw new ValidatorException(facesMessage);
      }
      if (reject != null && email.getHost().indexOf(reject) != -1) {
        throw new ValidatorException(facesMessage);
      }
    }
  }

  public Collection<String> getClientImportNames() {
    return null;
  }

  public String getClientLibrarySource(FacesContext ctx) {
    ExternalContext externalContext = ctx.getExternalContext();
    String path = externalContext.getRequestContextPath();
    return path + "/EmailValidator.js";
  }

  public String getClientScript(FacesContext context, UIComponent value) {
    return null;
  }
```

```
  public String getClientValidation(FacesContext context, UIComponent value) {
    return "new EmailValidator('" + accept + "','" + reject + "')";
  }

  public String getAccept() {
    return accept;
  }

  public void setAccept(String accept) {
    this.accept = accept;
  }

  public String getReject() {
    return reject;
  }

  public void setReject(String reject) {
    this.reject = reject;
  }
}
```

In Listing 4-40, all implemented methods, except `getClientValidation()`, are the same as for `ClientConverter`. Since `EmailValidator` has two attributes, we can pass them to the client side within the constructor. The `validate()` method executes the same logic on both the server and client sides, throwing `ValidatorException` and `TrValidatorException`, respectively, if validation fails; see Listing 4-41.

Listing 4-41. *EmailValidator.js*

```
EmailValidator = function(accept,reject) {
    this.accept = accept;
    this.reject = reject;
}

EmailValidator.prototype = new TrValidator();

EmailValidator.prototype.validate = function(value, label, converter) {
    if(value != null) {
        var email = value;

        var facesMessage = new TrFacesMessage("Validation Error",
        "Email cannot be accepted",
        TrFacesMessage.SEVERITY_ERROR);

        if(this.accept != null && email.host.indexOf(this.accept) == -1)
            throw new TrValidatorException(facesMessage);
```

```
        if(this.reject != null && email.host.indexOf(this.reject) != -1)
            throw new TrValidatorException(facesMessage);
    }
}
```

The last thing you have to do is to declare the validator and converter in your `faces-config.xml`; see Listing 4-42.

Listing 4-42. *Validator and Converter Declaration in faces-config.xml*

```
<converter>
  <converter-id>
    com.apress.myfaces.trinidad.EmailConverter
  </converter-id>
  <converter-class>
    com.apress.myfaces.trinidad.jsf.clientside.EmailConverter
  </converter-class>
</converter>
<validator>
  <validator-id>
    com.apress.myfaces.trinidad.EmailValidator
  </validator-id>
  <validator-class>
    com.apress.myfaces.trinidad.jsf.clientside.EmailValidator
  </validator-class>
</validator>
```

That is it! Now, the e-mail address conversion and validation can be used in our JSP pages; see Listing 4-43.

Listing 4-43. *Using the E-mail Converter and Validator*

```
<tr:inputText value="#{newCustomerBase.customer.email}"
              label="Contact Email"
              converter="emailConverter">
    <demo:emailValidator accept="apache.org" reject="hotmail.com,yahoo.com" />
</tr:inputText>
```

Note To provide a custom tag for your validator, you need to implement a `javax.faces.webapp.ValidatorTag` and create a Tag Library Descriptor (TLD) for it. You can find a complete example of this in the Source Code section of the Apress web site.

Exception and Message APIs

In the e-mail example, `TrConversionException` and `TrValidationException` are used together with `FacesMessage` to throw exceptions if conversion or validation fails. These client-side exceptions and FacesMessages are identical to their server-side counterparts except they are prefixed with Tr. The signatures for both exceptions are the same. Listing 4-44 shows the exceptions' signatures, and Table 4-8 lists and explains their parameters.

Listing 4-44. *Client-Side Exceptions*

```
function TrConverterException(facesMessage, summary, detail);
function TrValidatorException(facesMessage, summary, detail);
```

Table 4-8. *Client-Side Exception Parameters*

Parameter	Description
facesMessage	TrFacesMessage instance for displaying failure information
summary	Summary text used when facesMessage is null
detail	Detail text used when facesMessage is null

A client-side message (TrFacesMessage) has the same properties as its server-side counterpart. See Listings 4-45 and 4-46 and Table 4-9 for the TrFacesMessage signature, descriptions of its parameters, and how to use it.

Listing 4-45. *Client-Side Message Signature*

```
function TrFacesMessage(summary, detail, severity);
```

Table 4-9. *Client-Side Message Parameters*

Parameter	Description
summary	Summary text of the message
detail	Detail text of the message
severity	Seriousness of the message with the possible values SEVERITY_INFO (default), SEVERITY_ERROR, SEVERITY_WARN, and SEVERITY_FATAL

Listing 4-46. *Instantiating a Client-Side Message*

```
Var msg = new TrFacesMessage("Validation Error",
                             "E-mail cannot be accepted",
                             TrFacesMessage.SEVERITY_ERROR);
```

Note that the summary and detail texts are hard-coded. In order to bring some flexibility by supporting parameters and message formatting, Trinidad provides a handy class called TrFastMessageFormatUtils. TrFastMessageFormatUtils has a method called format that takes a parameterized message and a list of parameters to merge into the message. See Listings 4-47 and 4-48 and Table 4-10 for the TrFastMessageFormatUtils signature, descriptions of its parameters, and how to use it.

Listing 4-47. *Client-Side Message-Formatting Utility Signature*

```
function TrFastMessageFormatUtils()
TrFastMessageFormatUtils.format = function(messageString, parameters)
```

Table 4-10. *Client-Side Message-Formatting Utility Parameters*

Parameter	Description
`messageString`	Parameterized string to be formatted. A parameter is declared using curly braces and the number of the parameter to insert, for example, `{0}` to insert the first parameter declared in `parameters`.
`parameters`	Any number of comma-separated parameters to be used in formatting the message.

Listing 4-48. *Instantiating a Client-Side Message Using TrFastMessageFormatUtils*

```
var parameterizedDetail = "E-mail value: \"{1}\" for \"{0}\" cannot be accepted";
var detail = TrFastMessageFormatUtils.format(parameterizedMsg, label, value);
var msg = new TrFacesMessage("Validation Error",
                             detail,
                             TrFacesMessage.SEVERITY_ERROR);
```

Since the label and value are provided within the validate method in Listing 4-48, the output would be "Email value: invalid@invalid.com for Contact Email cannot be accepted".

Components

Trinidad provides over 100 components that are aimed at satisfying every requirement an application could face. As well as the simpler components like input texts, buttons, and labels, Trinidad also has an advanced set of UI components including tables, trees, and charts. A complete list of the components can be found in the demonstration application available for download on the Trinidad web site.

In the following sections, we will introduce the Chart and Table components.

Chart

The Chart component is a Scalable Vector Graphics (SVG)–powered component for creating graphical visualization of data model. The data model must be an implementation of `org.apache.myfaces.trinidad.model.ChartModel`. `ChartModel` is an abstract class used for providing chart data; other configuration is done declaratively with component attributes like `type` and `legendPosition`. Listings 4-49 and 4-50 show how to use the chart tag and define a chart model.

Listing 4-49. *Using the Chart Tag in JSP Documents*

```
<tr:chart value="#{demo.chartModel}" type="verticalBar" legendPosition="top" />
```

The chart in Listing 4-49 obtains the data model from a backing bean and renders an SVG vertical bar chart displaying the crop production per year. Listing 4-50 shows the managed bean that defines the chart model.

Listing 4-50. *Defining a Chart Model*

```
public class PopulationChartModel extends ChartModel{

  public List getGroupLabels() {
    List list = new ArrayList();
    list.add("2004");
    list.add("2005");
    list.add("2006");
    list.add("2007");
    return list;
  }

  public List getSeriesLabels() {
    List list = new ArrayList();
    list.add("corn");
    list.add("wheat");
    list.add("barley");
    return list;
  }

  public List getYValues() {
    List values = new ArrayList();

    for (int i = 0; i < getGroupLabels().size(); i++) {
      List series = new ArrayList();
      for (int j = 0; j < getSeriesLabels().size(); j++) {
        series.add(new Double(Math.random() * 1000));
      }

      values.add(series);
    }
    return values;
  }
}
```

There are three abstract methods of `ChartModel` that need to be implemented:

- `List getGroupLabels()`: Returns the labels for each group (years).
- `List getSeriesLabels()`: Returns the label for each of the series (crop types).
- `List getYValues()`: Returns the actual data.

In Listing 4-50, the data is a list of lists containing `double` values. For each group, there is an entry in the main values list. The entry itself is also a list of values corresponding to the production amount of each type of crop for that year. The output can be seen in Figure 4-5.

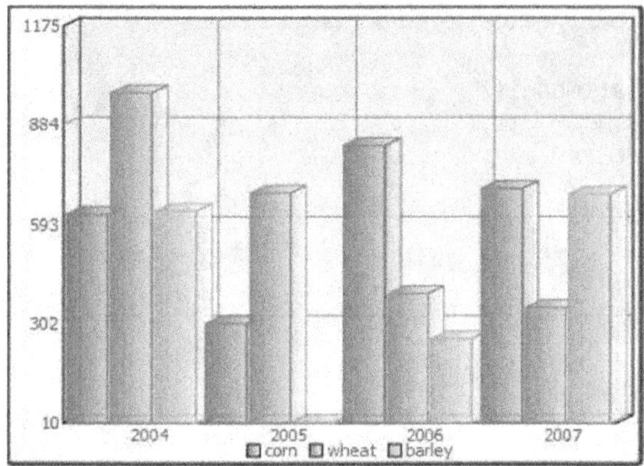

Figure 4-5. *Chart generated using the Trinidad Chart component*

Chart Customization

Most common chart types are supported, including pie, bar, line, and area. Consult the tag documentation on the Trinidad web site for the complete list of supported charts. The component has several customization attributes for labeling, animations, perspective, legend layout, and skinning. Refer to the tag documentation for the full list of customization options.

Handling Chart Events

To listen for events when the chart is clicked, the chart component provides an attribute for specifying a drill-down listener, which can be mapped to a method with the signature `public void methodName(org.apache.myfaces.trinidad.event.ChartDrillDownEvent)`; see Listings 4-51 and 4-52.

Listing 4-51. *Specifying a Drill-Down Listener*

```
<tr:chart value="#{demo.chartModel}"
          type="verticalBar"
          chartDrillDownListener="#{demo.onDrillDown}" />
```

Listing 4-52. *Implementing a Drill-Down Listener*

```
public void onDrillDown(ChartDrillDownEvent event) {
  int seriesIndex = event.getSeriesIndices()[0];
  int yValueIndex = event.getYValueIndices()[0];
```

```
    double value = event.getYValues()[0];
    String selectedCrop = (String)model.getSeriesLabels().get(seriesIndex);
    String selectedYear = (String)model.getGroupLabels().get(yValueIndex);

    //process selected data
}
```

Note When the chart is clicked, the event is passed through PPR, so the page is not reloaded.

Table

The Table component is an enhanced version of a regular HTML DataTable. What makes the table so powerful is the built-in support for paging, sorting, formatting, and detail toggling. The example used throughout this section gets a list of product objects to display and improves the display by adding features one by one.

Data and TableModel

The Table component uses `org.apache.myfaces.trinidad.model.CollectionModel` to access the underlying data to display. `CollectionModel` extends `javax.faces.model.DataModel` and adds support for row keys and sorting. You can still use regular Java lists, arrays, and the original faces `DataModel`.

Basic Table

In its simplest form, the Table component displays the data using the default look and feel, including the default page size of 25; see Listing 4-53.

Listing 4-53. *Basic Usage of the Table Component*

```
<tr:table var="customer" value="#{tableDemo.products}">
  <tr:column>
    <tr:outputText value="#{product.code}" />
  </tr:column>
  <tr:column>
    <tr:outputText value="#{product.name}" />
  </tr:column>
</tr:table>
```

Columns and Headers

`<tr:column />` enhances the regular JSF `<h:column />` by adding attributes for formatting and sorting.

There are two ways to specify the column headers: using the header facet (see Listing 4-54) and using the `headerText` attribute of the column (see Listing 4-55).

Listing 4-54. *Specifying a Column Header Using the Header Facet*

```
<tr:column>
  <f:facet name="header">
    <tr:outputText value="Code" />
  </facet>
  <tr:outputText value="#{product.code}" />
</tr:column>
```

Listing 4-55. *Specifying a Column Header Using the headerText Attribute*

```
<tr:column headerText="Code">
  <tr:outputText value="#{product.code}" />
</tr:column>
```

Nesting headers is also possible. The only change needed is adding a new parent column that spans the children columns; see Listing 4-56.

Listing 4-56. *Nesting Columns to Create Column Groups*

```
<tr:column headerText="Product Info">
  <tr:column headerText="Code">
    <tr:outputText value="#{product.code}" />
  </tr:column>
  <tr:column headerText="Name">
    <tr:outputText value="#{product.name}"/>
  </tr:column>
</tr:column>
```

Despite the `style` and `styleClass` support, the column component externalizes some common style attributes including `nowrap`, `align`, `width`, and `headerNoWrap` for convenience. Although the attribute names imply what they are useful for, consult the tag documentation for more information.

Pagination

Pagination is a must when presenting large datasets. Unlike the regular HTML DataTable, the Table component has built-in support for pagination. The number of rows to be displayed in a single page is specified using the `rows` attribute. The default number of rows to display is 25.

It is also possible to capture the moments when a page is changed by the user. When the page is changed, a `RangeChangeEvent` is fired. The event can be caught by specifying a listener method in the `rangeChangeListener` attribute. A sample use case would be to enabling caching for the viewed table ranges; see Listings 4-57 and 4-58.

Listing 4-57. *Specifying a Range Change Listener*

```
<tr:table rangeChangeListener="#{tableDemo.onRangeChange}">
```

Listing 4-58. *Implementing a Range Change Listener Method*

```
public void onRangeChange(RangeChangeEvent event) {
  int newStart = event.getNewEnd();
  int newEnd = event.getNewEnd();
  int oldStart = event.getNewEnd();
  int oldEnd = event.getNewEnd();

  //cache the data in old range
}
```

Sorting

Sorting is also a built-in feature of the Table component. Unlike pagination, sorting is not enabled by default. To enable sorting, a column needs to be configured using the `sortable` and `sortProperty` attributes; see Listing 4-59. Furthermore, the `DataModel` used must also support sorting.

Listing 4-59. *Enabling Column Sorting*

```
<tr:column sortable="true" sortProperty="code">
  <tr:outputText value="#{product.price}" />
</tr:column>
```

Note The `DataModel` used by the table must support sorting for the column sorting to work.

Enabling `sortable` provides an interactive UI to do sorting in ascending or descending order. On the other hand, `sortProperty` associates a `sortable` column with the property of the data to sort when the column is clicked. Sorting works for data types that implement `java.lang.Comparable` with no additional effort. For custom sorting mechanisms, the underlying `CollectionModel` must implement the following methods:

- `public boolean isSortable(String propertyName)`
- `public List getSortCriteria()`
- `public void setSortCriteria(List criteria)`

SortEvent and SortListener

It is possible to capture the moment when a column is sorted and add custom code to process. If a column is sorted, registered `SortListeners` are notified with the fired `SortEvent` that enables access to the sort property; see Listing 4-60 and 4-61.

Listing 4-60. *Specifying a Sort Listener of a Table*

```
<tr:table sortListener="#{tableDemo.onSort}" ...>
```

Listing 4-61. *Implementing a Sort Listener Method*

```
public void onSort(SortEvent sortEvent) {
  SortCriterion criteria = (SortCriterion)sortEvent.getSortCriteria().get(0);
  String property = criteria.getProperty();
  boolean asc = criteria.isAscending();

  //process custom
}
```

Row Selection

A common use case of tables is selecting a single row or multiple rows from the listed data. The Table component simplifies this requirement with the help of the `rowSelection` attribute. The `rowSelection` attribute supports two values: `single` for single row selection and `multiple` for multiple row selection.

In `single` mode, the selection is done via radio buttons, whereas check boxes are displayed for multiple selections. The example in Listings 4-62 and 4-63 shows how to enable the selection of multiple products from a table and add them to another table representing a shopping cart.

Listing 4-62. *Enabling Row Selection*

```
<tr:table var="product"
          value="#{tableDemo.products}"
          rowSelection="multiple"
          binding="#{tableDemo.table}" ...>

<tr:commandButton text="Add"
                  action="#{tableDemo.addToCart}" />
```

Listing 4-63. *Action Handler Copying Selected Rows*

```
public String addToCart() {

  // Iterate throught selected products
  for (Product product : (Product) table.getSelectedRowData()) {
    // Add the shopping cart table
    cart.add( product );
  }

  return null;
}
```

Detail Toggling

Detail toggling is a technique for displaying additional information about a row right below the row itself. By using the `detailStamp` facet, the Table component enables detail toggling. The facet content is rendered as hidden by default, and when the user chooses to display them, they show up. The example in Listing 4-64 uses `detailStamp` to display the detailed description of a product, since it may be too big to display in a separate column.

Listing 4-64. *Enable Detail Toggling*

```
<tr:table var="product" value="#{tableDemo.products}" …>
  ...
  <f:facet name="detailStamp">
    <h:outputText value="#{product.detailedDescription}" />
  </f:facet>
  ...
</tr:table>
```

■ **Note** A facet can have only one child component, but it's possible to add more by using that child as a container component, like a panel.

Look and Feel

Other than the `styleClass` attribute, there are a couple of attributes to change the look of the table. By default, the Table component draws vertical and horizontal lines for each cell. It is possible to manage these lines using the `horizontalGridVisible` and `verticalGridVisible` attributes. In addition, banding can be achieved by the `rowBandingInterval` and `columnBandingInterval` attributes. These attributes take integer values to specify the number of consecutive rows/columns that would have alternating styles. The default value is `0`, meaning every row and column looks the same. For advanced styling, continue reading the next section about component skinning.

Skinning

If you're familiar with Swing development, you have probably used or at least know about the Pluggable Look and Feel (PLAF) API. Using PLAF, different skins can be applied with little effort, and the same application can have various themes. Since JSF is built on reusable components just like Swing, skinning also makes sense although the JSF core does not support it at the moment. Without a central theme solution, a page author needs to go through all the components used in the application and use the `styleClass` and `style` properties, but applying styles this way is difficult to achieve and maintain. Trinidad, however, provides a solution that applies to all components; its skinning feature helps to manage the skins of all the components from a main control center and makes changing themes at runtime possible.

Creating a Custom Skin

Trinidad comes with a default skin called `simple skin`, but plugging in your own custom skin is easy with a little bit of configuration. `trinidad-skins.xml` is where you define your skins. As an example, we're going to create a custom skin called aqua and improve it throughout this section.

Skin Configuration

`trinidad-skins.xml` is located in the `WEB-INF` directory of your application. It could also, like `faces-config.xml`, be placed in the `META-INF` directory of your JAR, and it will automatically get picked up. The basic configuration of the `aqua` skin is displayed in Listing 4-65.

Listing 4-65. *Declaration of the Aqua Skin in trinidad-skins.xml*

```
<?xml version="1.0" encoding="ISO-8859-1"?>
<skins xmlns="http://myfaces.apache.org/trinidad/skin">
  <skin>
    <id>aqua.desktop</id>
    <family>aqua</family>
    <render-kit-id>
      org.apache.myfaces.trinidad.desktop
    </render-kit-id>
    <style-sheet-name>skins/aqua/aqua.css</style-sheet-name>
  </skin>
</skins>
```

Table 4-11 shows the description of the skin configuration tags.

Table 4-11. *Skin Configuration*

Configuration Tags	Description
`id`	Unique identifier of the skin.
`family`	Family name that the skin belongs to; used to enable the skin by specifying the `<skin-family>` in `trinidad-config.xml`.
`render-kit-id`	Used to determine in which environment (desktop or PDA) the skin would be employed. Possible values are `org.apache.myfaces.trinidad.desktop` and `org.apache.myfaces.trinidad.pda`.
`style-sheet-name`	CSS source file that contains the theme.
`bundle-name`	Internationalization bundle to use for labels and messages.
`extends`	Unique identifier of the skin for which to base the theme. If this is left empty, the skin will extend the simple skin.

Skin Style Sheet

Now that aqua skin is configured, the style sheet containing the theme needs to be provided. In `trinidad-skins.xml`, the CSS source is set to `skins/aqua/aqua.css`. For now, the CSS just contains a selector for setting the page backgrounds to aqua and two selectors for text fonts in the applications (see Listing 4-66).

Listing 4-66. *aqua.css*

```
body { background-color: aqua }
.AFDefaultFontFamily:alias { font-family: cursive; }
.AFDefaultFont:alias { font-size: 14px }
```

Turn On the Skin

Now that the skin is defined, it is time to enable it by defining the skin family in trinidad-config.xml as follows:

```
<skin-family>aqua</skin-family>
```

The skin-family configuration parameter also accepts EL expressions. This is a great way to change the skins dynamically at runtime without restarting the application with a hard-coded value.

That is it! Now, you can run any page of the application and observe that the background color is aqua and text font is 14-point Cursive. Although the selectors used in aqua.css are global selectors, meaning they affect more than one component, it's also possible to skin a single component.

Skinning a Single Component

A Trinidad component can be skinned in two ways: by defining the styleClass attribute or with general skinning.

The disadvantage of using styleClass is the amount of work required to apply the style manually to all components. Skinning solves this problem using the component-specific selectors. As an example, we are going to show you how to change the calendar icon and the title background color of the <tr:inputDate /> component (see Listing 4-67).

Listing 4-67. *Customizing Components Using CSS Selectors*

```
af|inputDate::launch-icon {
  content: url(/images/calendar/calendar_icon.gif);
}

af|inputDate::title {
        background-color: purple;
}
```

In Listing 4-67, we have customized the <tr:inputDate /> component using two selectors. All the <tr:inputDate /> components in the application will display a custom icon and a purple color title. To skin components, a CSS selector guide is necessary; the full list of available selectors is available online at http://myfaces.apache.org/trinidad/skin-selectors.html.

Platform-Specific Skinning

Satisfying the same look on different platforms might have been an issue if Trinidad did not provide browser compatibility features. The skin CSS file looks like a regular CSS file but actually has Trinidad-specific constructs that the skinning framework can interpret. For example, to manipulate the applied styles according to the operating systems and user agents, `@platform` and `@agent` are the two handy instructions (see Listing 4-68).

Listing 4-68. *Styling Based on the Platform and User Agent*

```
@platform windows, linux {

    @agent ie, netscape {
        af|inputDate::title {background-color: purple;}
    }

    @agent mozilla {
        af|inputDate::title { background-color: yellow;}
    }
}
```

In Listing 4-68, we have applied styling to browsers running on Windows and Linux. When the application is accessed via the Internet Explorer or Netscape browsers, the title color of an `<tr:inputDate />` will be purple. On the Mozilla Firefox browser, the title color will be yellow. The skin CSS is a great place for supplying agent-specific CSS attributes to achieve the same look and feel on different browsers.

In addition to platform and agents, skinning also supports RTL (right-to-left) languages. Selectors with the `:rtl` pseudoclass are applied when the browser works in RTL mode, so you can display flipped versions of the images to keep the RTL compatibility.

Skinning Tips

In the next sections, we will introduce some tips that are useful when developing skins.

CSS Compression

To save bandwidth and increase performance, the style sheets are compressed and not easily readable by default. However, in a development environment it would help a lot to disable the compression to debug style sheet resources; a context parameter is used to configure the content compression (see Listing 4-69).

Listing 4-69. *Context Parameter in web.xml to Disable Content Compression*

```
<context-param>
  <param-name>
    org.apache.myfaces.trinidad.DISABLE_CONTENT_COMPRESSION
  </param-name>
  <param-value>true</param-value>
</context-param>
```

Default Skin

When a skin is not defined explicitly, the simple base skin is selected as the default skin. If a custom skin is defined without the `<extends>` tag, it will extend the base skin by default. As a result of this, the base skin properties still apply to components. To avoid this, `-tr-inhibit` is used to block style sheet properties of the parent skin.

Listing 4-70 inhibits all the style properties of the base skin and sets custom properties afterward.

Listing 4-70. *Blocking Base Skin Properties*

```
af|inputNumberSpinbox::content {
    -tr-inhibit: all;
    width:50px;
}
```

Selector Composition

Reusing selectors helps reduce the amount of work required when creating selectors. The `-tr-rule-ref` rule can be used to include other selectors so that you don't have to write them again. As a result of composition, this leads to better maintainability and less code. Listing 4-71 includes another selector first to be applied and then specifies the width style.

Listing 4-71. *Creating a New Style Using Selector Composition*

```
af|inputText::content {
    -tr-rule-def: selector(".AFDarkBackground:alias");
    width:50px;
}
```

Aliases

Throughout this "Skinning" section, you may have noticed the selectors ending with the `:alias` suffix. Aliases are basically templates for reusing selectors based on the `-tr-rule-ref` described previously. Alias selectors do not make it directly to the generated style sheet; instead, the styles defined in them are used in the generation process.

Tuning and Configuration

In the previous sections, we have shown some configuration options via `trinidad-config.xml`. Actually, this configuration file is more than what you have seen so far. An example of a simple `trinidad-config.xml` file is displayed in Listing 4-72.

Listing 4-72. *A Simple trinidad-config.xml File*

```
<?xml version="1.0"?>
<trinidad-config xmlns="http://myfaces.apache.org/trinidad/config">

  <!-- Set to false in production environment -->
  <debug-output>true</debug-output>

  <skin-family>#{user.preferences.skin}</skin-family>

</trinidad-config>
```

Like the value of the `skin-family` parameter, most options can have EL expressions that would be evaluated per request. The complete list of configuration options is displayed in Table 4-12. In addition to the configuration in `trinidad-config.xml`, there are a couple of context parameters in `web.xml` related to performance configuration; see Table 4-13.

Table 4-12. *Trinidad Configuration Options in trinidad-config.xml*

Configuration Tags	Description
`debug-output`	In a development environment, Trinidad can render debug comments about HTML blocks rendered by components, indent, and even validate the HTML output.
`client-validation`	See the "Client-Side Conversion and Validation" section for the possible values.
`output-mode`	There are three output modes: `default` is the regular output mode; `printable` is useful for printable pages; and `email` suits pages that can be e-mailed.
`skin-family`	See the "Skinning" section.
`oracle-help-servlet-url`	Defines a URL to an Oracle Help for the Web (OHW) installation.
`accessibility-mode`	Determines the accessibility mode of the application. Possible values are `inaccesible`, which turns off accessibility, and `screenReader`, which adds support for screen readers.
`time-zone`	This option is mainly used in date and time conversion. If it's not set, the time zone is retrieved from the user agent's time zone.
`two-digit-year-start`	Base year value for years specified by their last digits like "95". The default value is `1950`.
`page-flow-scope-lifetime`	Maximum number of allowed `pageFlowScope` instances; the default value is `15`.
`number-grouping-separator`	Used in number conversion. If it's not set, the separator is resolved from the current locale.
`decimal-separator`	Same as `number-grouping-separator`.
`right-to-left`	Renders the pages from right-to-left for some languages, like Arabic.
`currency-code`	Used in currency field conversion when the field does not specify the currency explicitly.

Configuration Tags	Description
uploaded-file-processor	Full class name of an org.apache.myfaces.trinidad.webapp.UploadedFileProcessor implementation. This is a good place to plug in your own implementation other than the Trinidad's default UploadedFileProcessor.
formatting-locale	Used by converters when an explicit locale is not defined.

Note All options in trinidad-config.xml can be accessed programmatically via RequestContext.

Table 4-13. *Trinidad Context Parameters for Performance**

Context Parameter	Description
CACHE_VIEW_ROOT	Manages the unique token-based state-saving technique of Trinidad. Optimizes performance by caching the UIViewRoot.
CLIENT_STATE_METHOD	Trinidad provides two alternatives in case the state saving is set to client: default token mode enables token-based state saving, and all mode saves the state in a regular hidden input.
CLIENT_STATE_MAX_TOKENS	Number of client-side tokens that would be cached. The default value is 15.
USE_APPLICATION_VIEW_CACHE	Enables caching at application level for optimized performance; not suitable in development environment.
DEBUG_JAVASCRIPT	Turns off JavaScript obfuscation, which is enabled by default. Set it to true in the development process.
DISABLE_CONTENT_COMPRESSION	Disables the generated style sheet compression on the server side (which is the default). Set it to false when developing a custom skin.
CHECK_FILE_MODIFICATION	Checks the file modification dates of JSP and CSS files used in caching; suitable for development process.
ENABLE_LIGHTWEIGHT_DIALOGS	When pop-up dialogs are blocked, lightweight dialogs are handy, since they are based on modal IFRAMES.

** All parameters should be prefixed org.apache.myfaces.trinidad.*

Tuning Trinidad

In a production environment, first disable all the debug options that are only useful in development. These include

- debug-output in trinidad-config.xml
- org.apache.myfaces.trinidad.CHECK_FILE_MODIFICATION context parameter in web.xml
- org.apache.myfaces.trinidad.DEBUG_JAVASCRIPT context parameter in web.xml.

Second, turning off unique token-based client-side state saving also improves performance because of the decreased workload on the server during state saving/restoring process.

Summary

MyFaces Trinidad is a JSF framework providing a large number of product-quality components and extensions for tackling some of the limitations of the JSF specification. These extensions include the pageFlowScope for implementing wizard-like functionality, partial page rendering for implementing Ajax-based applications, the dialog framework for implementing pop-up dialogs, and client-side conversion and validation to increase performance by avoiding server-side trips.

On top of the extensions to the JSF specification, Trinidad also comes with a large number of product-quality components that greatly simplify end user interface. In this chapter, only a few of these components were introduced. Visit the Trinidad web page for a complete list of available components. As if this wasn't enough, Trinidad also provides skinning functionality to manage the look and feel of your application.

Unlike many other JSF frameworks, Trinidad is highly compatible with other JSF frameworks. You can use the individual JSF components of Trinidad without having to completely redo your application.

CHAPTER 5

Conversations and Scoping with Orchestra

Orchestra is a special project that truly reflects the dynamic nature of the MyFaces community and the open innovation it breeds. Orchestra was born out of the need to address conversation state for long-running wizard-based form interactions in MyFaces projects. While it is possible to achieve this in plain JSF, it is not efficient from a memory management standpoint. Additionally, Orchestra persistence management is an elegant way to avoid the inevitable lazy initialization exceptions every JSF newbie gets when managing persistence. We encourage you to incorporate Orchestra in your JSF project when the use case demands it.

Note Orchestra is a relatively new project and is actively updated. The goal of this chapter is to help you gain a clear understanding of Orchestra's capabilities and the situations when it is applicable. We will not be going into detailed examples like we have for Tomahawk and Trinidad, because the examples would likely be invalid by the time you read and try them. We want you to see the promise this framework provides and present it as a lightweight option (versus the more comprehensive Seam framework from JBoss).

Why Use Orchestra?

Orchestra addresses four major areas of JSF development. First, Orchestra addresses the need for a managed bean scope beyond request, session, and application. The scope is called conversation and provides an efficient way of keeping managed beans in memory until they are no longer needed. On top of the conversation scope, Orchestra also provides a conversation context that allows users to open multiple independent windows of your application.

In addition, Orchestra addresses the need of processing events that occur when a view is being initialized, before it is processed and rendered. This is done using `ViewController`, which can be coupled with conversations for managing timeouts.

Also, Orchestra offers easier management of persistence in the web tier. It provides the ability to manage the persistence context and entity manager on your behalf—no more exceptions like `OutOfMemory` and `LazyInitializationException` and no more reattach or merge operations.

■ Note Orchestra works at the web tier. Therefore, when dealing with persistence issues, Orchestra can only help if database access is being performed from the web tier. If you are using the full EJB (Enterprise JavaBean) stack, with all business logic and data IO carefully kept locked away from the presentation code, unfortunately, Orchestra's persistence support does not apply.

Finally, Orchestra provides a convenience component for generating forms for modifying database content.

In this chapter, we will start off by showing how to prepare your application for using Orchestra. Then we will look at the areas addressed by Orchestra: Conversations, `ViewController`, Persistence, and DynaForm. Finally, we will look at the architecture of Orchestra and show you its internal workings.

Creating an Application with Orchestra

The Orchestra distribution can be found on the Apache MyFaces Orchestra project page (`http://myfaces.apache.org/orchestra`). The download page contains two distributions: Core and Core15. The Core distribution is fully compatible with Java 1.4, whereas Core15 is an extension for providing enhancements for Java 5. Download both the Core and Core15 distribution for your platform; extract `myfaces-orchestra-core-VERSION.jar` and `myfaces-orchestra-core15-VERSION.jar` from the downloaded files; and place them in the `WEB-INF/lib` directory of your web application.

Dependencies

First, the Orchestra core distribution should be made available to the application. Orchestra relies on the Spring Framework for implementing conversation functionality. If this functionality is not required, the Spring Framework can be left out of the application. However, in most cases, you would want to use the conversation functionality, so you should, therefore, download the latest version of the Spring Framework from `http://www.springframework.org/download`, extract `spring.jar` from the downloaded file, and place it in the `WEB-INF/lib` directory of your web application.

If you are going to use the persistence functionality provided by Orchestra, you will need an implementation of the Java Persistence API (JPA), such as TopLink or Hibernate. Table 5-1 shows the Orchestra dependencies.

Table 5-1. *Orchestra Dependencies*

Dependency	Version	Description
MyFaces Orchestra Core15	1.0	Provides Orchestra enhancements for Java 5. Required only if you need the annotation enhancements for Java 5.
Spring Framework	2.x	J2EE Framework for simplifying enterprise programming. Required only if you need the conversion functionality.
Java Persistence API	1.0	Object relational mapping (ORM) framework for implementing object/relational database persistence.
commons-logging	1.1	Jakarta Commons library providing a wraparound for common Logging APIs.
Apache MyFaces or JavaServer Faces RI	1.1 or 1.2	Implements JSF 1.1 or 1.2.

Configuring the Web Descriptor (web.xml)

An Orchestra application is a standard web application and needs a web application descriptor (`WEB-INF/web.xml`). As a JSF application, the `web.xml` file has to include a servlet definition for the `FacesServlet` and a corresponding servlet mapping. Furthermore, an Orchestra listener is required to listen for conversation timeouts as well the Spring Framework listeners; see Listing 5-1.

Listing 5-1. *web.xml with Orchestra Configuration Highlighted in Bold*

```
<?xml version="1.0" encoding="UTF-8"?>
<!DOCTYPE web-app PUBLIC
    "-//Sun Microsystems, Inc.//DTD Web Application 2.3//EN"
    "http://java.sun.com/dtd/web-app_2_3.dtd">
<web-app>
  <listener>
    <listener-class>
      org.apache.myfaces.orchestra.conversation.servlet.➥
        ConversationManagerSessionListener
    </listener-class>
  </listener>
  <listener>
    <listener-class>
      org.springframework.web.context.ContextLoaderListener
    </listener-class>
  </listener>
  <listener>
    <listener-class>
      org.springframework.web.context.request.RequestContextListener
    </listener-class>
  </listener>
```

```
  <servlet>
    <servlet-name>Faces Servlet</servlet-name>
    <servlet-class>javax.faces.webapp.FacesServlet</servlet-class>
    <load-on-startup>1</load-on-startup>
  </servlet>
  <servlet-mapping>
    <servlet-name>Faces Servlet</servlet-name>
    <url-pattern>/faces/*</url-pattern>
  </servlet-mapping>
  <servlet-mapping>
    <servlet-name>Faces Servlet</servlet-name>
    <url-pattern>*.faces</url-pattern>
  </servlet-mapping>
</web-app>
```

■ Note Orchestra was designed to work with non-JSF applications. This requires setting up extra filters in `web.xml`. Instructions can be found on the Orchestra installation page at `http://myfaces.apache.org/orchestra/myfaces-orchestra-core/installation.html`.

Configuring the Spring Framework

In a web application environment, Spring reads its configuration by default from a file called `applicationContext.xml` located in the `WEB-INF` directory.

■ Tip It is possible to use an alternate name and location for this file through the `contextConfigLocation` context parameter in your `web.xml` file.

The Spring configuration file, shown in Listing 5-2, contains

- Initialization of Orchestra related modules
- Definition of the conversation bean scopes
- Persistence configuration
- Managed beans used by your application

Listing 5-2. *applicationContext.xml Spring Framework Configuration*

```
<?xml version="1.0" encoding="UTF-8"?>
<beans xmlns="http://www.springframework.org/schema/beans"
    xmlns:xsi="http://www.w3.org/2001/XMLSchema-instance"
    xmlns:tx="http://www.springframework.org/schema/tx"
    xmlns:aop="http://www.springframework.org/schema/aop"
    xsi:schemaLocation="
    http://www.springframework.org/schema/beans
    http://www.springframework.org/schema/beans/spring-beans-2.0.xsd
    http://www.springframework.org/schema/tx
    http://www.springframework.org/schema/tx/spring-tx-2.0.xsd
    http://www.springframework.org/schema/aop
    http://www.springframework.org/schema/aop/spring-aop-2.0.xsd">

  <!-- (1) Orchestra initilization -->
  <import resource="classpath*:/META-INF/spring-orchestra-init.xml" />

  <!-- (2) Bean scopes -->
  <bean class="org.springframework.beans.factory.config.CustomScopeConfigurer">
    <property name="scopes">
      <map>

        <entry key="conversation.manual">
          <bean class="org.apache.myfaces.orchestra.conversation.➥
                          spring.SpringConversationScope">
            <property name="timeout" value="30" />
            <property name="advices">
              <list>
                <ref bean="persistentContextConversationInterceptor"/>
              </list>
            </property>
          </bean>
        </entry>

        <entry key="conversation.access">
          <bean class="org.apache.myfaces.orchestra.conversation.➥
                        spring.SpringConversationScope">
            <property name="timeout" value="30" />
            <property name="advices">
              <list>
                <ref bean="persistentContextConversationInterceptor"/>
              </list>
            </property>
            <property name="lifetime" value="access"/>
          </bean>
        </entry>
```

```
    </map>
  </property>
</bean>

<!-- 3. Persistence configuration -->
<bean id="persistentContextConversationInterceptor"
      class="org.apache.myfaces.orchestra.conversation.➥
             spring.PersistenceContextConversationInterceptor">
  <property name="persistenceContextFactory" ref="persistentContextFactory"/>
</bean>

<bean id="persistentContextFactory"
      class="org.apache.myfaces.orchestra.conversation.spring.➥
             JpaPersistenceContextFactory">
  <property name="entityManagerFactory" ref="entityManagerFactory"/>
</bean>

<bean class="org.springframework.orm.jpa.support.➥
             PersistenceAnnotationBeanPostProcessor"/>

<tx:annotation-driven />

<bean id="transactionManager" class="org.springframework.orm.jpa.➥
                                     JpaTransactionManager">
  <property name="entityManagerFactory" ref="entityManagerFactory"/>
</bean>

<bean id="entityManagerFactory"
      class="org.springframework.orm.jpa.LocalEntityManagerFactoryBean">
  <property name="jpaProperties">
    <props>
      <prop key="toplink.logging.level">
        FINE
      </prop>
      <prop key="toplink.jdbc.driver">
        org.apache.derby.jdbc.EmbeddedDriver
      </prop>
      <prop key="toplink.jdbc.url">
        jdbc:derby:myfacesOrchestraDB;create=true
      </prop>
      <prop key="toplink.jdbc.user">
        sa
      </prop>
```

```
        <prop key="toplink.jdbc.password">
          foobar
        </prop>
        <prop key="toplink.target-database">
          oracle.toplink.essentials.platform.database.DerbyPlatform
        </prop>
        <prop key="toplink.ddl-generation">
          create-tables
        </prop>
      </props>
    </property>
    <property name="persistenceUnitName" value="default"/>
  </bean>

  <!-- 4. Managed beans -->
</beans>
```

Your application is now ready for using the functionality provided by Orchestra (we will explain the previous listing in detail later in this chapter).

Conversations

When you need to keep data in a managed bean throughout multiple requests or even multiple pages, you need a conversation. For example, in an order processing system, starting an order and adding items to it requires multiple steps. Having the managed bean available with its full state during this operation can make your life easier.

It does not matter if this involves only one page or many pages. In the end, any logical operation requires multiple requests.

JSF (like the Servlet API) is not much help with only three scopes for beans to be managed: application, session, or request (see Table 5-2).

Table 5-2. *Managed Bean Scopes Available in JSF*

Scope	Description
Application	Application-scoped beans are shared among all users of the application and available until the application is stopped.
Session	Session-scoped beans are available to the individual users from the time they access the application until they leave.
Request	The Request scope is short lived. After each request, the data is gone.

When using the session scope, you come close to having a conversation, as data is available between requests, but other traps await you:

- Holding data for the complete lifetime of the session not only wastes memory but also makes the data hard to release. Who knows what data is available and when it can be released?
- Starting over with a specific operation is difficult, since you cannot easily discard or reinitialize the beans in question.
- Last but not least, you'll never be able to allow your user to use multiple windows. The session scope will always be visible for all windows; no demarcation exists in the Servlet API or in JSF.

■ **Note** Most JSF implementations (including MyFaces and Sun RI) provide support for multiple concurrent windows, but this only means that the JSF components are safe for use with multiple windows; any application that uses only Request-scoped beans will work correctly, but applications with Session-scoped beans will still produce very strange results.

Some libraries, like Tomahawk, provide a partial solution to this problem with the `<t:saveState />` tag, as described in Chapter 2. This tag allows you to save the bean data from one request to the next but requires you to have your bean marked as `Serializable`, which requires a significant amount of work as you have to manage the conversation manually. On top of that, you will be struggling with exceptions if you are using persistence, as `<t:saveState />` will detach entities from the persistence context.

The Orchestra library provides a solution that works across all JSF implementations and was mainly built to work with Java 1.4 and later. When using Java 5, custom annotations are provided for ease of development. The conversation scope solution does require that the Spring Framework be used to declare Conversation-scoped managed beans rather than the standard JSF facility. However, there are many other good reasons for using Spring!

There are other projects addressing the conversation issue, like JBoss Seam, Apache Shale Dialog Manager, and Spring Web Flow. The Orchestra wiki (`http://wiki.apache.org/myfaces/Orchestra`) contains an up-to-date comparison of similar frameworks.

■ **Note** Objects stored in the Conversation scope are actually present in the HTTP session but grouped together as children of `Conversation` and `ConversationContext` objects. This makes it possible to discard data for a single conversation and to have multiple "conversation contexts" (independent windows).

Conversation Examples

Orchestra provides some example applications, including a rewrite of the Java Pet Store (`http://java.sun.com/developer/releases/petstore/`), to demonstrate its features. The source files of the example application can be downloaded from the MyFaces Subversion repository (`http://myfaces.apache.org/orchestra/source-repository.html`) and built using Maven, or you can download the precompiled, ready-for-deployment version at `http://people.apache.org/repo/m2-snapshot-repository/org/apache/myfaces/orchestra/myfaces-orchestra-examples-project`.

In the Java Pet Store application, the following scenarios may be considered different conversations:

- Buying a pet
- Registering for a pet training course

Something qualifies as a conversation if there are objects that need to be used over multiple requests, but for which there is a clear point in time at which the objects are no longer needed in memory—after a purchase has been completed or after a booking for a course has been made.

Objects that are stored in a conversation are typically JSF managed beans, that is, objects that are referenced by JSF EL expressions and that are expected to be created on demand when an EL expression first references them. We'll show you later how to configure which conversation a managed bean belongs to. However, you can also add other objects to a conversation from Java code.

■ Caution When using Orchestra's Conversation-scoped persistence, each conversation has its own persistence context. As a result, there are limitations on the sharing of persistent objects among objects in different conversations.

Sometimes, when you divide an application into conversations, you may discover that a particular managed bean is needed in more than one conversation. If it is truly necessary for the same managed bean instance to be present in multiple conversations, that bean can be configured as part of a third conversation whose lifetime spans both of the other conversations. However, more commonly, the instance does not need to be the same; in this case, just create two managed bean declarations. This keeps the lifetime of the managed bean instance short, and thereby minimizes memory usage.

■ Note Each conversation has a unique name. More than one conversation can be active at the same time, though of course, the fewer the better. Keeping conversations short saves memory!

You can retrieve an object representing a conversation with the Orchestra API. However, the name of a conversation is only relevant when configuring managed beans and when using Orchestra's `<o:endConversation />` tag (we will discuss this tag later in this chapter).

Conversation Lifetime

A conversation has a start and an end. The time between when a conversation starts and ends is called the conversation lifetime.

Conversations generally get started automatically when a JSF EL expression references a bean that is declared as being part of a particular conversation. Finding the end of a conversation is a little more complex and will be discussed in the "Access Lifetime" and "Manual Lifetime" sections.

Access Lifetime

An Access-scoped conversation ends if a JSF request completes without invoking any method on any of the objects stored in the access conversation. This applies remarkably often. A JSF view usually has one backing bean that EL expressions reference, and that backing bean holds the data needed for that page. When a user performs multiple operations on that page, the same backing bean gets used each time. Eventually, the user will select a command that navigates to some other page that does not use that same backing bean.

If the backing bean has been configured using an Access-scoped conversation, the same instance is used for each page render, like a Session-scoped managed bean. However, after the new page has been rendered, the no-longer-needed backing bean quietly and automatically vanishes.

Access conversations also work for sequences of views where each view uses the same basic data and therefore references the same managed bean.

Caution Watch out for Partial Page Rendering (PPR) and Ajax requests, which can cause only parts of pages to be rendered! In most cases, these operations will still retrieve data from some bean in the Access scope and therefore keep the Access scope alive, but if not, the Manual scope may be needed (see the "Manual Lifetime" section).

Manual Lifetime

When a conversation is more complex, a bean may be needed on only some of the views in a sequence. The friendly Access scope is too eager to discard data in this case.

As with Access-scoped conversations, a Manual-scoped conversation's lifetime typically starts automatically when some EL expression references the managed bean that is configured as part of a conversation.

Tip See the "The ConversationUtils Class" section for another way for a conversation to start.

A Manual conversation ends, however, only when code explicitly tells it to. This can be done via a call to the Orchestra API or by using a JSF component. In either case, the code that ends the conversation is expected to be an action method that causes a conversation to be invalidated; that is, the conversation ends after the user has asked the application to perform a particular operation that makes the data irrelevant.

Listing 5-3 is a snippet from the Orchestra Pet Store example showing how to invalidate a manual conversation after performing an action. Listing 5-4 shows how to invalidate a manual conversation using a JSF component.

Listing 5-3. *Invalidating a Manual Conversation in the Backing Bean*

```
public String saveAction() {
  ....
  topic.setOwner(getVoterDao().getByKey(getBallotState().getVoterId()));
  topicDao.save(topic);

  Conversation.getCurrentInstance().invalidate();
  return FacesConst.SUCCESS;
}
```

Listing 5-4. *Invalidating a Manual Conversation Using the JSF Component*

```
<h:commandButton value="" method="#{bean.saveAction}">
  <orchestra:endConversation name="topicConversation"/>
</h:commandButton>
```

When using the component approach to ending a conversation, the conversation name needs to be explicitly provided. In the backing bean approach, the `"current conversation instance"` can be retrieved, making the conversation name unnecessary.

Whether the code or component approach is better is up to you to decide. It could be argued that the concept of a conversation is not a presentation/view concept, so making the call from the code is perhaps cleaner. However, avoiding direct calls to Orchestra from within managed bean code is also nice.

Invaliding the conversation relies on the user using the application navigation: it works only when the sole way to leave a particular view is by causing an action method to be invoked (`<h:commandButton />` or `<h:commandLink />`). If a user walks away from the PC, the conversation is not discarded until the user session eventually times out. Similarly, if the view contains raw HTML links (`<h:outputLink />`), the conversation is only cleaned up by a timeout.

■ **Note** Orchestra provides the ability to time out a conversation earlier than the HTTP session timeout (see the "Configuring Conversation-Scoped Managed Beans" sections for details).

Managing Independent Windows

Some web users often open multiple windows of the same web application to perform multiple tasks on it. For example, while a time-consuming operation is in progress, they want to be working elsewhere in the application, or they would like to view some reference screens in one window while performing actions in another. In the most complex cases, they may want to use multiple windows to work concurrently on the same part of the web application.

A web application that uses only Request-scoped objects has a little problem with this: each window is naturally independent. The only potential issue is where data in a database changes such that when an HTTP form is submitted there is some kind of data conflict. However, that can happen even without multiple windows and must be handled by application code anyway.

When browser windows do not share an HTTP session, there is also a small problem; the situation is the same as Request-scoped. This is effectively the same as using two different PCs simultaneously.

However, when requests from two browser windows share the same HTTP session and the application cannot limit itself to just Request-scoped data things get tricky. JSF implementations typically perform some work to ensure that the components themselves work correctly in this situation, by encoding a hidden identifier into the data they render, even when the JSF component tree is stored in the session. However, data added to the session by the user is not protected in this way; there is only one instance of each managed bean in session scope, and both windows will be modifying that same instance.

If all beans are stored in the conversation scope rather than session scope, Orchestra can ensure that different windows see different copies of all these beans, removing any undesirable interactions.

When a web application is first accessed by a user (whether by clicking a link or selecting a bookmark), a new conversation context is created for that user. If the user then repeats this operation, the new window will have a different conversation context associated, although the HTTP session is the same. You can find more information about conversation contexts in the "Orchestra's Architecture" section.

BROWSER WINDOWS AND SESSIONS

Java web-servers usually use a cookie to associate an HTTP request to a particular HTTP session; if the cookies are shared between two windows, the same HTTP session is also used for requests coming from both browser windows.

With Microsoft Internet Explorer, selecting the Open New Window menu option (or pressing Ctrl+N) produces a new window that shares its cookies with the original, while clicking the application launcher (or starting the application from the command line) creates a window that does not share cookies with any other existing windows. Mozilla Firefox shares cookies in both cases; only if a different profile is used are cookies independent across windows.

The Role of Spring

Orchestra needs the ability for managed beans to declare that they are in a custom scope and to invoke the creation and lookup of those beans. JSF's managed bean declaration facility simply doesn't support extension; the format is fixed. Fortunately, JSF does allow the bean creation and lookup process to be customized.

The Spring project (`http://www.springframework.org`) provides excellent facilities for managing bean declarations and integrates well with JSF. Orchestra requires that Spring (version 2.0 or later) be used when declaring Conversation-scoped beans. This does not require you to make any code changes of any sort to the JSF application—just a few entries in the `web.xml` file and the addition of the Spring library to the classpath.

The presence of the Orchestra library on the Java classpath automatically configures the lookup of EL variables to be redirected to Spring when a match is not found by the standard implementation.

■ Note Orchestra is not tightly coupled to Spring; it should be possible to use any dependency-injection framework that provides the necessary hooks. See the "Orchestra's Architecture" section for further details.

Configuring Conversation-Scoped Managed Beans

Conversation-scoped managed beans are declared in `/WEB-INF/applicationContext.xml`. The first bean declaration in the configuration file configures the custom scopes (see Listing 5-5). The `bean` xml element adds the custom scopes `conversation.manual` and `conversation.access`. There are various properties configurable for the `SpringConversationScope` (see Table 5-3). The properties get applied to any conversation created with the respective scope. You can choose any names you like and add more scope definitions if you need different combinations, for example, different timeouts for some conversations.

Listing 5-5. *Custom Scope Configuration (Snippet from /WEB-INF/applicationContext.xml)*

```
<bean class="org.springframework.beans.factory.config.CustomScopeConfigurer">
  <property name="scopes">
    <map>
      <entry key="conversation.manual">
        <bean class="org.apache.myfaces.orchestra.conversation.➥
                         spring.SpringConversationScope">
          <property name="timeout" value="30" />
          <property name="advices">
            <list>
              <ref bean="persistentContextConversationInterceptor"/>
            </list>
          </property>
        </bean>
      </entry>
```

```
        <entry key="conversation.access">
          <bean class="org.apache.myfaces.orchestra.conversation.➥
                        spring.SpringConversationScope">
            <property name="timeout" value="30" />
            <property name="advices">
              <list>
                <ref bean="persistentContextConversationInterceptor"/>
              </list>
            </property>
            <property name="lifetime" value="access"/>
          </bean>
        </entry>
      </map>
    </property>
</bean>
```

Table 5-3. *Properties of SpringConversationScope*

Property	Description
`lifetime`	This may be set to either `manual` or `access`. If not specified, `manual` lifetime applies to all conversations created with this scope.
`timeout`	This may be set to a number of minutes. If managed beans belonging to the conversation have not been accessed within the specified timeout, the conversation is automatically ended by Orchestra. Because conversations are indirectly held by the HTTP session, they will be discarded when the HTTP session times out. However, the HTTP session timeout is refreshed on each request. If the user starts a conversation and leaves it inactive but continues working on some other part of the same application, the conversation will continue to take up memory indefinitely. If this is a concern for your application, a conversation timeout can be defined. If this property is not specified, no timeout applies to conversations created by this scope.

After the custom scope configuration, you can declare your conversation beans (see Listing 5-6). You can access beans declared here from a JSF EL expression, such as #{someBean}, just like a managed bean declared in the standard JSF configuration file. However, the bean will be stored in a conversation with name conv1, and when that conversation ends, the bean will be discarded even though the HTTP session remains. See Table 5-4 for details on the bean declaration attributes.

Listing 5-6. *Managed Conversation Bean (Snippet from /WEB-INF/applicationContext.xml)*

```
<bean name="someBean"
      class="example.SomeBackingBean"
      scope="conversation.manual"
      orchestra:conversationName="conv1">
</bean>
```

Table 5-4. *Bean Declaration Attributes*

Attribute	Description
scope	Declares the scope of the bean from the available scopes in applicationContext.xml. In Listing 5-5, conversation.manual and conversation.access are available. The bean in Listing 5-6 uses the conversation.manual scope and will, therefore, be kept alive until the conv1 conversation is explicitly closed or until the HTTP session timeout is reached. If the bean scope was declared as conversation.access, the conversation created to hold this bean would automatically be invalidated if a request did not use any data from the conv1 conversation.
conversationName	The conversationName attribute is optional, and it is quite useful to declare managed beans without an explicit conversationName. A view, or even a sequence of views, often needs just one non-request-scoped bean (i.e., the conversation only has one object in it). Note that it is not valid for two beans to declare themselves members of the same conversation but use different scopes.

Tip As you have already configured Spring for use with Conversation-scoped beans, you should think about defining all your JSF beans (Request-, Session- and Application-scoped) in Spring rather than the standard JSF configuration files. Spring provides some very nice additional features over basic JSF, yet integrates completely transparently into JSF.

Conversation-Related JSF Tags

The next sections will illustrate the conversation-related JSF tags in Orchestra.

<o:endConversation />

This tag can be added as the child of a command component to invalidate the conversation after the action has been performed (see Listing 5-7). Presumably, the action does something that means the beans in the conversation are no longer relevant. Table 5-5 shows the attributes for the endConversation tag.

Listing 5-7. *Ending a Conversation Using the JSF Component*

```
<h:commandButton value="" method="#{bean.saveAction}">
  <o:endConversation name="conv1"/>
</h:commandButton>
```

Table 5-5. *Attributes of the endConversation Tag*

Attribute	Description
`name`	Specifies the conversation that is to be invalidated. This attribute is mandatory.
`onOutcome`	Comma-separated list of navigation strings. If the action method returns a value that matches something in the list, the conversation is invalidated; otherwise, it remains active. This attribute is optional; if not specified, the conversation is ended regardless of the value returned by the action method, unless the action method throws an exception.
`errorOutcome`	A navigation string to use if the action method throws an exception. Instead of an error page being displayed, the user is navigated to the defined view. When the `errorOutcome` navigation occurs, the conversation is not ended.

<o:separateConversationContext />

This tag allows a pop-up window to be created that accesses the same web application completely independently of the original window, assuming all states are stored in conversation scope and not session scope. Window independence is achieved by grouping conversations together into a conversation context and associating different conversation contexts with different windows.

Orchestra manages this association by adding a conversation context identifier parameter to all URLs in a view. The `<o:separateConversationContext />` component suppresses this parameter for its nested components, so they trigger a new conversation context when used.

■ **Note** If you would like to start a new conversation context using a `<h:commandLink/>` or `<h:commandButton/>`, you will have to embed the whole JSF `<h:form/>` tree within the `<o:separateConversationContext/>` component.

Listing 5-8 shows an example of two output links. The first one maintains the conversation context URL parameter; the second one doesn't.

Listing 5-8. *Separating the Conversation Context*

```
<h:outputLink value="/">
  <h:outputText value="Home" />
</h:outputLink>
<o:separateConversationContext>
  <h:outputLink value="/" target="_blank">
    <h:outputText value="Home in new window" />
  </h:outputLink>
</o:separateConversationContext>
```

Tip Orchestra uses a URL parameter and not any magic view state trick. It is therefore possible to manipulate the conversation context ID from JavaScript. This allows for creating a JavaScript mouse button handler that traps right-button clicks on links and provides a custom "Open in New Window" menu that would open a new window with a URL that is identical to the original window URL except that the context ID parameter has been removed.

Managing Events with ViewController

One of the things that many people feel JSF lacks is the ability to invoke life cycle events on backing beans associated with the current view. Until now, there has been no standard way of implementing life cycle events. There are a handful of popular open source implementations, one of which is Orchestra's `ViewController`.

Note Support for life cycle events has been planned as a standard feature in JSF 2.0 (JSR 314). Information can be found at the Java Community Process web site: `http://jcp.org/en/jsr/detail?id=314`.

In a nutshell, `ViewController` enables a bean to be associated with one or more views. Once associated, the bean will receive life cycle events for the specified views. The bean receives events by either implementing the `ViewController` interface, shown in Figure 5-1, or specifying the callback methods using annotations.

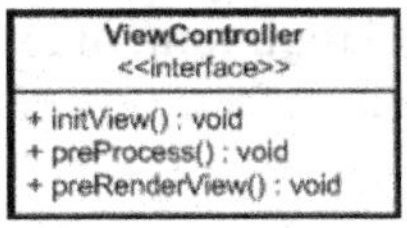

ViewController
<<interface>>
+ initView() : void
+ preProcess() : void
+ preRenderView() : void

Figure 5-1. *The ViewController interface*

The `ViewController` interface specifies the three callback methods described in Table 5-6.

Table 5-6. *Callback Methods in ViewController*

Method	Description
`initView()`	This is called when a request starts for a view that this bean is associated with. Note that `initView()` is called once for every user request to a view associated with the bean.
`preProcess()`	This is called before any JSF components invoke their action methods.
`preRenderView()`	This is called before view rendering starts.

Mapping Views to Beans

First of all you have to tell the system how the view name is related with a backing bean. By default (without the Core15 module), Orchestra maps views to beans automatically by their names; Table 5-7 shows an example. Note that it is not a requirement for all views to have a corresponding bean.

Table 5-7. *View-to-Bean Mapping Scheme Example*

View	Bean Class
`/userInfo.jsp`	`userInfo`
`/SecureArea/userPassword.jsp`	`secureAreaUserPassword`
`/1stStep.jsp`	`_1stStep`

■ **Note** Some parts of Orchestra take advantage of the `ViewController`'s ability to associate a bean with a view, regardless of whether the bean wants any callbacks; the `ConversationRequire` annotation and the JSF Converter support are two such examples.

Finding the Life Cycle Methods

Once the corresponding bean is located, Orchestra needs to determine which methods on that bean should receive the life cycle events.

The simplest approach is for the bean to implement the `ViewController` interface (from the `org.apache.myfaces.orchestra.viewController` package) as mentioned previously. However, as Orchestra uses reflection to look up the callback methods, the only real requirement is to use the same method names and signatures as those in the `ViewController` interface.

Mapping via Annotations

If you use Orchestra's Core15 extension, annotations can be used to map both views to beans and callback methods.

View mapping is done using the `@ViewController` annotation, and the `@InitView`, `@PreProcess`, and `@PreRenderView` annotations are used for specifying the callback methods; see Listing 5-9.

Listing 5-9. *Mapping with Annotations*

```
@ViewController(
  viewIds={"/page1.jsp", "/page2.jsp", "/page3.jsp"})
public class AnnotatedMultiViewBean {
```

```
  @InitView
  public void initialiseView() {
    ...
  }

  @PreProcess
  Public void beforeViewProcessing() {
    ...
  }

  @PreRenderView
  Public void beforeViewRendering() {
    ...
  }
}
```

■Note When using annotations, it is possible to map more than one view to the same class, which is not possible with the automatic, magical naming scheme.

Customizing the ViewController

`ViewController` can be customized by providing your own `ViewControllerManager`. A custom `ViewControllerManager` must extend the abstract class `AbstractViewControllerManager`, found in the `org.apache.myfaces.orchestra.viewController` package, as shown in Listing 5-10.

Listing 5-10. *Custom ViewController*

```
public class MyViewControllerManager extends AbstractViewControllerManager {

  private ViewControllerNameMapper viewControllerNameMapper =
      new DefaultViewControllerNameMapper();

  private ViewControllerExecutor viewControllerExecutor =
      new ReflectiveViewControllerExecutor();

  public DefaultViewControllerManager() {
  }

  protected ViewControllerNameMapper getViewControllerNameMapper() {
    return viewControllerNameMapper;
  }
```

```
  protected ViewControllerExecutor getViewControllerExecutor() {
    return viewControllerExecutor;
  }
}
```

Once the ViewControllerManager is implemented, you can activate it through the Spring configuration file as shown in Listing 5-11.

Listing 5-11. *Activating a Custom ViewController*

```
<bean
    name="org.apache.myfaces.orchestra.viewController.ViewControllerManager"
    class="com.apress.orchestra.MyViewControllerManager"
    scope="singleton" />
```

Requiring Conversations

The @ConversationRequire annotation allows you to issue an automatic redirect to the entry page of the conversation if a conversation is not running (see Listing 5-12). This gracefully handles situations where conversation timeouts are in use or the HTTP session has timed out. It also handles cases where users manipulate URLs directly or use bookmarks.

Listing 5-12. *Defining Conversation Requirements*

```
@ConversationRequire(
  conversationNames = "someConversation",
  entryPointViewIds = "/Page1.jsp",
  redirect = "/Page1.faces")
@ViewController(viewIds={"/Page1.jsp", "/Page2.jsp", "/Page3.jsp"})
public class MyViewControllerWithConversation {}
```

When using the @ConversationRequire annotation, you need to tell Orchestra which views the bean is associated with, so that before processing begins, the appropriate beans can be checked for required conversation annotations.

The Orchestra ViewController has a number of other features, but only the view-to-bean mapping is necessary to enable the @ConversationRequire annotation.

Whenever the system is going to view one of the specified pages Orchestra will check if the conversation someConversation is running. If not, a redirect to /Page1.faces will be issued. Note that you have to tell Orchestra which of the ViewController pages is the entry point (entryPointViewIds) to avoid endless loops.

As an alternative to the redirect attribute, you can also use the navigationAction attribute of the @ConversationRequire annotation. In this case, the navigation will be issued through the JSF navigation handler.

Note @ConversationRequire currently has no equivalent that isn't an annotation. The closest you can get is for the class to define itself as ViewController and the initView callback method to check for the existence of the conversation manually.

Managing Persistence in Orchestra

If you try to write applications without a framework that provides conversations that link to the persistence layer, you'll get exceptions from the persistence framework you'll wish you had never seen. As an example, you'll get `LazyInitializationException` if the reference in a one-to-many relationship has not been fetched prior to closing the persistence session. Likewise, if you use serialization to keep data between requests (remember `<t:saveState />`) and try to persist the entity again, you'll get `NonUniqueObjectException`, because the persistence layer would not be able to determine if the entity needs to be inserted or updated in the database.

These problems happen when using a new persistence session for each HTTP request. The solution is to keep the persistence session open exactly as long as required (no more, no less).

The Java Persistence API provides the concept of an extended persistence context, whose lifetime is not tied to a single HTTP request. However, there is no standard support for determining exactly when such an extended context should be closed. Using Orchestra's conversation scope, you can define this time span. You simply declare your managed beans in the conversation scope and let Orchestra set up the system in a way that any database access from within this Conversation-scoped managed beans uses the same persistence context. Ending the conversation will close the persistence context, too.

Quick Overview of the Java Persistence API

In case you are new to persistence frameworks, this section provides a quick overview of the important concepts.

A persistence context mainly holds the data you have loaded from the database and keeps track of this data to be able to issue SQL `INSERT` or `UPDATE` statements as required.

This data is called an "entity." For each and every record loaded from the database, such an entity will be created for you. You can add entities to the persistence context by calling the persist operation with the new object. When flushing the persistence context, the data will be kept in sync with the database again (see Figure 5-2).

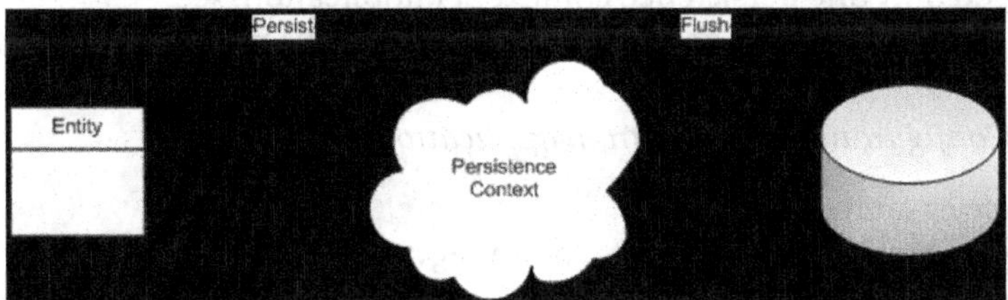

Figure 5-2. *Overview of persistence*

Since the object relationships can be complex and refer to many different tables, it makes sense to define some relationships as lazy (in contrast to eager). Lazy relations will be fetched from the database on demand, for example, when using the bean accessor to get the data. Lazy loading objects save memory and, with complex graphs of data that are not used often, avoids time-consuming database joins.

On the other hand, defining a relationship used often to be eagerly loaded can also be a time saver, especially if you iterate through a collection of entities and have to fetch data from the relations, too.

Sometimes, choosing whether to use lazy or eager loading isn't easy, but you'll definitely have to use lazy relations, which might result in `LayzInitializationException` if not used carefully.

A persistence context can be closed. Closing it will release all the memory it used and make any reference to an entity that you stored in your managed bean a detached entity. "Detached" means that there is no persistence context responsible for this entity. Changes on the entity will no longer result in an SQL `UPDATE`. Persisting it again will result in duplicate key exceptions from the database or the persistence layer, depending on the configuration of the entity. Also, fetching noninitialized lazy relations will fail, too.

As a side note, it is good to know that some persistence layers allow you to partially remove objects from the persistence context, which is useful if you have to batch process many thousand entities. If you remove entities that are no longer being used from the context, you can help avoid `OutOfMemory` exceptions and speed up some of the operations of the persistence context.

■ Note The Java Persistence API is an API developed under the Java Community Process to standardize the interface for ORM providers.

Using Orchestra's Persistence Support

Orchestra can tie an ORM's persistence context to a conversation. To get rid of the `LazyInitializationException` and related issues, the persistence context is kept open as long as the conversation, and this is what Orchestra does automatically for you.

First, you configure Orchestra for the persistence context to use in `/WEB-INF/applicationContext.xml`. You need only one persistence context per application; see Listing 5-13 (this configuration assumes that you have already set up your JPA provider).

Listing 5-13. *Persistence Context Configuration (Snippet from applicationContext.xml)*

```
<bean id="persistentContextConversationInterceptor"
      class="org.apache.myfaces.orchestra.conversation.spring.➥
             PersistenceContextConversationInterceptor">
  <property name="persistenceContextFactory" ref="persistenceContextFactory"/>
</bean>

<bean id="persistenceContextFactory"
      class="org.apache.myfaces.orchestra.conversation.persistenceContexts. ➥
             JpaPersistenceContextFactory">
  <property name="entityManagerFactory" ref="entityManagerFactory"/>
</bean>
```

```
<bean id="entityManagerFactory"
      class="org.springframework.orm.jpa.LocalContainerEntityManagerFactoryBean">
  <property name="dataSource" ref="managedDataSource"/>
</bean>
```

The `persistentContextConversationInterceptor` has been configured as an advice and, with the help of the `persistenceContextFactory`, ensures that the execution of any method of a Conversation-scoped bean has this interceptor configured. Obtaining an `EntityManager` from a conversation bean will access the `entityManager` bound to bean.

Finally, the `persistenceContextFactory` is responsible for maintaining the `entityManager` and telling Spring about the existence of the persistence context. Spring has extensive support for persistence, which Orchestra is simply enhancing by coupling it to the concept of a conversation.

Your code then uses standard facilities for accessing the persistence context, for example, Spring's JPA template or JPA's `@Transactional` and `@PersistenceContext` annotations.

■ **Note** The term "advice" comes from the aspect-oriented programming world. It means that certain methods on a class get intercepted so that other code can run before and after the call, potentially changing the behavior of the class being intercepted.

Using Persistence with Annotations

When using Java 1.5 or later, simply annotate your Data Access Objects (DAO) with standard transactional annotations; see Listing 5-14.

Listing 5-14. *Data Access Object*

```
import javax.persistence.PersistenceContext;

public class ShopCustomerDao {

  @PersistenceContext
  private EntityManager entityManager;

  public ShopCustomer getByKey(long customerId) {
    return entityManager.find(ShopCustomer.class, Long.valueOf(customerId));
  }

  public void save(ShopCustomer shopCustomer) {
    entityManager.persist(shopCustomer);
  }
}
```

If you are used to writing persistence code with JPA, this will look very familiar.

Caution Passing loaded entities from one conversation to another is not allowed: the `entityManager` might complain that the entity is already bound to another `entityManager`. It's best to just pass the primary key between conversation boundaries and reload the entity within the conversation.

While Orchestra works with JPA by default, it should be possible to plug any persistence layer in via a few appropriate adapter classes—even custom persistence implementations you've rolled yourself!

Using Persistence Without Annotations

There are a number of ways to access the `EntityManager` without using annotations to specify injection. Listing 5-15 shows how this can be injected into a DAO.

Listing 5-15. *Injecting the Entity Manager Factory into a DAO*

```
<bean name="productDao"
      class="org.apache.myfaces.examples.mops.dao.ProductDao">
  <property name="entityManagerFactory" ref="entityManagerFactory"/>
</bean>
```

The most convenient way to handle the `entityManagerFactory` is by subclassing the Spring helper class `JpaDaoSupport`, as shown in Listing 5-16.

Listing 5-16. *Extending Spring's JpaDaoSupport*

```
public class ProductDao extends JpaDaoSupport {

  public Product getByKey(Long productId) {
    return getJpaTemplate().find(Product.class, productId);
  }
}
```

Transaction Management

Transaction management can be handled using Spring's JPA template or the standard `@Transactional` annotation.

In case of annotation, each method of your backing bean that is going to issue a database update has to be annotated using `@Transactional`. In other case, you'll simply use no annotation. There is no need to use a specific read-only transaction: `@Transactional(readOnly=true)`.

Note You are often required to throw away the `entityManager` once an exception has occurred during the flush or commit operation. To achieve this, you'll have to invalidate the conversation and start over. Whether there is a way around this inconvenience depends on the ORM you use.

Using Non-JPA Persistence Implementations

You can use non-JPA persistence implementations by providing your own implementations of `PersistenceContextFactory` and `PersistenceContext` (from the package `org.apache.myfaces.orchestra.conversation.spring`) (see Figure 5-3).

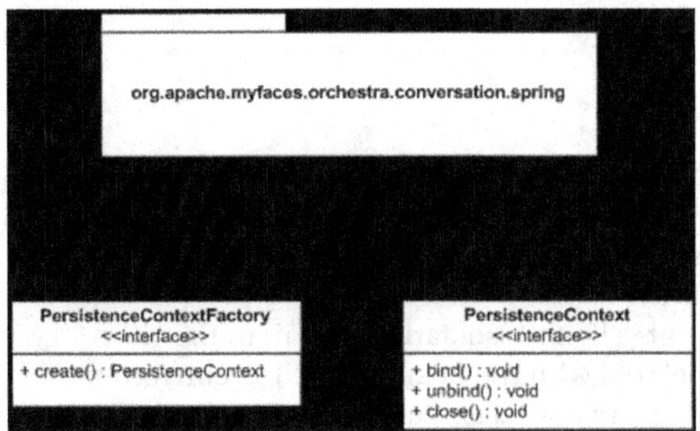

Figure 5-3. *Interfaces to implement for providing a non-JPA persistence implementation*

The factory simply has to return a new instance of your `PersistenceContext` every time the `create()` method is invoked.

The `PersistenceContext` has to bind the resource to the current thread once its `bind()` method is invoked. For our JPA implementation, this means that the `entityManager` is set up using Spring's `TransactionSynchronizationManager`.

On `unbind()`, `PersistenceContext` has to free this resource again.

■ **Note** You have to maintain a stack of resources, as you might have recursive calls or calls from one conversation into another. Please refer to the `JpaPersistenceContextFactory` implementation for an example.

In `close()`, you finally have to close the resource—this should be the one and only place where the close operation should happen. Again, our JPA implementation will close the `entityManager` here.

Normally, `close()` will only be called at the end of a conversation.

ConnectionManagerDataSource

If you are going to use a persistence layer that is not JPA compliant, you might find Orchestra's `ConnectionManagerDataSource` handy. It ensures, with the help of the `OrchestraServletFilter`, that any open database connection will be closed at the end of the request.

Simply wrap your `dataSource` into a `managedDataSource` and use the `managedDataSource` in any subsequent configuration; see Listing 5-17.

Listing 5-17. *Using the ConnectionManagerDataSource*

```
<bean id="managedDataSource"
      class="org.apache.myfaces.orchestra.connectionManager. ➥
             ConnectionManagerDataSource">
  <property name="dataSource" ref="dataSource"/>
</bean>
```

JSF Converters and Persistence

Sometimes, a JSF converter is required to access the database. Normally, you would like this access to happen within your current conversation. While managed beans are associated with a conversation, JSF components are not. A custom converter is called from a JSF component and therefore has no "current conversation" either.

A way out of this dilemma is to use ViewController. Associating a bean to the view allows Orchestra to use the conversation associated with the bean for the JSF converter, too. Listing 5-18 shows the persistence-friendly JSF converter class CustomerGroupPkConverter. Listing 5-19 shows how to use the converter, and Listing 5-20 shows how to declare the converter in the applicationContext.xml.

Listing 5-18. *Persistence-Friendly JSF Converter*

```
public class CustomerGroupPkConverter implements Converter {

  private CustomerGroupDao customerGroupDao;

  public CustomerGroupDao getCustomerGroupDao() {
    return customerGroupDao;
  }

  public void setCustomerGroupDao(CustomerGroupDao customerGroupDao) {
    this.customerGroupDao = customerGroupDao;
  }

  @Transactional(readOnly=true)
  public Object getAsObject(FacesContext context, UIComponent component,
    String value) throws ConverterException {

    if (StringUtils.isEmpty(value)) {
      return null;
    }

    long id = Long.parseLong(value, Character.MAX_RADIX);
    return customerGroupDao.getByKey(id);
  }
```

```
  public String getAsString(FacesContext context, UIComponent component,
    Object value) throws ConverterException {

    if (value == null){
      return "";
    }

    return Long.toString(((CustomerGroup) value).getId().longValue(),
      Character.MAX_RADIX);
  }
}
```

Listing 5-19. *Using an Orchestra Converter*

```
<o:converter beanName="prZoneConverter" />
```

Listing 5-20. *Declaring the Converter in applicationContext.xml*

```
<bean name="customerGroupPkConverter"
      class="org.apache.myfaces.examples.mops.lib.CustomerGroupPkConverter"
      scope="viewController"
      autowire="byName"
</bean>
```

The DynaForm Component

With Orchestra's Core15 module, you'll get a JSF component called DynaForm. This component is quite powerful when it comes to creating simple (data-entry–style) JSF pages. It doesn't solve every problem (you can't create a whole application using DynaForm), but in some situations, it will be very helpful.

You still have to handle all the backing bean requirements manually. DynaForm is not developed to provide a full rapid-application workflow, although, chances are that we will see a generator in the future that will create these backing bean templates. The basic idea of the DynaForm component is to create the form part of the JSF view dynamically at runtime based on, for example, the EJB annotation of your entities.

Assume that you have the `ShopCustomer` entity from Listing 5-21 and a JSF view defined like Listing 5-22: you'll get a simple two-column data-input form for the `ShopCustomer` entity (see Figure 5-4).

Listing 5-21. *JPA Entity Representing a Customer*

```
@Entity
public class ShopCustomer {

  @Id
  @GeneratedValue(strategy = GenerationType.TABLE)
  private Long id;
```

```
  @Basic(optional=false)
  private String firstName;

  @Basic(optional=false)
  private String lastName;

  @Basic(optional=false)
  private String email;

  @ManyToOne(
    fetch = FetchType.LAZY,
    cascade = CascadeType.ALL,
    optional = false)
  @DataProvider(
    description = "#{customerGroupSuggest.getDescription}",
    value = "#{customerGroupSuggest.getCustomerGroupsByFulltext}",
    converterId="customerGroupPkConverter")
  private CustomerGroup customerGroup;

  @Version
  private Long version;
}
```

Listing 5-22. *JSF View Using DynaForm*

```
<ox:dynaForm id="customer"
             uri="org.apache.myfaces.examples.mops.model.ShopCustomer"
             valueBindingPrefix="mopsCustomerLogin.shopCustomer">
  <h:panelGrid id="customer-layout"
               columns="2" />
</ox:dynaForm>
```

Notice the customerGroup row. Based on the `@ManyToOne` annotation, the DynaForm component will automatically use the `InputSuggestAjax` component and configure it using the `@DataProvider` annotation.

Also, the `@Basic` attribute had some influence to the required attribute of the created component.

In contrast to the single-row input panel, you could also have a data-table-like output; see Listing 5-23 and Figure 5-5.

Listing 5-23. *JSF View Using DynaForm with a Data Table*

```
<ox:dynaForm id="customerGroups"
             uri="org.apache.myfaces.examples.mops.model.CustomerGroup">
  <h:dataTable id="customerGroups-layout"
               var="entity"
               value="#{mopsEditCustomerGroup.customerGroups}" />
</ox:dynaForm>
```

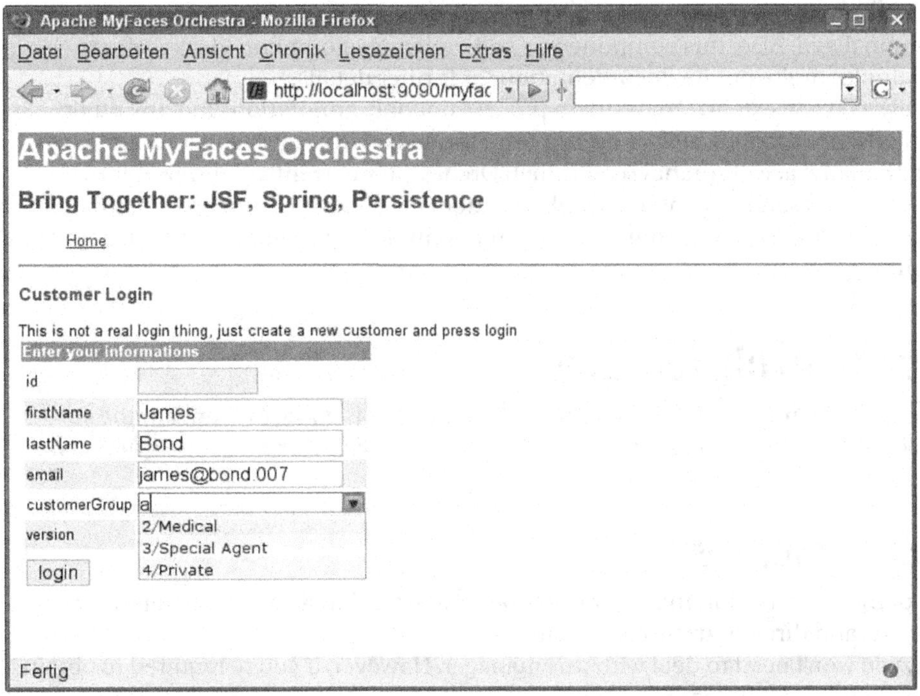

Figure 5-4. *The DynaForm component in action*

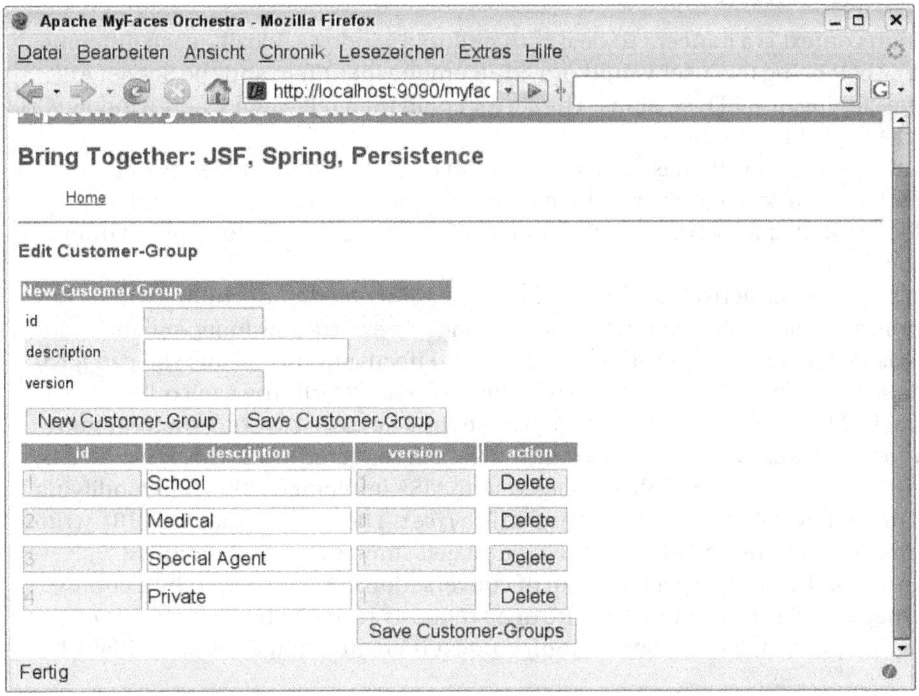

Figure 5-5. *Using DynaForm with a data table*

This section has provided just a quick overview; there is not enough room here to explain the component in detail. Also, this component is still under development. Please refer to Orchestra's examples or the online documentation for further details.

Additionally, you can extend Orchestra to process not only annotations but any other metadata storage that describes how to build a form. And there are ways to use component libraries other than MyFaces Tomahawk, although Orchestra is currently optimized for MyFaces. In Orchestra's sandbox, there are enhancements to allow the DynaForm GuiBuilder to use some nice-looking MyFaces Tomahawk components, like the calendar and the input suggestion components.

Orchestra's Architecture

To use a library, it is often useful to know a little bit about what is going on beneath the surface. In this section, we present a very rapid tour of the major widgets and gadgets that make Orchestra run.

ConversationManager

One instance of the conversation manager exists per HTTP session and handles all the conversation contexts and through it the conversations.

Normally, you won't need to deal with this manager. However, if you're required to obtain it, you can use `ConversationManager.getInstance()`.

ConversationContext

The conversation context is a concept to deal with multiple windows. Ideally, each different browser window belonging to a user would provide a unique identifier, and the Servlet API would allow the cloning of HTTP sessions. The server could then tell when a new window was opened and take appropriate action.

Unfortunately, old Santa still hasn't made that wish come true. But Orchestra does its best to emulate this. Via a sneaky trick, every URL included in a page has a context ID query parameter added to it. Requests from new windows will not have this ID, so requests from new windows can be detected.

Orchestra stores all the active conversations for a session together as children of a `ConversationContext` object. All that is necessary to make a new window independent of the old data is to ensure it uses a new `ConversationContext`. Effectively, this means you can navigate within the same application in multiple windows without interfering each other.

To keep track of this conversation context, we use the `RequestParameterProvider` framework to add a `conversationContext` URL parameter to each rendered URL. This is invoked by overriding the `HttpServletResponse` object passed to the JSF implementation and modifying the `encodeURL` method to call the `RequestParameterProvider`. The result is that any URL written to the servlet response by any code within the request gets intercepted and modified.

For each user, Orchestra maintains a map of conversation contexts keyed by a context ID, which is expected to be present in the URL of all requests received by the web server. When this ID is not present, a new conversation context is created that does not initially have any Conversation-scoped objects in it. On page render, the context ID is appended to every link's URL and every form's action attribute. Therefore, whatever action the user selects will pass the same context ID back to the server. This does have the side-effect of making it difficult to output normal links, which do not have this ID set, and outputting links that open a pop-up window to access the same web application using a new conversation context would be particularly challenging. A JSF component is provided (`separateConversationContext`) that can be wrapped around links to suppress the automatic transfer of the context ID.

FrameworkAdapter

One thing we had in mind while creating Orchestra was to avoid any hard dependency on either JSF or Spring.

As you might have noticed, a lot of JSF-specific things are provided, as JSF is expected to be the UI framework of the majority of Orchestra users.

However, the inner core of Orchestra does not require JSF at all; all dependencies have been abstracted out into a `FrameworkAdapter` interface. To use Orchestra with other frameworks, simply provide a custom implementation suitable for your environment.

In addition, the Spring dependency could be replaced. If you are using a dependency injection framework that allows external code to manage scopes like Spring does, you should be able to port Orchestra to this framework, too. If the framework also supports aspect-oriented programming and some kind of persistence handling, you'll be finished within hours.

RequestParameterProvider

`RequestParameterProvider` is a framework that allows you to instruct the servlet engine to add an additional URL parameter to each URL it encodes.

Even if it is possible to get access to this framework, please do not use it, as it is likely to be moved to a more general MyFaces project later. It is meant to be used just by the Orchestra internals.

RedirectTrackerNavigationHandler

This is a very useful optional feature that we use to store JSF messages from one request to another one. What is this good for? Well, think about the use case where we check if a conversation is running, and, if not, issue a redirect to the start page of the conversation. During this process, we add some messages that normally are lost due to the subsequent redirect.

The handler will keep track of this use case and prepares for not losing them by storing the messages in session.

To enable this feature, you have to add the code in Listing 5-24 to your `faces-config.xml` file.

Listing 5-24. *Enabling the RedirectTrackerNavigationHandler*

```
<navigation-handler>
  org.apache.myfaces.custom.redirectTracker.RedirectTrackerNavigationHandler
</navigation-handler>
```

UrlParameterNavigationHandler

You know the bookmarkable URL problem in JSF? `UrlParameterNavigationHandler` is a first step toward a solution to it. After enabling the handler in `faces-config.xml` (see Listing 5-25), you'll be able to have a new special navigation rule (see Listing 5-26).

Listing 5-25. *Enabling UrlPatameterNavigationHandler*

```
<navigation-handler>
  org.apache.myfaces.orchestra.urlParamNav.UrlParameterNavigationHandler
</navigation-handler>
<view-handler>
  org.apache.myfaces.orchestra.urlParamNav.UrlParameterViewHandler
</view-handler>
```

Listing 5-26. *Enabling a Special Navigation Rule*

```
<navigation-case>
  <from-outcome>EditSelectedProduct</from-outcome>
  <to-view-id>/mops/EditProduct.jsp?productId=#{anyBean.productId}</to-view-id>
  <redirect/>
</navigation-case>
```

Before issuing the redirect navigation, any EL expression within the `<to-view-id>` tag will be replaced. In your backing bean, you can use the well-known request parameter map to read this parameter; see Listing 5-27.

Listing 5-27. *Obtaining the Product ID from the Parameter Map*

```
String productId =
  (String) FacesContext.getCurrentInstance().getExternalContext()
                      .getParameterMap().get("productId");
```

Application Programming Interface

A number of classes in Orchestra provide methods useful for applications to call. They aren't very heavily used, because Orchestra doesn't require your code to be filled with calls to Orchestra classes, but they are there when needed.

Unless noted otherwise, the classes in the following sections are all in the namespace `org.apache.myfaces.orchestra`.

The Conversation Class

Each conversation that is currently active has an instance of the `Conversation` class, and the instance holds all of the objects that are in that conversation.

The getCurrentInstance Method

Calling the static method `Conversation.getCurrentInstance()` from within the Conversation-scoped bean allows you to get access to the conversation object associated with the calling code. If the caller is not actually a Conversation-scoped bean itself, what is returned is the conversation associated with the nearest Conversation-scoped bean on the call stack.

The invalidate Method

At the end of an action method, you'd typically end the conversation, which can be done by simply calling `Conversation.getCurrentInstance().invalidate()`.

On the next request to this bean or any other bean configured for this conversation, the conversation will be started again.

The alternative to calling this API is to use the `endConversation` JSF component.

The setAttribute and getAttribute Methods

You can attach any additional attribute to the conversation by using the `setAttribute` and `getAttribute` methods, similar to the way you can with the HTTP session object. The objects are stored within the conversation and will be discarded when that conversation is invalidated.

The ConversationManager Class

The most important method to know in the `ConversationManager` class is the `getConversation(name)` method. This method allows code to access any conversation currently running within your conversation context. It's not expected to be extensively used, though; normally, retrieving the current conversation (via the `Conversation` class) is sufficient.

The ConversationUtils Class

Sometimes, it is useful to throw away the current conversation and at the same time create a new one. We can accomplish this using the `invalidateAndRestartCurrent` method. For example, processing a particular action may cause a large number of database queries and cause the current persistence context to become large. After the action (e.g., saving), you may only need a small subset of this data. The solution is to invalidate the current conversation, start a new one, and copy across any data that is still needed. Of course, persistent objects cannot be copied directly, because the new conversation has a new persistence context, but there are a number of obvious solutions to this issue. Listing 5-28 demonstrates how to invalidate and restart the current conversation.

As you can see, after we've committed all data we get the current entity ID, invalidate the current conversation, and start a new instance of it. The new instance is then initialized with just the minimum data we need to retain. Sneaky, isn't it?

Listing 5-28. *Invalidating and Restarting the Current Conversation*

```
public class EditCustomerGroup {

  public String saveAction() {
    SpringUtils.commit(transactionManager);

    long customerGroupId = getCustomerGroup().getId();
    EditCustomerGroup newConversation = (EditCustomerGroup)
    ConversationUtils.invalidateAndRestartCurrent();
    newConversation.initWithCustomerGroup(customerGroupId)

    return "success";
  }
}
```

Useful Interfaces

In Orchestra, there are some useful interfaces you should be aware of. The following sections will illustrate them.

ConversationAware

Beans implementing the `ConversationAware` interface will be informed of the conversation they belong to.

ConversationMessager

A `ConversationMessager` implementation is used by Orchestra to inform the user about any problems related to conversation management.

Summary

Apache MyFaces Orchestra implements a conversation scope in addition to the request and session scope you'd normally use in your web application. This conversation scope will make it easy to develop applications connected to a persistence layer. Due to the modularity of Orchestra, you can use any JPA implementation such as Hibernate, or by providing your own adapter, virtually any persistence framework.

Even if you do not use any of the persistence features provided by Orchestra, its conversation scope and the other features allow you to easily build solid backing beans to provide your nifty-looking Ajax components with the necessary data with reasonable response time.

Once you start working with Orchestra, you might find yourself asking how you ever wrote programs without it.

To keep up with the latest development efforts, you can visit the Orchestra home page at `http://myfaces.apache.org/orchestra` or join the vibrant community on the MyFaces mailing list.

CHAPTER 6

Layouts and Themes with Tobago

Tobago aids you in creating web applications with a consistent look and feel by providing you with a collection of comfortable, high-level components, which can be positioned with a layout manager. The goal is to approximate the appearance of classic desktop applications. Tobago is based on a strict separation of structure and design. You describe the structure of a page and which controls it contains; the representation of the page and its style are handled by Tobago.

You can customize the design and style through themes. Currently, Tobago contains only themes for HTML clients. To achieve output independence, the views should be developed without any HTML, CSS, or JavaScript. A Tobago page normally contains only JSF and Tobago tags. Features, styling, and design via HTML, CSS, or JavaScript are handled by the theme.

The development of Tobago started in 2002. With the introduction of the JSF standard, it was decided to base Tobago on JSF. By 2005, Tobago was released as an open source project and became a subproject of Apache MyFaces in 2006. We will be referencing a simple address book application throughout this chapter to demonstrate the various features of Tobago.

Trying Out Tobago

The Tobago project (`http://myfaces.apache.org/tobago/`) contains the demo and address book examples, as well as the blank example. The demo example illustrates many of the important features of Tobago and acts as the online documentation. The address book example is a small, self-contained web application. Finally, there is the blank example, which is a minimal Tobago application that can act as a starting point for a new application.

You can download the Tobago examples at the following URLs:

- *Demonstration example*: `http://people.apache.org/repo/m2-snapshot-repository/org/apache/myfaces/tobago/tobago-example-demo/`
- *Address book example*: `http://people.apache.org/repo/m2-snapshot-repository/org/apache/myfaces/tobago/tobago-example-addressbook/`
- *Blank example*: `http://people.apache.org/repo/m2-snapshot-repository/org/apache/myfaces/tobago/tobago-example-blank/`

Online Demo

The Tobago demonstration page links to an already deployed version of the latest demonstration application. You can access the page online at `http://tobago.atanion.net/tobago-example-demo/`.

Creating an Application with Tobago

The Tobago distribution can be found on the Apache MyFaces Tobago project page (`http://myfaces.apache.org/tobago`). The download page contains the latest distribution and example application for Windows and Unix. Download the latest distribution: `myfaces-tobago-version-dist.tar.gz` or `myfaces-tobago-version-dist.zip` where `version` is the current version of Tobago and extract the distribution in a directory on your PC.

Dependencies

A Tobago web application needs to package many libraries. First of all, the Tobago core JAR and theme JARs should be made available in the application. Some themes depend on each other; for example, to be able to use the Speyside theme, the Scarborough theme and Standard theme have to be included as well. These dependencies are defined in the `META-INF/tobago-theme.xml` files inside the theme JARs.

All dependencies are packaged inside the Tobago distribution and should be copied from `libs/` directory to the `WEB-INF/libs/` directory of your web application. Table 6-1 shows all the Tobago dependencies.

Table 6-1. *Tobago Dependencies*

Dependency	Version	Description
commons-beanutils	1.7.0	Jakarta Commons library for easy usage of the Reflection and Introspection APIs
commons-collections	3.1	Jakarta Commons library for easy usage of the Java Collections Framework
commons-digester	1.8	Jakarta Commons library for mapping XML and Java objects
commons-fileupload	1.2	Jakarta Commons library providing file uploading capabilities for servlets and web application
commons-io	1.1	Jakarta Commons library providing a collection of I/O utilities
commons-lang	1.2	Jakarta Commons library providing extensions for the `java.lang` classes
commons-logging	1.1	Jakarta Commons library providing a wraparound for common logging APIs
Apache MyFaces or JavaServer Faces RI	1.1 or 1.2	Implements JSF 1.1 or 1.2

Configuring the Web Descriptor (web.xml)

A Tobago application is a standard web application and needs a web application descriptor (`WEB-INF/web.xml`). As a JSF application, the `web.xml` file has to include a servlet definition for the FacesServlet and a corresponding servlet mapping. During development, it is convenient to serve the resources for Tobago-like images, scripts, and style sheets directly out of the theme JARs. To accomplish this, the `web.xml` file needs to contain the definition for the Tobago ResourceServlet and the corresponding servlet mapping (see Listing 6-1). For a production environment, we advise extracting the theme resources and letting the servlet container or web server serve these resources directly; see the "Advanced Assembly" section.

Listing 6-1. *web.xml with Tobago Configuration Highlighted in Bold*

```
<?xml version="1.0" encoding="UTF-8"?>
<web-app version="2.5" xmlns="http://java.sun.com/xml/ns/javaee"
    xmlns:xsi="http://www.w3.org/2001/XMLSchema-instance"
    xsi:schemaLocation="http://java.sun.com/xml/ns/javaee
        http://java.sun.com/xml/ns/javaee/web-app_2_5.xsd">
  <filter>
    <filter-name>multipartFormdataFilter</filter-name>
      <filter-class>
        org.apache.myfaces.tobago.webapp.TobagoMultipartFormdataFilter
      </filter-class>
  </filter>
  <filter-mapping>
    <filter-name>multipartFormdataFilter</filter-name>
    <url-pattern>/faces/*</url-pattern>
  </filter-mapping>
  <servlet>
    <servlet-name>Faces Servlet</servlet-name>
    <servlet-class>javax.faces.webapp.FacesServlet</servlet-class>
    <load-on-startup>1</load-on-startup>
  </servlet>
  <servlet>
    <servlet-name>ResourceServlet</servlet-name>
    <servlet-class>
      org.apache.myfaces.tobago.servlet.ResourceServlet
    </servlet-class>
  </servlet>
  <servlet-mapping>
    <servlet-name>Faces Servlet</servlet-name>
    <url-pattern>/faces/*</url-pattern>
  </servlet-mapping>
  <servlet-mapping>
    <servlet-name>ResourceServlet</servlet-name>
    <url-pattern>/org/apache/myfaces/tobago/renderkit/*</url-pattern>
  </servlet-mapping>
```

```
  <welcome-file-list>
    <welcome-file>faces/Welcome.jsp</welcome-file>
  </welcome-file-list>
</web-app>
```

Configuring Tobago (tobago-config.xml)

The JSF-specific configuration for Tobago is contained in the `faces-config.xml` file inside the Tobago core JAR. To make the configuration available for JSF, the `tobago-core.jar` has to be placed into the web application. The Tobago-specific configuration is defined in the `WEB-INF/tobago-config.xml` file. A minimal configuration should at least specify the default theme for the Tobago application (See Listing 6-2).

Listing 6-2. *tobago-config.xml*

```
<?xml version="1.0" encoding="UTF-8"?>
<!DOCTYPE tobago-config PUBLIC
    "-//The Apache Software Foundation//DTD Tobago Config 1.0//EN"
    "tobago-config_1_0.dtd">
<tobago-config>
  <theme-config>
    <default-theme>speyside</default-theme>
  </theme-config>
  <resource-dir>tobago-resource</resource-dir>
  <resource-dir>org/apache/myfaces/tobago/renderkit</resource-dir>
</tobago-config>
```

Creating a Basic Tobago Page

To use JSP as a rendering technology, Tobago provides two tag libraries that contain the definition of available JSP tags: the Tobago core library and the extension library. The Tag Library Descriptor (TLD) for these libraries contains documentation for the tags and defines the available required and optional attributes. IDEs can leverage this information to help the developer construct JSP pages. Listing 6-3 shows a basic Tobago page.

Listing 6-3. *Basic Tobago Page*

```
<%@ taglib uri="http://java.sun.com/jsf/core" prefix="f" %>
<%@ taglib uri="http://myfaces.apache.org/tobago/component" prefix="tc" %>
<%@ taglib uri="http://myfaces.apache.org/tobago/extension" prefix="tx" %>
<%@ page contentType="text/html;charset=UTF-8" language="java" %>
<f:view>
  <tc:page>
    <f:facet name="layout">
      <tc:gridLayout/>
    </f:facet>
    <tc:out value="Hello World"/>
  </tc:page>
</f:view>
```

Controls

Tobago makes use of the extensibility of JSF to achieve its decoupling from the rendering tier. It provides its own tag library, components, and render kit. Besides the JSP tag library, Facelets view definitions (see Chapter 3) are also supported. The extension folder in the Tobago distribution contains the support library to use Facelets instead of JSP.

Because of the strict separation between structure and design, you can use different themes for your application. This allows you to execute applications that can render different corporate designs for different portals while keeping the view source unchanged. This mechanism is easier than adapting plain CSS, in the sense that various style sheet themes/skins have to be referenced and loaded based on environmental parameters.

Besides the basic input controls HTML provides, Tobago offers additional high-level controls that traditional desktop application developers would recognize. These controls will be described in the following sections.

Tobago also contains a deprecated tree control. The API of this tree control does not really fit to the other controls. But the sandbox already contains a version of the future tree control, which will be introduced in Tobago 1.1.

Basic Controls

HTML offers a large set of input controls that form the basis of Tobago's controls. This base includes single-line text-input fields, text areas, labels, radio buttons, checkboxes, links, buttons, and so on. The Tobago example demonstration in the "Trying out Tobago" section shows these controls in action; see Figure 6-1.

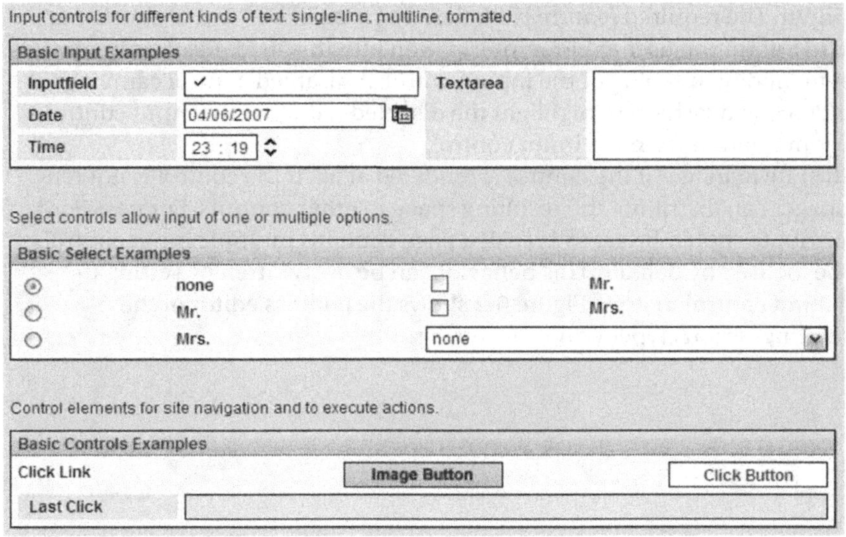

Figure 6-1. *Basic controls*

Input Control

A single-line input control can be rendered with the <tc:in> tag. The extended version can be accessed with <tx:in>. In general, the extension library, which is usually referenced by the tx prefix, provides convenience variants of controls. For the <tc:in> control, the extended version <tx:in> contains boilerplate code for rendering labels. For form-like input views, nearly every input control has a corresponding label. The label is connected to the input control. If the label is clicked, the input control gains focus. Listing 6-4 shows an example of using the extended input control.

Listing 6-4. *Example Usage of the Extended Input Control*

```
<tx:in
    label="#{bundle.name}"
    value="#{address.name}"
    required="false" readonly="false"
    disabled="false" rendered="true" />
```

The label attribute determines the textual description for the control. It is laid out with a grid layout manager. The theme specifies the default label width, but it can be overwritten with the labelWidth attribute. If the label contains an underscore character, the character following it will become an access key. This is represented in the user interface by underlining the access key character. If the access key is pressed together with the Alt key, the corresponding input field gains focus.

The value attribute contains the content of the input control.

The required attribute controls validation and allows the theme to render a special marker for required input. The required feature is rendered as a small box with a check mark inside the input field to inform the user to enter information into this field. Read-only controls do not allow the user to modify the value of the input control. A disabled control cannot gain focus; the label is rendered in a fashion to highlight the disabled nature of the input control, and the user cannot copy content from the input control.

The rendered attribute manages if the control is rendered at all. If the control is not rendered, the layout manager can distribute the resulting space to other controls. For password fields, the password attribute should be set to true. If a page contains multiple input controls, the first control will be focused by default. This behavior can be overwritten by setting the focus attribute of an input control to true. Figure 6-2 shows the address editor of the addressbook example using various types of input controls.

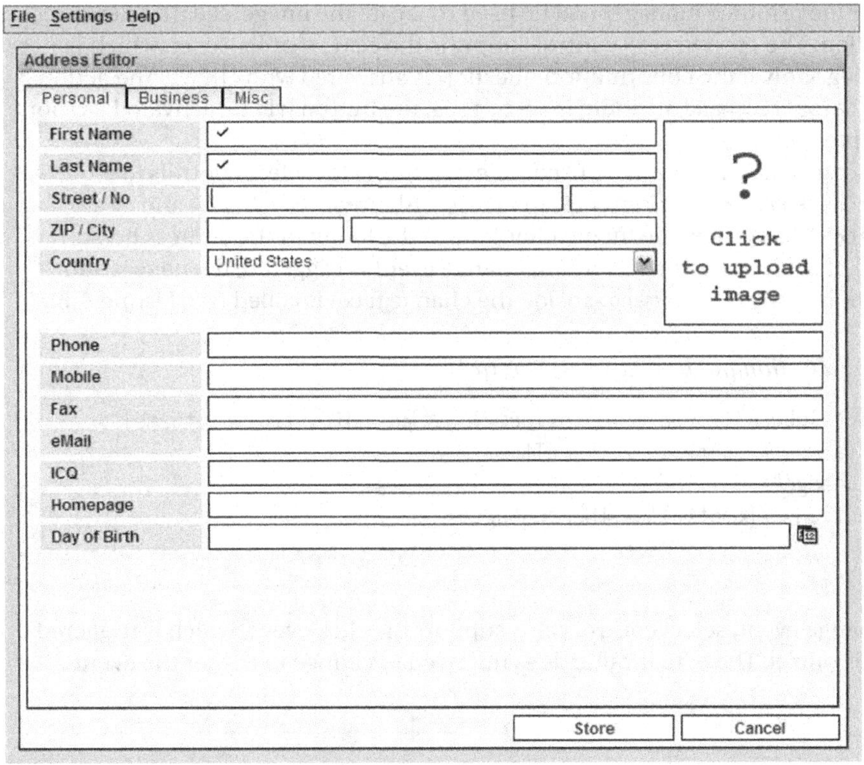

Figure 6-2. *Address editor*

Commands

Tobago supports different ways to use commands. The basic versions are `<tc:button>` and `<tc:link>`; others include toolbars and menus, which are described in later sections.

Listing 6-5 shows an example of executing a command when clicking a button.

Listing 6-5. *Conditional Execution of a Command*

```
<tc:button label="Delete" action="#{controller.delete}"
           image="image/delete.png" defaultCommand="false">
  <f:facet name="confirmation">
    <tc:out value="Do you want to delete it?" />
  </f:facet>
</tc:button>
```

In Listing 6-5, the `label` attribute defines the text on the button. The `action` attribute points to the method that is executed if the button is clicked. By means of the `image` attribute, the button can be decorated with an icon. The image can be placed relatively to the root of the web application, or the resource manager can be used to locate the image; see the "Resource Management" section. The `<tc:button>` control supports the `confirmation` facet, which generates a message dialog. Only if the confirmation question is answered with OK will the action be executed. If the `defaultCommand` attribute is set to `true`, the button will be activated as soon as the Enter key is pressed.

A generic `<tc:command>` control can be used for event facets for select controls like `<tc:selectBooleanCheckbox>`, `<tc:selectOneRadio>`, `<tc:selectManyCheckbox>`, and `<tc:selectOneChoice>`. This is how the theme changing in the footer of the address book example is realized. If a new theme is selected, a change event is triggered; the page is submitted; and the action of the `<tc:command>` inside the change facet is called (see Listing 6-6).

Listing 6-6. *Executing a Command from a Select Control*

```
<tx:selectOneChoice label="#{bundle.footerTheme}" value="#{controller.theme}">
  <f:selectItems value="#{controller.themeItems}" />
  <f:facet name="change">
    <tc:command action="#{controller.themeChanged}"/>
  </f:facet>
</tx:selectOneChoice>
```

Besides the change event, select controls also support the click event, which is triggered if someone clicks the control. The actual value does not need to change to trigger the event.

■ **Note** Tobago includes a double request prevention mechanism. After a button or link is clicked in the client, the page is blocked to avoid duplicate clicks. If the server request takes longer than expected a transitioning effect is shown. First the page is faded out, and later, a progress animation is presented. To turn off this effect, the transition attribute can be set to `false`.

Sheet Control

The `<tc:sheet>` component allows you to display tabular data. The address book example uses it to provide an overview of all stored addresses, as shown in Listing 6-7 and Figure 6-3.

Listing 6-7. *Sheet Control for Entering a Person's Basic Details*

```
<tc:sheet columns="1*;1*;1*" value="#{controller.currentAddressList}"
          var="address" state="#{controller.selectedAddresses}"
          sortActionListener="#{controller.sheetSorter}" rows="25"
          showRowRange="left" showPageRange="right" showDirectLinks="center">

  <tc:column id="firstName" label="#{bundle.listFirstName}" sortable="true"
             rendered="#{controller.renderFirstName}">
    <tc:out value="#{address.firstName}" />
  </tc:column>
```

```
  <tc:column id="lastName" label="#{bundle.listLastName}" sortable="true"
             rendered="#{controller.renderLastName}">
    <tc:out value="#{address.lastName}" />
  </tc:column>

  <tc:column id="dayOfBirth" label="Birthday" sortable="true"
             rendered="#{controller.renderDayOfBirth}">
    <tc:out value="#{address.dayOfBirth}">
      <f:convertDateTime pattern="#{bundle.editorDatePattern}" />
    </tc:out>
  </tc:column>
</tc:sheet>
```

The `value` attribute links to a list model in the controller providing the data for the sheet. The `<tc:sheet>` contains three `<tc:column>` tags, which describe the columns of the sheet. The `label` of the column is rendered as a header cell. The `var` attribute of `<tc:sheet>` defines a local variable `address`, which refers to a row in the data model and can be used in the definition of the columns.

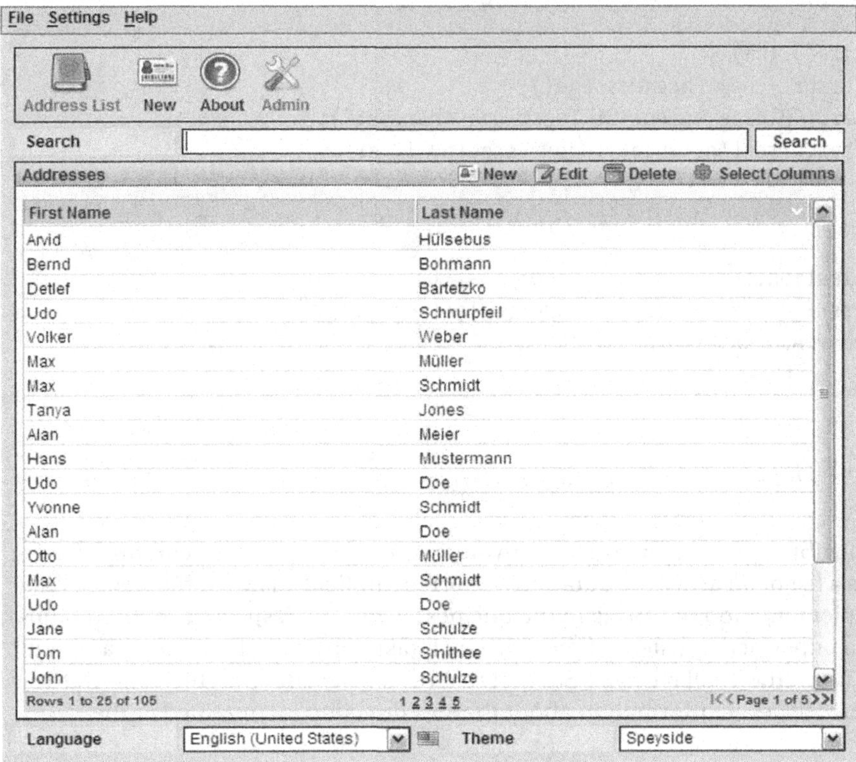

Figure 6-3. *Address list*

In Listing 6-7, each column uses a `<tc:out>` tag to render the data for the sheet cell by accessing the appropriate property of the row object. Instead of `<tc:out>`, arbitrary input controls like `<tc:in>`, `<tc:selectBooleanCheckbox>`, and `<tc:selectOneChoice>` can be used.

The various attributes of the sheet that start with `show` configure the navigational elements of the sheet; `showDirectLinks`, for example, allows the user to directly jump to the desired page of the sheet.

The `state` attribute refers to a `SheetState` object. Tobago binds information about the state of the sheet to this object, like which rows are selected. This allows the developer to react based on the selection inside the business logic. In the address book example, there is a toolbar above the sheet. The toolbar contains a delete action, among others, and this delete action is dependent on the selected rows in the sheet. The `selectable` attribute of the sheet controls the selection mode for the sheet. Possible values are `none`, `single`, and `multi`. The default value is `multi`; it allows multiple rows to be selected. Listing 6-8 show the method bound to the delete button and describes how to access the selected rows.

Listing 6-8. *Method Bound to the Delete Button*

```
public String deleteAddresses() throws AddressDaoException {
  List<Integer> selection = selectedAddresses.getSelectedRows();

  if (selection.size() < 1) {
    FacesMessage error = new FacesMessage();
    error.setSummary("Please select at least one address.");
    FacesContext.getCurrentInstance().addMessage(null, error);
    return null;
  }

  for (int i = selection.size() - 1; i >= 0; i--) {
    Address address = currentAddressList.get(selection.get(i));
    addressDao.removeAddress(address);
  }
  // ...

  return OUTCOME_LIST;
}
```

The `sortable` attribute of the `<tc:column>` activates sorting for the related column. If the data for the sheet is a list or an array, the data can be sorted implicitly. The `sortActionListener` attribute allows implementation of sorting in the business logic. The respective method binding has to point to a public action listener method, which takes an `ActionEvent` as a parameter and returns `void`. The method will receive a `SortActionEvent`, which denotes the column triggering the sort event. However, information about the sort direction is contained in the `SheetState`.

TabGroup Control

The <tc:tabGroup> control renders different content on the same area of the view via tab panels. The switching behavior of the panels can be controlled with the switchType attribute. The panels can be switched on the client or the server. If the switching is performed on the server, Tobago can be instructed to only partially exchange the content of the page making use of Ajax. Switching done on the client is faster, but the content of the page is bigger, because the rendering information of all tab panels has to be transferred to the client at once.

In Listing 6-9, two of the tab panels are rendered only if a certain condition is met in the controller. These particular tab panels are only rendered if the application is in the expert mode.

Listing 6-9. *Tab Groups for Switching Between Personal, Business, and Miscellenous Information*

```
<tc:tabGroup switchType="reloadTab" immediate="true">
  <tc:tab label="#{bundle.editorTabPersonal}">
    <jsp:include page="tab/personal.jsp"/>
  </tc:tab>

  <tc:tab label="#{bundle.editorTabBusiness}" rendered="#{!controller.simple}">
    <jsp:include page="tab/business.jsp"/>
  </tc:tab>

  <tc:tab label="#{bundle.editorTabMisc}" rendered="#{!controller.simple}">
    <jsp:include page="tab/misc.jsp"/>
  </tc:tab>
</tc:tabGroup>
```

Menu Control

To mimic the appearance of a desktop application, it is common to place a menu bar at the top of the page. This can be done with the <tc:menuBar> tag inside the menuBar facet of the <tc:page>. A menu bar can contain <tc:menu> tags, which can be nested to produce submenus. Actions can be bound with method bindings to <tc:menuItem> tags. A menu item can be disabled and can encapsulate icons. An underscore in the label marks the character following as an access key, which can be activated by pressing it together with the Alt key.

In the address book example in Listing 6-10, the settings menu contains single selections created by <tx:menuRadio> to choose the current theme and language. Additionally, it demonstrates how to use a checkbox menu item <tc:menuCheckbox> to change the mode of the application.

Listing 6-10. *Menu Bar with Various Types of Controls*

```
<tc:menuBar id="menuBar">
  <tc:menu label="_File">
    <tc:menuItem label="_New" action="#{controller.createAddress}"
                 image="image/contact-new.png"/>
    <tc:menuItem label="_Add Dummy Addresses"
                 action="#{controller.addDummyAddresses}"/>
    <tc:menuSeparator/>
    <tc:menuItem label="_Logout"
                 image="image/system-log-out.png"/>
  </tc:menu>

  <tc:menu label="_Settings">
    ...
    <tc:menu label="_Theme">
      <tx:menuRadio action="#{controller.themeChanged}"
                    value="#{controller.theme}">
        <f:selectItems value="#{controller.themeItems}"/>
      </tx:menuRadio>
    </tc:menu>
    <tc:menuCheckbox label="Simple _Mode" value="#{controller.simple}"/>
  </tc:menu>
  ...
</tc:menuBar>
```

Toolbar Control

The `<tc:toolBar>` tag renders a group of buttons. The toolbar can be configured to render a textual description of the action or an icon in different standard sizes. The buttons are created with the `<tc:toolBarCommand>` tag, which is a slightly limited version of the standard button tag.

In the address book example in Listing 6-11, the first toolbar button navigates to the address list. If the address list is already the current view, the button is disabled. There is a naming convention to provide disabled versions for image resources by adding an additional `Disabled` before the file extension. The disabled version has to reside in the same folder as the original image. In Listing 6-11, the resource manager can find a black-and-white icon `x-office-address-bookDisabled.png` as a disabled version of the normal address book icon.

Listing 6-11. *Toolbar with a Command for Showing the Address List*

```
<tc:toolBar iconSize="big">
  <tc:toolBarCommand
    label="#{bundle.toolbarAddressList}"
    action="#{controller.search}" immediate="true"
    image="image/x-office-address-book.png"
    disabled="#{facesContext.viewRoot.viewId == '/application/list.jsp'}"/>
  ...
</tc:toolBar>
```

Pop-ups

A pop-up is a small modal dialog that is displayed in the context of the current page. General use cases for a pop-up are entering new data and confirming or canceling the new data. Pop-ups can be activated by adding a popup facet to commands. Alternatively, a pop-up can be activated programmatically by setting the rendered attribute to true; in this way, you can use a pop-up as a message box.

In the address book example in Listing 6-12, the displayed columns for the address list can be controlled via a pop-up. This pop-up is bound to a button in the toolbar for the sheet.

Listing 6-12. *Displaying a Pop-up Confirmation Dialog*

```
<tc:button label="Open Popup">
  <f:facet name="popup">
    <tc:popup width="300" height="270">
      <tc:box label="Popup Title">
        ...
        <tc:panel>
          <f:facet name="layout">
            <tc:gridLayout columns="*;fixed;fixed"/>
          </f:facet>

          <tc:cell/>

          <tc:button label="OK">
            <tc:attribute name="popupClose" value="afterSubmit"/>
          </tc:button>

          <tc:button label="Cancel">
            <tc:attribute name="popupClose" value="immediate"/>
          </tc:button>
        </tc:panel>
      </tc:box>
    </tc:popup>
  </f:facet>
</tc:button>
```

The typical semantics of the confirmation and cancel buttons can be controlled via a <tc:attribute> with the name popupClose. This attribute can have two different values: afterSubmit or immediate. Both buttons close the pop-up, but only the afterSubmit variant stores the entered data into the model.

File Upload

A file select control can be created with <tc:file>. The uploaded file is stored inside a FileItem object bound to the value attribute. The class FileItem is provided by commons-fileupload.

The address book allows the user to store photographs associated with the contacts. The user can click an empty image placeholder to open a pop-up with the file select control that is created by the code fragment in Listing 6-13.

Listing 6-13. *Uploading a Photo*

```
<tc:file value="#{controller.uploadedFile}" required="true">
  <tc:validateFileItem contentType="image/*"/>
</tc:file>
```

With the validator `<tc:validateFileItem>` the content type or maximum size of the uploaded file can be restricted. For security reasons, the style of an HTML file select control (input field of type file) can only be customized in a very limited way. Therefore, the input control for the file name and the upload button may not optimally fit to the theme.

To handle multipart form data requests from the browser, either the `TobagoMultipartFormdataFilter` servlet filter has to be configured in `web.xml` or the `tobago-fileupload.jar` has to be added to the classpath. The address book demonstration uses the latter approach, which is based on a `FacesContextFactory` defined in the included `faces-config.xml` of the JAR. The context factory can be configured with two different `<env-entry>` tags in the `web.xml` to control maximum upload limit and the directory for uploaded files. See the JavaDoc of `FileUploadFacesContextFactoryImpl` for more information.

Layout Management

The placement of components on a page is done with the help of a layout manager. The functionality of a layout manager is similar to those found in Swing. The standard layout manager for Tobago is `<tc:gridLayout>`. It can be bound to a container tag with a `layout` facet.

The grid layout manager divides the area of the page into a rectangular grid. This grid can be controlled with the `rows` and `columns` attributes of the `<tc:gridLayout>` tag. The syntax is similar to the multilength notation from HTML and consists of a semicolon-separated list of layout tokens.

A layout token may be an absolute length in pixels like `100px`, a percentage length like `50%`, a relative length like `2*` or `*` as a shorthand for `1*`, or the value fixed. Relative lengths are served by layout manager from the remaining available space, which is distributed proportionally based on the number before the *.

If the layout manager has 400 pixels to lay out the columns with the layout tokens `2*;*;100px`, it first claims 100 pixels for the third column and distributes the remaining 300 pixels in the ratio 2:1, ending up with 200 pixels for the first column and 100 pixels for the second column. The layout token `fixed` instructs the layout manager to take the required pixel size of the contained control. A `<tx:in>` control normally has a fixed height. To place multiple `<tx:in>` controls one below the other without superfluous spacing, the layout manager can be instructed with fixed layout tokens to use exactly the required vertical space for a `<tx:in>`. For a more concrete example, see Listing 6-14, which is based on the editor view of the address book.

Listing 6-14. *Layout of the Editor View of the Address Book*

```
<tc:panel>
  <f:facet name="layout">
    <tc:gridLayout columns="*" rows="fixed;fixed;fixed;*"/>
  </f:facet>

  <tx:in ... />
  <tx:in ... />
  <tx:in rendered="#{! controller.simple}" ... />
  <tx:textarea ... />
</tc:panel>
```

The grid consists of one column and four rows. The first three rows use a fixed height that is implied by the theme and contained controls. The fourth row takes the remaining vertical space.

One of the main reasons to use a layout manager is its ability to optimally manage the available space. The layout manager knows, for example, if controls have a fixed height and which controls can grow if there is enough space.

Since the layout manager is targeted specifically at JSF, it can flexibly react to the `rendered` attribute of components. If the address book application is in simple mode, some of the components are not rendered; see Figure 6-4. The layout manager automatically distributes the newly available space to the remaining dynamic components, which are laid out with relative or percentage lengths.

If a control should utilize multiple adjacent grid cells, it can be wrapped with a `<tc:cell>` tag. With the `spanX` and `spanY` attributes of a `<tc:cell>` control, the layout manager can be instructed to make the contained control span multiple cells in the X and Y directions.

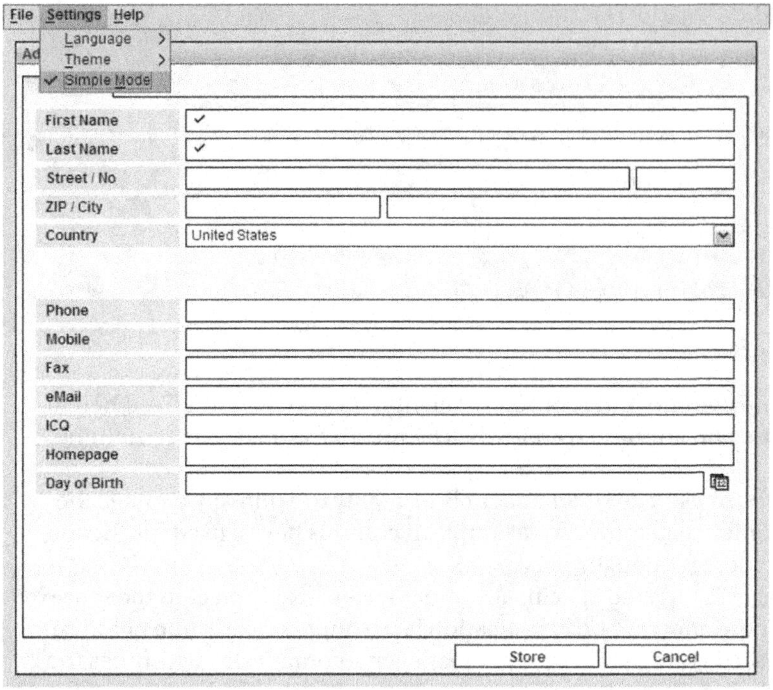

Figure 6-4. *Address editor in simple mode automatically distributing available space*

Themes

Tobago allows you to specify the structure of a page. Additionally, the look of a page is controlled by the selected theme. A theme defines the colors, dimensions, behavior, and graphics of controls. Tobago comes with a selection of themes. These are Speyside, Richmond, Charlotteville, and Scarborough—named after settlements on Tobago. Speyside is the main theme, where most development focus is targeted. You will want to use this theme to start a new web application; see Figure 6-5. The remaining themes, Richmond and Charlotteville, are variations of Speyside, as shown in Figures 6-6 and 6-7. Scarborough is the basic theme, and it tries to directly rely on the standard features of HTML, as shown in Figure 6-8.

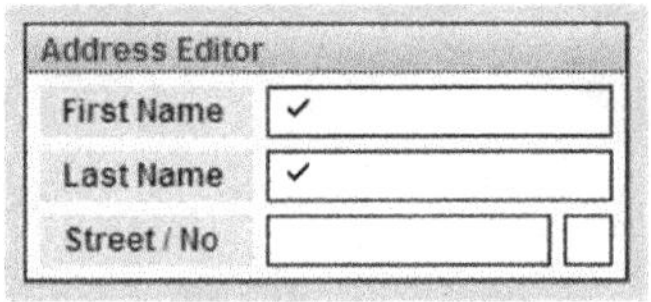

Figure 6-5. *The Speyside theme*

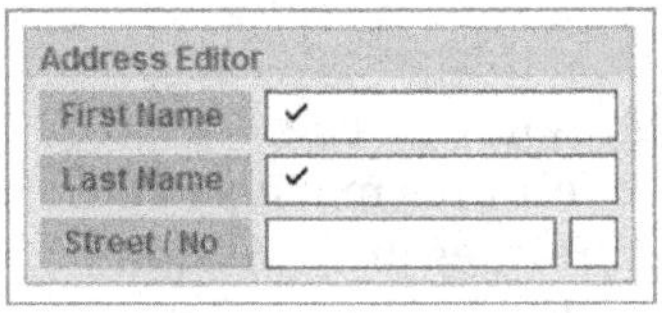

Figure 6-6. *The Richmond theme*

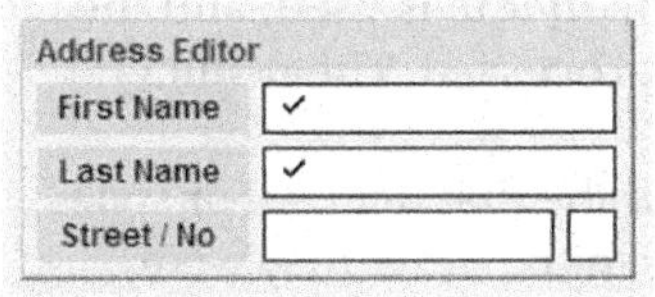

Figure 6-7. *The Charlotteville theme*

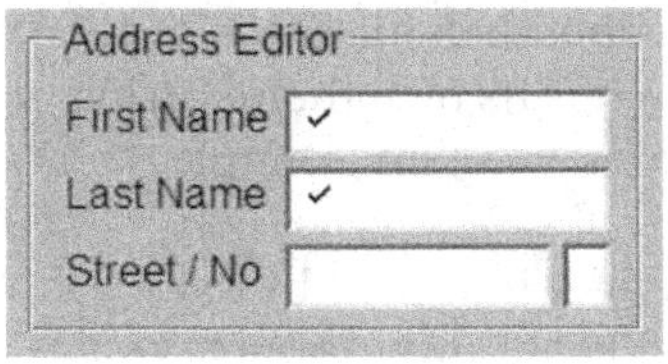

Figure 6-8. *The Scarborough theme*

Themes can be used to make an application follow the corporate design of a company or give users the ability to change the look and feel of an application to their preferences. The address book example demonstrates how to make the theme selectable by the user. A select box displays the available themes, which are configured in the `tobago-config.xml` file, and a button triggers an action in the controller to set the theme in the Tobago `ClientProperties` object. See Listing 6-15.

Listing 6-15. *Changing the Theme Programmically*

```
public String themeChanged() {
  FacesContext facesContext = FacesContext.getCurrentInstance();
  ClientProperties client = ClientProperties.getInstance(facesContext);
  client.setTheme(theme);
  return null;
}
```

Resource Management

For Tobago, resources are images, style sheets, scripts, and string resources. These resources can be dependent on the locale, browser, or theme. The resource manager collects all resource locations, and when a resource is requested, determines the inclusion order. A resource can be available in different themes and multiple locales. The resource manager first looks under the selected theme with the used browser and locale. If the resource is not found, the fallback locale is used to continue the search. After all fallback locales are examined, the fallback for the browser is used, and the locales are searched again. After all fallback browsers are searched, the fallback for the theme is used, and the search starts again with the locales until all fallback themes are processed. The result is cached for later reuse.

For resources such as images, the resource manager stops with the first match. For style sheets and scripts, the resource manager returns a list of resources in the order they were found. This establishes a powerful defaulting mechanism.

By relying on the resource manager, you can provide localized images with different text values for a button. The locale of the view is used to determine the correct language version of the image. The resource manager supports the XML format for property files, easing the use of special characters in string resources. The evaluation of the theme in inclusion order can be used to support different corporate wordings. If each client has its own theme string resources for the different themes can arrange the words in different ways, for example, "email", "e-mail", or "eMail".

In the `tobago-config.xml` file, additional paths can be specified for inclusion by the resource manager, as shown in Listing 6-16. In this way, you can add your own resources or even overwrite or extend existing resources. But changing existing themes this way may result in compatibility issues when switching to a newer version of Tobago, since the theme files are not stable yet and do not count as an official external API.

Listing 6-16. *Specifying Additional Paths for Inclusion by the Resource Manager*

```
<tobago-config>
  <theme-config>
    <default-theme>speyside</default-theme>
  </theme-config>
  <resource-dir>tobago-resource</resource-dir>
</tobago-config>
```

The resource directory denotes a folder inside the WAR relative to the root. Paths for resources follow the pattern in Listing 6-17.

Listing 6-17. *Pattern for Locating Resource Paths*

```
<content-type>/<theme>/<browser>/<directory>/<resource-name>(_<locale>)?.<extension>
```

Currently, only HTML is supported as a content type, although the sandbox contains the beginnings for WML support. The address book example has two variants of an empty portrait with instructions how to upload a real portrait:

```
tobago-resource/html/standard/standard/image/empty-portrait.png
tobago-resource/html/standard/standard/image/empty-portrait_de.png
```

The first image is the default image with instructions in English. In the second image, the instructions are localized in German. The first standard in the path denotes the fallback theme, and the second standard represents the fallback browser. The directory part in the pattern stands for an arbitrary subpath, in this example, for the folder image.

Adding Markup

Several controls like `<tc:in>`, `<tc:panel>`, or `<tc:column>` support the `markup` attribute. It allows the developer to apply logical styles to a control. Which markup values are supported is defined for each theme in the `theme-config.xml` file. If a theme does not define supported markup for a renderer, that theme inherits the markup from the fallback theme. The Standard theme defines `number` for `<tc:in>` and `<tc:out>`, and `strong` and `deleted` for `<tc:out>`. The markup `number` is usually used to make numbers right aligned; `strong` is used to emphasize content; and `deleted` marks text as no longer available normally by crossing it out. The visual representation of markup is up to the theme, so the markup will fit to the overall look and feel of the theme.

To add new markup, you can write your own theme. Choose the theme you want to extend, and specify the selected theme as fallback theme. The Example theme in Listing 6-18 extends Speyside and adds markup for columns.

Listing 6-18. *Extending an Existing Theme and Adding Markup*

```
<tobago-theme>
  <name>example</name>
  <deprecated-name>
    org.apache.myfaces.tobago.context.ExampleTheme
  </deprecated-name>
  <resource-path>org/apache/myfaces/tobago/renderkit</resource-path>
  <fallback>speyside</fallback>
  <renderers>
    <renderer>
      <name>Column</name>
      <supported-markup>
      <markup>new</markup>
      </supported-markup>
    </renderer>
  </renderers>
</tobago-theme>
```

To realize the visualization of the markup, Tobago will add certain CSS style classes into the generated HTML for the marked control. The theme has to provide the styling information. The style class name results from the following naming rule `"tobago-" + rendererName.toLower() + "-markup-" + markupName`; see Listing 6-19.

Listing 6-19. *Style for the Supported Markup*

```
.tobago-column-markup-new {
  background-color: yellow;
}
```

For the Example theme, it was decided to render a new column with a yellow background.

The address book example uses a different way to add markup. In this case, three markup values—`ok`, `warn`, and `error`—are defined for the `<tc:progress>` control directly in the `tobago-config.xml` file. The administration area contains a progress bar to visualize the memory utilization of the virtual machine. Depending on the percentage value of the memory usage, the business logic assigns different markup values for the progress bar to classify the state of the memory utilization; see Figure 6-9.

Figure 6-9. *Progress control with markup*

The resource directory contains style sheets for visualizing the markup values as different background colors: green for `ok`, yellow for `warn`, and red for `error`. The Speyside theme, for example, is extended by the `html/speyside/standard/style/style.css` file.

Creating Your Own Tobago Control

The ideal place to start when you want to create your own Tobago control is the sandbox. To access the sandbox, you have to check it out using Subversion:

```
svn checkout \
    http://svn.apache.org/repos/asf/myfaces/tobago/tags/tobago-1.0.14/sandbox \
    sandbox-1.0.14
```

Alternatively, if you have checked out the complete Tobago source tree, you can find the sandbox directory right under the root directory. In this section, we will create an HTML control in the sandbox as an example. The new control will be a slider for entering integer numbers.

This control consists of a slider bar with an attached number input field. If you move the slider, the number field is changed accordingly, and vice versa. Figure 6-10 shows a preview of the control. You can find the complete code in the Tobago sandbox.

Figure 6-10. *Slider control for entering numbers*

The UIComponent

We are starting with the user interface component of the control and will name it `org.apache.myfaces.tobago.component.UIInputNumberSlider`. Like all JSF components, Tobago components must extend `javax.faces.component.UIComponent`. Because we want to create an input component, we can extend `javax.faces.component.UIInput`, which is a nondirect subclass of `javax.faces.component.UIComponent`. The class `UIInput` is already an implementation of `javax.faces.component.EditableValueHolder`, which saves you a lot of work.

The JSF runtime environment needs the component type as an identifier for creating instances of components. Tobago components need to store this information in the component itself in the constant `COMPONENT_TYPE`. This constant is processed by the Tobago annotation visitor that is used in the build process to create the `faces-config.xml` file.

We also implement some additional properties into our component: `min`, `max`, `readonly`, and `disabled`. The `min` property specifies the smallest number that can be entered, and the `max` property specifies the largest. With the `readonly` property set, the user cannot modify the value of the slider; the same is true for the `disabled` property, but in this case, the complete control appears deactivated. All properties should be value binding enabled, which makes their getters a little bit more complicated. To ensure that our component state is saved between requests, we have to override the state holder methods of `UIInput`. Listing 6-20 illustrates some parts of our component class.

Listing 6-20. *Component Class for the Number Slider*

```
public class UIInputNumberSlider extends javax.faces.component.UIInput {

  public static final String COMPONENT_TYPE =
      "org.apache.myfaces.tobago.InputNumberSlider";

  private Boolean readonly;
  private Boolean disabled;
  private Integer min;
  private Integer max;

  public Boolean isReadonly() {
    if (readonly != null) {
      return readonly;
    }

    ValueBinding vb = getValueBinding(TobagoConstants.ATTR_READONLY);

    if (vb == null) {
      return false;
    } else {
      return (Boolean.TRUE.equals(vb.getValue(getFacesContext())));
    }
  }
```

```
  public void setReadonly(Boolean readonly) {
    this.readonly = readonly;
  }

  ...

  public void restoreState(FacesContext context, Object state) {...}
  public Object saveState(FacesContext context) {...}
}
```

The Renderer

There are two ways in JSF to render a component. The first one is to implement the encoding and decoding between UI component and the view in the UI component directly. This is called the direct implementation programming model. The second method is to delegate the task to an appropriate renderer, which is called the delegating programming model. The delegated programming model keeps your components independent from the view technology and is preferred for Tobago components.

A renderer in JSF must be a subclass of `javax.faces.render.Renderer`, but Tobago components' renderers must also implement the interface `org.apache.myfaces.tobago.renderkit.LayoutInformationProvider` to get the renderer to work with the Tobago layout management. With this interface, Tobago renderers provide the layout manager with certain information about the sizing of the component that is rendered. The required methods have a default implementation in the `org.apache.myfaces.tobago.renderkit.RendererBase` class, which uses properties that are provided by the theme configuration of the theme used (`tobago-theme-config.properties`). We name our renderer `InputNumberSliderRenderer` and extend from `LayoutableRendererBase`. Following the Tobago naming convention, the renderer must end with "Renderer".

When subclassing `LayoutableRendererBase`, the theme configuration is a good place to provide the information needed for the layout. The implementation searches the configuration for properties with the following pattern: `render name without "Renderer" + "." + key`. All values are interpreted as pixels. Table 6-2 specifies some of the recognized keys.

Table 6-2. *Recognized Keys for LayoutableRendererBase*

Key	Description
`fixedWidth, fixedHeight`	This is the preferred and normal size of a control. It is used if the value fixed is specified within the layout properties of a layout manager.
`paddingWidth, paddingHeight`	The padding attributes add empty space between the control and its surroundings.
`headerHeight`	Some controls, like the `<tc:box>` control, use this property to specify extra space for the header.

If `LayoutableRendererBase` does not find a value for a renderer, it searches for default properties: `"Tobago." + key`. We could (but will not) specify a width padding of 5 pixels for our control by adding the property `InputNumberSlider.paddingWidth=5` in the theme configuration of the sandbox theme. Please note that the resource location mechanism as described in the section "Resource Management" is used to find a property.

The Tobago theme configuration is not only used by `RendererBase`, but properties of our renderers can be specified there. For example, we define the percentage of the width of the slider of our control in the `tobago-theme-config.xml`: `InputNumberSlider.sliderWidthPercent=66`. This means that the slider gets 66 percent of the width of our control, and the input field, 34 percent. The value can be accessed in the renderer with the code in Listing 6-21.

Listing 6-21. *Obtaining Theme Configuration Programmatically*

```
int width = ThemeConfig.getValue(facesContext, component, "sliderWidthPercent");
```

The Tobago theming mechanism locates renderers by their locations in the package structure. Normally, all Tobago renderers are located under the root package `org.apache.myfaces.tobago.renderkit`. Below this, the location depends on the output technology: the theme and browser.

We use the `html.sandbox.standard.tag` subpackage, because we are writing an HTML control for the sandbox theme. Package `standard` means that all browsers (Mozilla, Internet Explorer, etc.) will be served by this renderer. The last package tag is obligatory for historical reasons.

The code for encoding/decoding in the renderer is quite long, so only some interesting fragments are shown in Listing 6-22. All encoding is done in the method `encodeEnd`. First, the properties of the component are retrieved. Next, the response writer is used to generate the HTML input field of our control. The response writer for Tobago components is `org.apache.myfaces.tobago.webapp.TobagoResponseWriter`, which is created by the Tobago render kit. It provides the component developer with additional convenience methods and handles escaping. The decoding is done in the method `decode` and retrieves the value of the input field back from the HTTP request.

Listing 6-22. *Rendered for the Number Slider Component*

```
package org.apache.myfaces.tobago.renderkit.html.sandbox.standard.tag;

public class InputNumberSliderRenderer extends RendererBase {

  public void encodeEnd(FacesContext facesContext, UIComponent component)
        throws IOException {

    String currentValue = getCurrentValue(facesContext, component);
    boolean readonly =
          ComponentUtil.getBooleanAttribute(component, ATTR_READONLY);
    boolean disabled =
          ComponentUtil.getBooleanAttribute(component, ATTR_DISABLED);
    TobagoResponseWriter writer =
          HtmlRendererUtil.getTobagoResponseWriter(facesContext);
    ...
```

```
    writer.startElement(HtmlConstants.INPUT);
    String inputIdAndName = getIdForInputField(facesContext, component);
    writer.writeNameAttribute(inputIdAndName);
    writer.writeIdAttribute(inputIdAndName);

    if (currentValue != null) {
      writer.writeAttribute(HtmlAttributes.VALUE, currentValue, false);
    }

    writer.writeAttribute(HtmlAttributes.READONLY, readonly);
    writer.writeAttribute(HtmlAttributes.DISABLED, disabled);
    writer.endElement(HtmlConstants.INPUT);
    ...
  }

  public void decode(FacesContext context, UIComponent component) {
    UIInput uiInput = (UIInput) component;
    ...
    String inputId = getIdForInputField(context, component);
    Map requestParameterMap =
          context.getExternalContext().getRequestParameterMap();

    if (requestParameterMap.containsKey(inputId)) {
      String newValue = (String) requestParameterMap.get(inputId);
      uiInput.setSubmittedValue(newValue);
    }
  }

  private String getIdForInputField(FacesContext context, UIComponent component){
    ...
  }
}
```

When the HTML output in the renderer is generated the question how to size the elements arises. It is not a good idea to hard-code static width or height information, because the layout manager determines how much space the control should occupy. But how can a renderer know how much space it should use?

Tobago creates a style map for each component and adds it to the components attributes. This style map contains values for the width and the height of the control determined by the layout manager. In the renderer, this map can be accessed and the values can be taken into account when creating HTML elements. Listing 6-23 demonstrates the use of the style map.

Listing 6-23. *Using the Style Map*

```
HtmlStyleMap style = (HtmlStyleMap) component.getAttributes().get("style");
int width = style.getInt("width");
```

The Tag and the Tag Declaration

All JSF implementations must support JSP as the page description language for JSF pages. This is also standard for writing Tobago pages. A different view technology that does not depend on JSP is also available—Facelets. To allow an author to use our control, we need to define a JSP tag, a custom action, by writing one class and one interface: the tag class itself and a tag declaration interface that is Tobago-specific.

We start with the tag class. All JSP custom actions in JSF that correspond to a UI component in the component tree must either subclass `javax.faces.webapp.UIComponentTag` or `javax.faces.webapp.UIComponentBodyTag` depending on whether they need support for body content functionality or not. Our action has no body content, so we want to subclass `UIComponentTag`. Again, there is an opportunity to save some effort if we extend from `org.apache.myfaces.tobago.taglib.component.TobagoTag`, which extends from `UIComponentTag`. This class already implements the handling for the `readonly` and `disabled` properties.

Our tag is named `org.apache.myfaces.tobago.taglib.sandbox.InputNumberSliderTag` and consists of four new properties (`min`, `max`, `value`, and `valueChangeListener`) with their getter/setters, an implementation of `getComponentType`, a `release` method, and a `setProperties` method.

Tag classes in Tobago are unintelligent gateways between the view technology (JSP) and the render independent UI component. No output should be generated in the JSP tag directly. Output should be produced only in appropriate renderers. The advantage with this approach is that we can use a different view technology like Facelets without changing our code.

Next comes the declaration of the tag, so the declaration implements an interface, `org.apache.myfaces.tobago.taglib.sandbox.InputNumberSliderTagDeclaration`. This interface describes our tag and its attributes with annotations. Tobago's build process uses this declaration to generate a `faces-config.xml` file and a TLD for our component with the help of the annotation processing tool (APT). The interface is annotated with an `@Tag` annotation with a name attribute. The specified value, `numberSlider`, is the name of the JSP tag. The next annotation, `@UIComponentTag`, clarifies that the tag belongs to a component with an associated renderer. The `rendererType` and `uiComponent` attributes specify the type of the renderer and the class of the UI component. Please note that the Tobago render kit will add the suffix "Renderer" to the renderer type to find a matching renderer class.

After the interface, the properties that are defined for the tag are annotated. By convention, the setter of the property is used. The `@TagAttribute` annotation describes a property that is part of the JSP tag. The `@UIComponentTagAttribute` annotation specifies a component property. Our properties appear in both the tag and the component. With the additional annotation attribute type, as shown in Listing 6-24, we define the type of the properties.

Tobago has many predefined tag attribute declarations. We make use of them by extending the needed interfaces like `IsReadonly` or `HasValue`; see Listing 6-24.

Listing 6-24. *Tag Declaration Using Annotations*

```
@Tag(name = "numberSlider")
@UIComponentTag(
    rendererType = "InputNumberSlider",
    uiComponent = "org.apache.myfaces.tobago.component.UIInputNumberSlider")

public interface InputNumberSliderTagDeclaration extends
    HasIdBindingAndRendered, IsReadonly, IsDisabled,
    HasValue, HasValueChangeListener {

  @TagAttribute()
  @UIComponentTagAttribute(type="java.lang.Integer", defaultValue="0")
  void setMin(String min);

  @TagAttribute()
  @UIComponentTagAttribute(type="java.lang.Integer", defaultValue="100")
  void setMax(String max);
}
```

Building and Using the Control

After obtaining all four elements needed to create a Tobago control (the UI component, renderer, tag, and tag declaration), we are ready to build. This is done with a simple `mvn install` in the sandbox directory: the classes are compiled; the `faces-config.xml` and the tag library descriptions are generated; and everything is packaged and stored in the target directory. Depending on the Tobago version, the package is called something like `tobago-sandbox-1.0.17.jar`. Put this JAR file in the classpath of your web application, and the control can be used on a JSP page (see Listing 6-25). It is important to switch to the Sandbox theme in the Tobago configuration.

Listing 6-25. *Using the Custom Control*

```
<%@ taglib uri="http://myfaces.apache.org/tobago/sandbox" prefix="tcs" %>
<%@ taglib uri="http://java.sun.com/jsf/core" prefix="f" %>
<f:view>
  ...
  <tcs:numberSlider value="#{controller.value}" min="0" max="200"/>
  ...
</f:view>
```

Security

To enable security for a Tobago application, you can either write your own log-in mechanism or use the standard way provided by the servlet specification. The standard way has a small drawback, because the name attribute for an HTML input control normally cannot be controlled via JSF or Tobago. For form-based authentication, the Servlet Specification requires the input fields of a login dialog to have the names j_username and j_password, respectively. Since we cannot influence the names of <tc:in> controls directly, we have to resort to a hack. We subsequently change the rendered field names with JavaScript inside the browser; see Listing 6-26.

Listing 6-26. *Enabling Form-Based Authentication*

```
<tx:in id="j_username" label="Username"/>
<tx:in id="j_password" password="true" label="Password"/>
...
<tc:script onload="initLoginForm();">
  function initLoginForm() {
    var user = document.getElementById("page:j_username");
    user.name = "j_username";
    var pass = document.getElementById("page:j_password");
    pass.name = "j_password";
    var form = document.getElementById("page::form");
    form.action = "${pageContext.request.contextPath}/j_security_check";
  }
</tc:script>
```

The onload attribute instructs Tobago to execute the passed JavaScript function after the HTML page was loaded.

Tobago provides an extension package, tobago-security, to secure method bindings with annotations. Currently, including the JAR in the classpath is not sufficient for using tobago-security, since the order in which the faces-config.xml files from libraries in the classpath are evaluated depends on the JSF implementation. The faces-config.xml file of tobago-security defines alternatives for command components with security handling. The easiest way is to copy the component redefinitions into the faces-config.xml file of the web application.

With the tobago-security package, a method can be marked with @RolesAllowed to designate the necessary roles for a business functionality. The method binding will only be evaluated if the user has the appropriate role. Likewise, the class can be marked with @RolesAllowed to secure all methods. In the address book example in Listing 6-27, the Admin toolbar button points to a method in AdminController that is annotated with the required role admin.

Listing 6-27. *Using Annotations to Security Methods*

```
@RolesAllowed("admin")
public String admin() {
  return OUTCOME_ADMIN;
}
```

If the user of the application does not have the admin role, the button is disabled, and the method binding will not be evaluated. Additionally, the @DenyAll and @PermitAll annotations are supported. These security annotations are part of the Common Annotations specification (JSR 250).

Virtual Forms

The <tc:page> tag acts as a global form. Therefore, for simple pages without control dependencies, no explicit form has to be used. The <tc:form> control allows nesting of forms and creates dependencies between controls.

If a form is submitted, only the contained model references are updated; other values are temporarily stored. With <tc:form>, partial validation can be realized, because validation is limited to controls inside a <tc:form> tag. As a result, subforms provide an alternative to immediate for input controls. In the address book example in Listing 6-28, changes to the theme and the language are isolated to subforms to avoid conflicts with validations elsewhere on the page.

Listing 6-28. *Using Virtual Forms to Change Themes*

```
<tc:form>
  <tx:selectOneChoice label="Theme" value="#{controller.theme}">
    <f:selectItems value="#{controller.themeItems}" />
    <f:facet name="change">
      <tc:command action="#{controller.themeChanged}"/>
    </f:facet>
  </tx:selectOneChoice>
</tc:form>
```

Partial Rendering

To avoid the reloading of complete pages, Tobago has a renderedPartially attribute to update only parts of the page. For <tc:tabGroup> controls, this can be achieved by configuring the switching type to reloadTab. Tobago also supports a more generic way to update container controls like <tc:panel>, <tc:box>, <tc:popup>, or <tc:sheet> using <tc:attribute> with the name renderedPartially and a value with a comma-separated list of identifier paths of the respective containers. An identifier path is a colon-separated list of IDs of nested naming containers. An absolute path of IDs has to begin with a colon character followed by the ID of the <tc:page> control. A path that does not start with a colon is a relative path from the current naming container. By using multiple colon characters at the beginning of the path, parent naming containers can be accessed. The action of the command has to return null as an outcome, because the current view has to be used again. Only a subtree of the view is updated.

Listing 6-29 shows a simple example where an input control is enabled depending on the state of a checkbox.

Listing 6-29. *Enabling Input Controls Without Reloading*

```
<tc:page id="page">
  <tc:box label="Container" id="box">
    <tx:selectBooleanCheckbox label="Enable" value="#{controller.miscEnabled}">
      <f:facet name="change">
        <tc:command>
          <tc:attribute name="renderedPartially" value=":page:box"/>
        </tc:command>
      </f:facet>
    </tx:selectBooleanCheckbox>
    <tx:in label="Misc." disabled="#{!controller.miscEnabled}"/>
  </tc:box>
</tc:page>
```

Instead of reloading the whole page, only the surrounding container `<tc:box>` of the `<tx:in>` control is updated, if the value of the checkbox changes. The absolute ID path of the box, which should be updated, is set as the `renderedPartially` attribute of the command.

Additionally, `<tc:panel>` controls can be reloaded on a regular basis to be able to display changes over time. To accomplish this, the panel has to be provided with a `reload` facet. This facet has to contain a `<tc:reload>` tag to specify the frequency for the reload in milliseconds; see Listing 6-30.

Listing 6-30. *Specifying Reload Frequency*

```
<tc:panel>
  <f:facet name="reload">
    <tc:reload frequency="5000"/>
  </f:facet>
  ...
</tc:panel>
```

The address book uses the reload facility on an administration page to regularly display the memory utilization of the virtual machine.

Advanced Assembly

As described in the "Configuring the Web Descriptor (web.xml)" section, themes can be served directly out of the theme JARs with the help of a special servlet. Generally, streaming static resources poses a slight overhead, but using the servlet also provides a simple way to define HTTP expire headers for the static resources. The expiration period can be specified in seconds as an `init-param` for the servlet; see Listing 6-31.

Listing 6-31. *Specifying an Expiration Period for Resources*

```
<servlet>
  <servlet-name>ResourceServlet</servlet-name>
  <servlet-class>
    org.apache.myfaces.tobago.servlet.ResourceServlet
  </servlet-class>
  <init-param>
    <param-name>expires</param-name>
    <param-value>14400</param-value>
  </init-param>
</servlet>
```

Instead of streaming the resources with a servlet, your resources can be unpacked and supplied by the servlet container directly. Alternatively, a web server like the Apache HTTP Server can be set up in front of the servlet container. The web server can intercept the URLs for the static resources and serve them instead of the servlet container. If the themes are unpacked, only the resources should be unpacked, not the class files or property files. But the JARs still have to be put into the classpath to provide the necessary implementation files for the theme.

Besides the MyFaces JSF implementation, Tobago also works with other JSF implementations like the Reference Implementation (RI) from Sun. The POM for the address book example provides three profiles for different JSF implementations. The default is MyFaces, but there is an additional profile for the Sun RI. The third profile assumes that the container provides an implementation for JSF.

Summary

Tobago allows you to develop rich web applications with a fantastic set of controls. The development is easy and independent of the view technology. And, even better, the web application makes use of technologies like Ajax without making any effort. The ease of development enables Tobago to be used for rapid prototyping, because the views can be designed without the need to program any lines of Java code.

In the near future, the tree component from the sandbox will become part of the standard Tobago distribution, and you can expect other useful controls to follow. With MyFaces focusing on fulfilling the JSF 1.2 specification, Tobago is aiming for JSF 1.2 compatibility as well. Another goal is to attain a form of integration with other component sets like Tomahawk. Currently, your ability to add such controls to a Tobago application is limited, partly because there is no way to add the necessary layout and theming information for external controls.

CHAPTER 7

Antipatterns and Pitfalls

This chapter covers antipatterns and pitfalls of day-to-day JSF development. Many of these issues have kept us up at night, and most of these are old problems with new faces: performance, tight coupling, cache management, thread safety, security, and interoperability.

N Plus One

The N Plus One antipattern typically finds its way into web applications in a scenario like this: You want to render a web page of purchase orders along with some data about the customer of each order. This data must be read from a database. An efficient approach would be to pull a single dataset by joining the `Customer` table and the `Order` table. A far less efficient approach would be to read a dataset from the `Order` table, iterate over this dataset, and go back to the database for detailed customer information related to that order. The first approach costs one round-trip; the second approach costs *N* plus one round-trips, where *N* is the number of orders. Let's look at how this antipattern can find its way into JSF applications.

The powerful Open Transaction in View pattern has grown popular among application developers using object-relational mapping (ORM) frameworks. In the Hibernate community, the pattern often goes by a slightly different name, Open Session in View. This pattern begins by opening a transaction in a servlet filter as the request arrives and closing the transaction before the response is sent. The `OpenTransactionInViewFilter` class (OTVF) is an implementation of this pattern:

```
public class OpenTransactionInViewFilter implements Filter {

        public void doFilter(ServletRequest request,
                                ServletResponse response, FilterChain chain) {

                try {

                        ObjectRelationalUtility.startTransaction();
                        chain.doFilter(request, response);
                        // commits transaction, if open
                        ObjectRelationalUtility.commitTransaction();

                } catch (Throwable throwable) {
```

```
                                try {

                                        ObjectRelationalUtility.rollback➥
Transaction();

                                } catch (Throwable _throwable) {
                                        /* sans error handling */
                                }

                        }
                }

                public void init(FilterConfig config) throws ServletException { }

                public void destroy() { }
}
```

The beauty of this pattern is the convenience of querying the ORM framework in an action method, placing a persistent object in request scope, and letting the navigation handler forward the request to the appropriate view template. The page developer has the luxury of pulling data to the response via JSF EL expressions. Data can be lazily loaded as the page renders and each JSF EL expression walks the Request-scoped object graph.

We once assisted with a project where this pattern was applied. The project was on time and under budget, but the application had performance problems. During the first six months of development, the application had developed a very loud conversation with the database. The primary culprits were view templates like this:

```
<!-- One trip to the database for the projects ... -->
<h:dataTable value="#{projectBean.projects}" var="project">
        <h:column>
                <h:commandLink action="#{projectBean.viewProject}"
                        value="view project"/>
        </h:column>
        <h:column>
        <!-- ... and plus N trips for each project manager record -->
                <f:facet name="header">Project Manager</f:facet>
                #{project.manager.name}
        </h:column>
        <h:column>
                <f:facet name="header">Project Name</f:facet>
                #{project.name}
        </h:column>
        <h:column>
                <f:facet name="header">Start Date</f:facet>
                #{project.startDate}
        </h:column>
```

```
        <h:column>
                <f:facet name="header">End Date</f:facet>
                #{project.endDate}
        </h:column>
</h:dataTable>
```

The data for this form could be retrieved with a single trip to the database. Instead, a single persistent instance of the domain model was being passed to the view template, and the JSF EL Resolver was triggering an additional trip to the database for each row to be rendered. The action methods in the managed beans weren't digging deeply enough into the database and were causing the well-known N Plus One antipattern.

An architectural decision was made to isolate all database transactions to the application invocation phase with the `OpenTransactionInApplicationPhaseListener` class (OTAPL), which accomplishes everything provided by the OTVF with finer transaction demarcation.

The OTVF scopes a transaction to the life cycle of the request, while the OTAPL scopes a transaction to a single phase in the request life cycle. This subtly makes the difference between a web page that renders in O(n) and a web page that renders in O(1).

```
public class OpenTransactionInApplicationPhaseListener
        implements PhaseListener {

        public void beforePhase(PhaseEvent event) {

                try {

ObjectRelationalUtility.startTransaction();

                } catch (Throwable throwable) {

/* sans error handling */
                }
        }

        public void afterPhase(PhaseEvent event) {

                try {

// commits transaction, if open
                        ObjectRelationalUtility.commitTransaction();

                } catch (Throwable throwable) {

                        try {

                                ObjectRelationalUtility.rollback➥
Transaction();
```

```
                                    } catch (Throwable _throwable) {

                                                /* sans error handling */
                                    }

                                    /* sans error handling */
                        }
            }

            public PhaseId getPhaseId() {
                        return PhaseId.INVOKE_APPLICATION;
            }
}
```

The OTVF was replaced with the OTAPL, and the tests were run. View templates triggering read operations to the database could be smoked out by closing the transaction before the response rendering phase. Pages with exceptions could be used to trace which data-access objects needed to be fine-tuned. Every unit test passed; more than half the integration tests failed.

Not only had this simple PhaseListener highlighted a performance issue, it raised the awareness of risk. There is a special time in the request processing life cycle for risk: the application invocation phase. A great number of JSF applications place risk later in the life cycle, in the response rendering phase, by performing most of the database trips after the action phase as the page is rendering, with no chance to recover from the unexpected. This is the worst time to do something risky; even logging options are limited. This behavior defeats one of the purposes of the MVC pattern: keep the view concerned about display. Hitting the database during the response rendering phase dilutes the value of your `try/catch` blocks in action methods. Would you write an action method like this?

```
public String doAction() {

            String outcome = "success";

            try {

                        getDao().goToTheDataBase();

            }catch(Exception e) {

                        handleException();

                        outcome = "failure";

            }finally {
```

```
// Exception uncaught
                        getDao().goToTheDataBaseAgain();

            }

            return outcome;

}
```

We are not suggesting that the OTVF itself is an antipattern or a pitfall. It is great for production systems, when exceptions are obviously not desired. The OTAPL, however, is better for day-to-day development and testing, when failing fast is desired—fixing a mistake costs less when the mistake is discovered earliest.

There is a time and place for risk in the JSF request processing life cycle: the invoke application phase. This phase is composed of two parts: action listeners and actions. Any action source can have zero or more action listeners and a single action method. Action listeners are always invoked first, followed by the action method. Action listeners and action methods have different properties and trade-offs. Action listeners provide the application developer with an `ActionEvent` reference. The `ActionEvent` provides useful information such as a reference to the `ActionSource` component from where the event originated. This information is not as easily available in an action method, where there is no `ActionEvent` reference. Action methods, on the other hand, are different from action listeners, because each one has a return type, something the view navigation handler can react to.

If you are using a file handle, queue, remote method, web service, or database, consider doing so in an action method, where you can declaratively react to the unexpected, rather than an action listener. There will always be corner cases, but you should try to avoid risk in an action listener, a PhaseListener, a managed bean constructor, custom converter, custom validator, or while the page is rendering.

The Map Trick

The Map Trick antipattern is a hack used to invoke business methods from view templates via an obscure limitation in the JSP and JSF specifications. By invoking business methods from a template, the view and model become tightly coupled.

JSF EL and Unified EL do not support parameterized method invocation. You get ternary logic, and you can call getters, but that's about it. Tapestry developers, or anyone else familiar with the Object-Graph Navigation Language (OGNL) expression language, are often disappointed to learn this because OGNL supports parameterized method invocation. The closest thing to parameterized method invocation is static method invocation via JSP EL or Facelets.

The `Map` interface is the only exception to this rule. JSP EL, JSF EL, and Unified EL all support invocation of the get method, a parameterized method of the `Map` interface:

```
#{myManagedBean.silvert} // pulls 'silvert' from managed bean Map
#{param['lubke']}        // pulls 'lubke' request parameter
            Some developers have implemented their own Map to take advantage of ➥
this.
public class MapTrick implements Map {
```

```
            public Object get(Object key) {

                        return new BusinessLogic().doSomething(key);

            }

            public void clear() { }
            public boolean containsKey(Object arg) { return false; }
            public boolean containsValue(Object arg) { return false; }
            public Set entrySet() {return null; }
            public boolean isEmpty() { return false; }
            public Set keySet() { return null; }
            public Object put(Object key, Object value) { return null; }
            public void putAll(Map arg) { }
            public Object remove(Object arg) { return null; }
            public int size() { return 0; }
            public Collection values() { return null; }

}
```

When the EL Resolver invokes the get method the parameter is then used by business logic. We once saw a project where an entire miniature framework was built around the map trick. Needless to say, the view and model were severely tightly coupled. There are always better alternatives to the map trick using plain methods and value expressions.

The Déjà Vu PhaseListener

The JSF request life cycle is broken into phases. The beginning and end of each phase is considered an event, and these events can be subscribed to via a PhaseListener. If a PhaseListener subscribes to the restore view phase of the request life cycle, MyFaces will invoke a callback method on the PhaseListener instance each time the restore view phase begins and ends for a request. When PhaseListener callback methods are invoked twice, it is a referred to as a Déjà Vu PhaseListener, an old problem that often crops up on the MyFaces mailing list.

Tip One of the most active mailing lists for the Apache Software Foundation is `users@myfaces.apache.org`. It is a wonderful place for exchanging new ideas, trading technical solutions, and engaging in flame wars. After all these years, MyFaces remains an open source project where the development team still interacts with application developers.

Let's look at how PhaseListeners are registered at start-up time. PhaseListeners can be registered in any JSF configuration file:

```
<lifecycle>
<phase-listener>
org.apache.myfaces.PhaseListenerImpl
</phase-listener>
</lifecycle>
```

JSF configuration files are specified via the javax.faces.CONFIG_FILES context parameter in the deployment descriptor:

```
<context-param>
    <description>comma separated list of JSF conf files</description>
    <param-name>javax.faces.CONFIG_FILES</param-name>
    <param-value>
                    /WEB-INF/faces-config.xml,/WEB-INF/burns.xml
    </param-value>
</context-param>
```

Per the JSF specification, MyFaces automatically parses /WEB-INF/faces-config.xml as well as all files specified in the comma-separated list of the javax.faces.CONFIG_FILES context parameter. When /WEB-INF/faces-config.xml is specified in the javax.faces.CONFIG_FILES context parameter it is parsed twice. The PhaseListeners configured in this file are consequently registered twice at start-up and invoked twice at runtime. MyFaces tries to warn you about this in the log files:

```
WARN  org.apache.myfaces.config.FacesConfigurator - /WEB-INF/faces-config.xml has ➥
been
specified in the javax.faces.CONFIG_FILES context parameter of the deployment ➥
descriptor.
This should be removed, as it will be loaded twice.  See JSF spec 1.2, 10.1.3
```

XML Hell++

JSF 1.1 and 1.2 are compatible with Java 1.4. This requirement limits the JSF specification from using Java annotations to declare things such as navigation rules or dependency injection. These things are declared in XML instead.

We once looked at a project in development with a configuration file similar to the following. The "contact us" page was to be accessible from just about every page on the site, and a separate action rule was used for each page.

```
<navigation-rule>
        <from-view-id>/home.xhtml</from-view-id>
        <navigation-case>
                <from-outcome>contact_us</from-outcome>
                <to-view-id>/contact.xhtml</to-view-id>
        </navigation-case>
</navigation-rule>
```

```
<navigation-rule>
        <from-view-id>/site_map.xhtml</from-view-id>
        <navigation-case>
                <from-outcome>contact_us</from-outcome>
                <to-view-id>/contact.xhtml</to-view-id>
        </navigation-case>
</navigation-rule>
<navigation-rule>
        <from-view-id>/about_us.xhtml</from-view-id>
        <navigation-case>
                <from-outcome>contact_us</from-outcome>
                <to-view-id>/contact.xhtml</to-view-id>
        </navigation-case>
</navigation-rule>
<!-- continued ... -->
```

A global navigation rule was used to reduce the configuration file by more than a hundred lines:

```
<navigation-rule>
        <from-view-id>*</from-view-id>
        <navigation-case>
                <from-outcome>contact_us</from-outcome>
                <to-view-id>/contact.xhtml</to-view-id>
        </navigation-case>
</navigation-rule>
```

The Myth of Static Typing

Java gives us type safety, but J2EE takes some of it away. Your first "Hello World" Java program was simple: you, the compiler, and the runtime. As applications grow in size and complexity, the compiler and the type system begin to matter less. JNDI lookups, JSP and JSF EL evaluation, object relational mappings, JMS message selectors, and XML configuration parsing all occur at runtime. Let's look at how the myth of static typing applies to JSF.

The heavy use of XML in JSF leaves a lot of room for configuration headaches. To demonstrate this, let's look at what happens when we use XML in a JSF configuration file with some serious problems. Included in the following XML code are a misspelled class name, several broken file system paths to view templates, two managed beans with the same name, and a cyclical managed bean reference. None of these mistakes will be caught by the compiler or parser at build or deploy time; all of these errors will occur at runtime.

```
<managed-bean>
  <managed-bean-name>invalid</managed-bean-name>
  <!-- misspelled class name throws ClassNotFoundException -->
  <managed-bean-class>
            org.apache.myfaces.book.misspelled.Invalid
  </managed-bean-class>
```

```
  <managed-bean-scope>session</managed-bean-scope>
  <managed-property>
                        <!-- one side of cyclical reference -->
                      <property-name>incorrect</property-name>
                      <value>#{incorrect}</value>
  </managed-property>
</managed-bean>

<managed-bean>
  <managed-bean-name>incorrect</managed-bean-name>
  <managed-bean-class>
            org.apache.myfaces.book.validate.Incorrect
  </managed-bean-class>
  <managed-bean-scope>session</managed-bean-scope>
  <managed-property>
                        <!-- other side of cyclical reference -->
                      <property-name>invalid</property-name>
                      <value>#{invalid}</value>
  </managed-property>
</managed-bean>

<managed-bean> <!-- first duplicate -->
  <managed-bean-name>duplicate</managed-bean-name>
  <managed-bean-class>
            org.apache.myfaces.book.validate.FirstDuplicate
  </managed-bean-class>
  <managed-bean-scope>session</managed-bean-scope>
</managed-bean>

<managed-bean> <!-- second duplicate -->
  <managed-bean-name>duplicate</managed-bean-name>
  <managed-bean-class>
            org.apache.myfaces.book.validate.SecondDuplicate
  </managed-bean-class>
  <managed-bean-scope>application</managed-bean-scope>
</managed-bean>

<navigation-rule>
         <from-view-id>/missing.jsp</from-view-id>
         <navigation-case>
                   <from-outcome>failure</from-outcome>
                   <to-view-id>/absent.jsp</to-view-id>
                   <redirect />
         </navigation-case>
</navigation-rule>
```

MyFaces has a built-in validation feature to catch many of these mistakes. You can install the MyFaces validation feature by placing the following context parameter in your servlet deployment descriptor:

```
<context-param>
    <description>Runs validation routine at startup</description>
    <param-name>org.apache.myfaces.VALIDATE</param-name>
    <param-value>true</param-value>
</context-param>
```

When deploying the previous configuration file with the MyFaces validation feature, the following appears in the logs:

```
WARN More than one managed bean w/ the name of 'duplicate' - only keeping the last

WARN File for navigation 'from id' does not exist
C:\work\apache-tomcat-6.0.10\webapps\book\missing.jsp

WARN File for navigation 'to id' does not exist
C:\work\apache-tomcat-6.0.10\webapps\book\absent.jsp

WARN Could not locate class org.apache.myfaces.book.misspelled.Invalid for managed
bean 'invalid'
```

One limitation of the validation feature is that it does not detect the cyclical managed bean reference between the invalid managed bean and the incorrect managed bean. You should keep in mind that recursive dependency injection is not supported. Per the JSF specification, MyFaces throws an exception at runtime when this is detected.

MyFaces must also throw an exception at runtime if it encounters a managed bean with a subscoped managed property. In the following example, the Session-scoped managed bean is not valid because it refers to a Request-scoped managed bean:

```
<managed-bean>
        <managed-bean-name>requestScopeManagedBean</managed-bean-name>
        <managed-bean-class>
                org.apache.myfaces.book.RequestScopeManagedBean
        </managed-bean-class>
        <managed-bean-scope>request</managed-bean-scope>
</managed-bean>

<managed-bean>
        <managed-bean-name>sessionScopeManagedBean</managed-bean-name>
        <managed-bean-class>
                org.apache.myfaces.book.SessionScopeManagedBean
        </managed-bean-class>
```

```
            <managed-bean-scope>session</managed-bean-scope>
            <managed-property>
                    <property-name>requestScopeManagedBean</property-name>
                    <value>#{requestScopeManagedBean}</value>
            </managed-property>
    </managed-bean>
```

Most of the functionality provided by the MyFaces validation feature has recently been reimplemented as generic reusable JUnit tests under the JBoss JSFUnit project (see `http://www.jboss.org/jsfunit/`).

Thread Safety

Some parts of your application will need to be thread safe; others will not.

You never have to worry about the `FacesContext` class. Calls to `FacesContext.getCurrentInstance()` return a thread-local data structure, the `FacesContext` instance. This means that while `getCurrentInstance` is a static method, calls to this method will never result in a race condition.

PhaseListeners and Renderers must be thread safe. Each PhaseListener is global to the application, and it subscribes to at least one phase event for every request. The relationship between component instances and renderer instances is many-to-one: components of the same type share the same renderer instance.

Custom tag handlers do not need to be thread safe, but the servlet container can reuse the tag instance. Always reset the field values by implementing the release method.

Session- and Application-scoped managed beans obviously have to be thread safe; Request- and None-scoped managed beans do not.

You may or may not need to make a custom converter thread safe. Registering a converter and using a converter tag will never introduce a race condition. The component will get a new converter instance each time it is needed.

```
<h:inputText value="#{managedBean.value}" >
        <f:converter converterId="threadUnsafeConverter" >
</h:inputText>

<converter>
  <converter-id>threadUnsafeConverter</converter-id>
<converter-class>
        org.apache.myfaces.book.ThreadUnsafeConverter
</converter-class>
    </converter>
```

Using the `converter` attribute, however, does introduce a race condition, because it is possible the same `Converter` instance will be used simultaneously by more than once request.

```
<h:inputText value="#{managedBean.value}"
                    converter="#{threadUnsafeConverter}" />

<managed-bean>
            <managed-bean-name>threadUnsafeConverter</managed-bean-name>
            <managed-bean-class>
                        org.apache.myfaces.book.ThreadUnsafeConverter
            </managed-bean-class>
            <managed-bean-scope>session</managed-bean-scope>
</managed-bean>
```

Custom validators have the same thread safety constraints as custom converters. Registered validators do not need to be thread safe, because they are created and used by one thread. Nonregistered validators in session or application scope do need to be thread safe.

Facelets Migration Challenge: Tags with Behavior

Java developers have long been able to create their own JSP tags. JSF developers inherited this ability, because the default view technology for JSF is built on top of JSP. JSF hooks into JSP by invoking the `setProperties` method when the JSP tag is first rendered. This is the tag handler's one chance to pass the tag attribute values on to the `UIComponent` mapped to the tag. However, behavior placed in the `setProperties` method is lost when using Facelets, because Facelets replaces JSP as the rendering layer altogether.

```
public class WidgetTag extends UIComponentELTag{

            private String styleClass = "default_class";
            private String title;

            public String getComponentType() {
                        return "org.apache.myfaces.book.widget";
            }

            public String getRendererType() {
                        return "org.apache.myfaces.book.widget";
            }

            public void setStyleClass(String styleClass) {
                        this.styleClass = styleClass;
            }

            public void setTitle(String title) {
                        this.title = title;
            }
```

```
        public void release() {
                super.release();
                styleClass = null;
                title = null;
        }

        protected void setProperties(UIComponent component) {

                super.setProperties(component);

                Widget span = (Widget) component;

                span.setStyleClass(styleClass);
                span.setTitle(title == null ? "no title" : title);

                FacesContext ctx = FacesContext.getCurrentInstance();
                Map sessionMap = ctx.getExternalContext().getSessionMap();
                span.setStyle((String) sessionMap.get("style"));

        }

}
```

An experienced JSF developer will notice a few things wrong with this picture. The `styleClass` field defaults to `default_style`, the value of the `title` field depends on ternary logic, and one of the component values is derived from a value expression. Unfortunately, all three of these behaviors have been implemented in the tag handler, so all are lost when the component is used with an alternative view technology such as Facelets.

When we develop custom JSF components, it is important to place this kind of logic out of a tag handler. The MyFaces code base is a good example of this. The source code for 25 components and 25 tag handlers of the JSF 1.2 implementation are generated from metadata at build time, with no behavior.

The `WidgetTag` class also has a bug. The `setProperties` method is not invoked for post-backs to the server; it's invoked only the first time the page is rendered. When the page is rendered for the first time, the style value is pulled from the session and passed to the component. If the session value changes during the workflow, the component will not reflect the new value on subsequent postback requests.

The Law of Demeter

The Law of Demeter is a core principle in object-oriented programming design. It stresses the importance of encapsulation with one simple rule: objects should only talk to their immediate neighbors.

Here's a demonstration of the Law of Demeter. Once upon a JavaOne conference, Mathias needed to borrow some money from the guy sitting next to him, Craig.

"Craig," said Mathias, "I owe Martin a beer. Can I borrow five bucks?"

Craig obliged, and Mathias took his wallet and removed five dollars.

"Mathias," said Craig, "if I started storing my money in my shoe or a purse, you would have to change the way you borrow money from me."

"You're right," said Mathias, "my money borrowing logic is coupled to your money hiding logic. Next time, I'll ask you for the money, and let you be concerned about where it is stored."

Craig knew Mathias was a smart guy and dismissed the incident as a harmless cultural misunderstanding. It wasn't; it was a classic demonstration of the Law of Demeter.

We have had the opportunity to partner with some very bright engineers over the years, and we are still blown away at how often this principle gets overlooked. Everyone would agree that people should not reach into each other's pockets for money, but many think it's acceptable for objects to do this:

```
employee.getDepartment().getManager().getOffice().getAddress().getZip()
 <!-- highly sensitive to changes of the domain model -->
#{employee.department.manager.office.address.zip}
<!-- encapsulated, insensitive to changes -->
#{employee.departmentalManagerOfficeZip}
```

Few experienced developers need to be convinced that the preceding Java method chain, or train wreck, does not observe a basic object-oriented principle. But some do not recognize that the equally long EL expression is worse. The luxury of a compilation error is not available, because the view template is loosely typed. `MethodNotFoundError` and `NullPointerException` are common with view templates like this. Refactoring is a pain, because EL is loosely typed. When EL expressions become five or six segments long, the view template becomes coupled to the model. To avoid violating the Law of Demeter in this way, use encapsulation with EL, not just plain Java.

Master-Detail

Master-detail is commonly used to refer to a common user interface design whereby a one-to-many relationship is displayed. Business requirements for a master-detail screen are common and are usually like this: as a salesperson, I need to pull up a customer on my screen and see a list of all purchase orders for that customer.

Before we delve into several different ways of creating a master-detail screen using JSF, let's take a look at a design decision that will drive many of the trade-offs between each implementation: the managed bean scope. A managed bean can be placed in four levels of scope: none, request, session, and application. The easiest decisions are those involving none and application scopes. Use cases for the none scope are about none; it is self-documenting. Use cases for Application-scoped managed beans typically involve read-only data. It is acceptable to perform write operations on Application-scoped managed beans as long as the operation is atomic (i.e., assigning a value to an `Integer`, `Boolean`, `Short`, etc.).

The most difficult scoping decisions involve request and session scopes, where the real work is typically done. The relevant decision factors are no different than when developing applications in ASP.NET, PHP, or Ruby on Rails: memory consumption, thread safety, state management, and so on.

There is no hard-and-fast rule for deciding between request scope and session scope, and it's a decision that can be made only by the people developing the application. This decision is a very important, because some Request-scoped solutions in JSF are not interchangeable with Session-scoped solutions; moving managed beans from one scope to another can be painful. Designing managed beans that work in both request and session scopes is both a way to avoid this pain as well as a way to learn the fundamentals.

The following view template consists of a `dataTable` tag and several columns. The value attribute of the `dataTable` tag evaluates to a `DataModel` property of the `masterDetail` managed bean.

```
<h:dataTable value="#{masterDetail.details}" var="detail">
            <h:column>
                        <h:commandLink action="#{masterDetail.viewDetail}"
                                    value="view details"/>
            </h:column>
            <h:column>
                        <f:facet name="header">Name</f:facet>
                        #{detail.name}
            </h:column>
            <h:column>
                        <f:facet name="header">Description</f:facet>
                        #{detail.description}
            </h:column>
            <h:column>
                        <f:facet name="header">Date</f:facet>
                        #{detail.date}
            </h:column>
</h:dataTable>
```

The `masterDetail` managed bean has a dependency injected reference to the `detail` managed bean:

```
<managed-bean>
            <managed-bean-name>masterDetailBean</managed-bean-name>
            <managed-bean-class>
                        org.apache.myfaces.book.masterDetail.MasterDetailPage
            </managed-bean-class>
            <managed-bean-scope>request</managed-bean-scope>
    <managed-property>
                <property-name>detailPage</property-name>
                        <value>#{detailBean}</value>
    </managed-property>
</managed-bean>
```

```
<managed-bean>
        <managed-bean-name>detailBean</managed-bean-name>
        <managed-bean-class>
                org.apache.myfaces.book.masterDetail.DetailPage
        </managed-bean-class>
        <managed-bean-scope>session</managed-bean-scope>
</managed-bean>

public class MasterDetailPage {

        private DataModel details ;
        private DetailPage detailPage;

        public DataModel getDetails() {
                return details;
        }

        public void setDetailPage(DetailPage detailPage) {
                this.detailPage = detailPage;
        }

        public String viewDetail() {

                Detail detail = (Detail) details.getRowData();

                detailPage.setDetail(detail);

                return "success"; // forward to the detail display template
        }
}
```

The `DataModel` wraps a `Collection` of `Detail` instances. Each item in the collection will be rendered as a row in the table. When an end user clicks `commandLink` in the left column the browser will `POST` an HTTP request back to the server. This request is commonly called a postback request. The `viewDetails` action method on the `masterDetail` managed bean is invoked before the server sends the response. Within the action method, the `getRowData` method of the `DataModel` instance is invoked to obtain a reference to a `Detail` instance. The `Detail` reference returned by the `getRowData` method corresponds to the row in which the `commandLink` was clicked. The `Detail` reference is passed to the `DetailPage` instance, and the request is forwarded to a template that will display the `Detail` properties:

```
<navigation-rule>
        <from-view-id>/master.xhtml</from-view-id>
        <navigation-case>
                <from-outcome>success</from-outcome>
                <to-view-id>/detail.xhtml</to-view-id>
        </navigation-case>
</navigation-rule>
```

This would be a good solution if the data were synchronized. However, we do not recommend using synchronization for managed bean access. Often, moving the managed bean down to request scope is less painful in the long run. This approach is not without its challenges, either.

In request scope, the action method will not be invoked when the end user clicks the `commandLink` because `commandLink`, and every other child of `dataTable`, does not exist during the postback request. The `dataTable` has no children, because the `value` attribute evaluates to `null`. `DataModel` and the wrapped `Collection` of `Detail` instances are not persistent across requests.

One approach is to lazily load the collection from within the managed bean. This approach is not ideal (there is no ideal way to solve this problem), because it introduces an additional database trip each time the page renders. Finally, there is often no guarantee that the table data hasn't changed since the previous request: the same synchronization problem is now across a network.

These arguments would, of course, apply to a similar approach of loading the data in a managed bean constructor:

```
public javax.faces.model.DataModel getDetails() {

        if (details == null) // lazy load
                details = getDetailFromDataBase();

        return details;
}
```

This puzzle illustrates the need for conversation scope (see Chapter 5) or for the MyFaces Tomahawk `saveState` tag (see Chapter 2). Let's see how we can solve this problem using the `saveState` tag:

```
<t:saveState value="#{masterDetail.details.wrappedData}"/>
```

Per the JSF specification, the `DataModel` class does not implement `Serializable`. Consequently, the expression `#{masterDetail.details}` will throw a `NotSerializableException` each time the page renders with client-side state saving. This problem can be solved by simply changing the value attribute expression of the `saveState` tag to the actual `List` wrapped by the `DataModel`, as shown in the preceding code line.

The collection can be preserved across requests once the `saveState` tag is added to the view template. Behind the scenes, MyFaces serializes and deserializes the collection. Consequently, the `Detail` class must now implement `Serializable` if the application is configured for the client-side state saving. The user can now invoke the `viewDetails` action method when clicking the `commandLink`. Unfortunately, the managed bean must still be refactored before it can be used in both request and session scopes.

You may have difficulties with Conversation-scoped recursive object graphs, because the underlying persistence mechanism saving for client-side states is Java serialization. If objects A and B both point to C before the page renders, they will point to separate copies of C on subsequent postback requests.

Another valid approach is to drop DataModel altogether and to transport the selected Detail instance identifier. The action method will use the identifier to query an object-relational mapping framework for the appropriate persistent instance. This is often the case when business requirements call for a data refresh as the work flow transitions to a new page.

There are several ways to obtain the identifier value in the action method. One approach to obtaining the identifier is to nest a param tag beneath commandLink:

```
<h:dataTable value="#{masterDetail.details}" var="detail">
         <h:column>
                  <h:commandLink action="#{masterDetail.viewDetail}"
                          value="view details">
                          <f:param value="#{detail.id}" name="id" />
                  </h:commandLink>
         </h:column>
         <h:column>
                  <f:facet name="header">Name</f:facet>
                  #{detail.name}
         </h:column>
         <h:column>
                  <f:facet name="header">Description</f:facet>
                  #{detail.description}
         </h:column>
         <h:column>
                  <f:facet name="header">Date</f:facet>
                  #{detail.date}
         </h:column>
</h:dataTable>
```

When an end user clicks the commandLink, the identifier is mapped to an HTTP parameter key of id and sent with the postback request. The value can then be retrieved from the request object within the viewDetails action method.

```
public String viewDetail() {

    FacesContext ctx = FacesContext.getCurrentInstance();
    ServletRequest request = (ServletRequest)
                    ctx.getExternalContext().getRequest();
    String id = request.getParameter("id");

    // sans try catch block
    Detail detail = new DetailDAO().findById(new Long(id));

    // inform the other managed bean
    detailPage.setDetail(detail);

    return "success"; // forward to the detail display template
}
```

A value expression is another way of obtaining the identifier value:

```
public String viewDetail() {

    FacesContext ctx = FacesContext.getCurrentInstance();
    Application app = ctx.getApplication();
    String id = (String)
app.evaluateExpressionGet(ctx, "#{param.id}", String.class);

    // sans try catch block
    Detail detail = new DetailDAO().findById(new Long(id));

    // inform the other managed bean
    detailPage.setDetail(detail);

    return "success"; // forward to the detail display template
}
```

But neither of these approaches is effective. JSF provides a component-based approach to web application development. Some developers have a difficult time letting go of the `javax.servlet.http.HttpServletRequest` object, and it is natural for those of us coming from an action framework like Struts to view each challenge in terms of request parameters. There is certainly nothing wrong with the Servlet API, but when we find ourselves writing a lot of request-bound code in JSF, our solution is probably not optimal.

The view and managed beans are coupled, because both maintain the parameter key, `id`—one cannot be changed without changing the other. The view template can only be reused with other managed beans that look for the `id` parameter. The managed bean can only be reused with other view template forms that send the `id` parameter with the request. The identifier needs to be manually converted to an integer before it is given to the ORM because request parameters are strings. The identifier value still has to be manually converted, and the managed bean has gained a little weight.

Another approach is to replace the request object or the value expression with dependency injection. This can be accomplished by adding a managed-property element to the manage bean declaration:

```
<managed-bean>
            <managed-bean-name>masterDetailBean</managed-bean-name>
            <managed-bean-class>
            org.apache.myfaces.book.masterDetail.MasterDetailPage
            </managed-bean-class>
            <managed-bean-scope>request</managed-bean-scope>
    <managed-property>
                <property-name>detailPage</property-name>
                        <value>#{detail}</value>
    </managed-property>
```

```
    <managed-property>
            <property-name>id</property-name>
                <value>#{param.id}</value>
    </managed-property>
</managed-bean>
```

The id parameter value can be declaratively read from the request and passed to the managed bean after it is created and before the action is invoked. The value is injected via a new id setter method:

```
public void setId(String id) {
            this.id = id;
}

public String viewDetail() {

            Long id = new Long(this.id);

            Detail detail = new DetailDAO().findById(id); // sans try catch

            // inform the other managed bean
            detailPage.setDetail(detail);

            return "success"; // forward to the detail display template
}
```

This approach is not ideal either: it introduces minor coupling between the view template and configuration file, because both maintain the same parameter key, id. Again, one cannot be changed without changing the other. The managed bean is not reusable, because every time the managed bean is created, MyFaces looks to the request for this parameter key. This is a problem because the id parameter key may be mapped to something entirely different within the context of other workflows. A null value will be injected if no parameter is found, wiping away any preexisting field value. Additionally, the JSF specification mandates automatic type conversion for component values, not dependency injection. The id property, therefore, has to be a String and its value still has to be converted internally by the managed bean. Finally, the problem is still defined in terms of request parameters.

The param tag, request object, programmatic expression evaluation, and dependency injection can all be replaced with a simple and powerful component introduced by the JSF 1.2 specification—setPropertyActionListener:

```
<h:dataTable value="#{masterDetailBean.details}" var="detail">
            <h:column>
                        <h:commandLink action="#{detailBean.load}"
                                    value="view details">
                                    <f:setPropertyActionListener
value="#{detail.id}"
                                                target="#{detailBean.id}" />
                        </h:commandLink>
            </h:column>
```

```
        <h:column>
                <f:facet name="header">Name</f:facet>
                #{detail.name}
        </h:column>
        <h:column>
                <f:facet name="header">Description</f:facet>
                #{detail.description}
        </h:column>
        <h:column>
                <f:facet name="header">Date</f:facet>
                #{detail.date}
        </h:column>
</h:dataTable>
```

The setPropertyActionListener tag moves data from one place to another on the JSF EL landscape and registers a server-side event handler for the postback request of the commandLink. During the application invocation phase, before the action method is called, the event handler invokes the getter method represented by the EL expression of the value attribute. The returned value is converted if necessary. Finally, the event handler sets the value on the setter property represented by the EL expression of the target attribute:

```
<f:setPropertyActionListener value="#{detail.id}"
                                target="#{detailBean.id}" />

public class Detail {

        public Long getId() { // from value attribute …
                return id;
        }

        /* getters and setters omitted */

}

public class DetailPage {

        public void setId(Long id) { // … to the target attribute
                this.id = id;
        }

        /* controller logic omitted */

}
```

The problem's solved with one line of template code. JSF conversion is realized without compromising reusability, and the view, managed bean, and configuration have been decoupled.

The JSF 1.2 implementation added a new tag to the standardized tag libraries: setPropertyActionListener. The setPropertyActionListener component behaves nearly identically to a component found in MyFaces Tomahawk: updateActionListener. It also provides an excellent opportunity for transitioning into the next section of this chapter, vendor lock-in.

Vendor Lock-In

J2EE standards aim to insulate application developers from vendor lock-in. JSF is a standard, but in a few corner cases, an application developer can inadvertently couple the application to a single vendor.

The setPropertyActionListener tag is unique among all tags defined by the JSF specification. It is a part of the standard JSF tag libraries, just like the form and view tags. However, the JSF component mapped to the setPropertyActionListener tag is not a part of the JSF API—there is no javax.faces.listener.SetPropertyActionListener in the JSF specification. The implementation must be instantiated in order to programmatically register or deregister the event handler for an action source such HtmlCommandButton. The ActionListenerExample class demonstrates this:

```
/* Apache MyFaces JSF 1.2 implementation */
import org.apache.myfaces.event.SetPropertyActionListener;

/* Sun RI JSF 1.2 implementation */
import com.sun.faces.taglib.jsf_core.SetPropertyActionListenerImpl;

/* Apache MyFaces Tomahawk */
import org.apache.myfaces.custom.updateactionlistener.UpdateActionListener;

/* Apache MyFaces Trinidad */
import org.apache.myfaces.trinidadinternal.taglib.listener.SetActionListener;

public class ActionListenerExample {

  public void attachListener(ActionSource actionSource) {

   actionSource.addActionListener(new SetPropertyActionListener() );
   actionSource.addActionListener(new SetPropertyActionListenerImpl());
   actionSource.addActionListener(new UpdateActionListener() );
   actionSource.addActionListener(new SetActionListener() );

  }

}
```

Applications using the first or second implementations are locked into one JSF implementation. This is ironic: the MyFaces Tomahawk or Trinidad components are the interoperable solutions, because UpdateActionListener and SetActionListener work across both implementations, as well as working on JSF 1.1 and 1.2.

Another form of vendor lock-in comes in the form of various tag attributes that have made it into the MyFaces core tag libraries of the 1.1.x releases, such as the `size` attribute of the `commandButton` tag or the `align` attribute of the `inputText` tag. These attributes are not found in the corresponding tags for the JSF reference implementation. This issue has fueled debate within the MyFaces team. What is best for users: vendor interoperability or backward compatibility? None of these attributes were moved forward to the MyFaces 1.2.x releases.

Facelets is another point worth mention when it comes to vendor lock-in. We have helped many organizations migrate from JSP to Facelets. Some have done this eagerly, and others have dragged their feet, but none of them have looked back. Some naysayers resist this change by waving the vendor lock-in flag: JSP is a standard; Facelets is not. Don't ever let anyone win this argument. Although Facelets is not a standard, HTML is. HTML is more mature than JSP, has a lower learning curve, and has a fairly higher market penetration. Facelets brings Java web developers closer to ASP.NET and Rails, in a good way.

AJAX 101

In this section of the chapter, we'll look at several ways to implement the requirements using JSF and AJAX, with an emphasis on the trade-offs that go hand in hand with each approach. We'll begin by introducing our running example and a couple of use cases.

The table shown in Figure 7-1 displays a list of employees. When a user clicks a "delete" link in the leftmost column, the employee is removed from the database as well as the page. When a user clicks a "view details" link, the browser retrieves employee details from the server. The `div` tag to the right of the table displays the employee details once they are received by the browser. Deleting an employee and reading an employee's details are done without a full-page refresh.

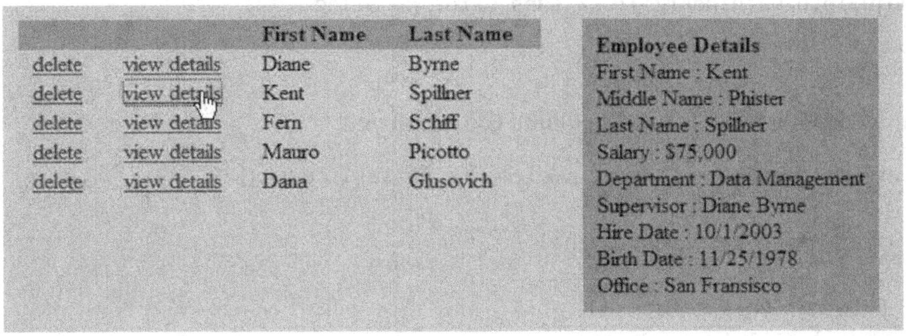

Figure 7-1. *List of employees table*

The relevant view template code for the employee table consists of a `dataTable` element and a plain `div` tag:

```
<h:dataTable value="#{employeeBean.employees}" var="employee">
  <h:column>
<a onclick="deleteEmployee(#{employee.id}); return false;"
   href="." >delete</a>
  </h:column>
```

```
  <h:column>
<a onclick="viewDetails(#{employee.id}); return false;"
   href="." >view details</a>
  </h:column>
  <h:column>
<f:facet name="header">First Name</f:facet>
#{employee.firstName}
  </h:column>
  <h:column>
<f:facet name="header">Last Name</f:facet>
#{employee.lastName}
  </h:column>
</h:dataTable>

<div id="employeeDetails" />
```

Let's begin by looking at how employees are deleted. The `deleteEmployee` event handler uses Dojo to send an HTTP request back to the server:

```
function deleteEmployee(id){ /* client side event handler */

   bindArgs = {
                url: "employees.jsf?deleteEmployeeId=" + id,
                load: deleteEmployeeCallback,
                method: "GET"
   };

   dojo.io.bind(bindArgs); // sans error handling

}
```

On the server, a PhaseListener is used to delete the employee:

```
public class DeleteEmployeePhaseListener implements PhaseListener {

    public void afterPhase(PhaseEvent event) {

                 ExternalContext ectx =
event.getFacesContext().getExternalContext();
                 HttpServletResponse response =
(HttpServletResponse) ectx.getResponse();
String id = (String)
            ectx.getRequestParameterMap().get("deleteEmployeeId");

               if (id != null)
                   deleteEmployee(response, id);

    }
```

```
    private void deleteEmployee(HttpServletResponse response,
String id) {

        boolean success = false;

        try {

            new EmployeeDAO().deleteById(new Long(id));

            success = true;

        } catch (Exception e) {

            handleError(e);

        } finally {

            try {

             // return JSON to the browser
             response.getWriter().print("{'success':" + success + "}");

            } catch (IOException e) {

                handleError(e);
            }

        }
    }

    /* sans other methods */

}
```

The `deleteEmployeeCallback` event handler is used to make the user interface reflect the outcome of the delete action:

```
/* client side response handler */

function deleteEmployeeCallback(type, data, xhr){

            var response = eval('(' + data + ')');

            if( response.success )
                        programmaticallyRemoveRowElementFromDOM();
            else
                        handleFailure();

}
```

The deleteEmployee event handler is a poor implementation for employee deletion. Deleting an employee is not safely repeatable, because doing so changes the state of the server. Such a request should use a POST or DELETE request rather than an idempotent GET request. POST and DELETE requests cannot be cached by the browser, which is obviously not desired in this use case. Furthermore, the bindArgs variable should be scoped with the JavaScript keyword, var.

```
/* client side event handler */

function deleteEmployeeRefactored(id){

   var bindArgs = {
                  url: "employees.jsf?deleteEmployeeId=" + id,
                  load: deleteEmployeeCallback,
                  method: "DELETE" /* ... or POST */
   };

   dojo.io.bind(bindArgs); // sans error handling

}
```

If you are developing an application that must be used with a wide array of browsers, you may have to compromise here. Some older browsers do not support the DELETE method for asynchronous HTTP requests. In that case, a POST request will work just fine.

Now, let's look at several different ways to implement the "view details" functionality. One implementation begins with a JavaScript onclick event handler for the employee name column:

```
<a onclick="viewDetails(#{employee.id}); return false;"
   href="." >view details</a>
```

The viewDetails event handler uses Dojo to send an HTTP request back to the server:

```
function viewDetails(id) { /* client side event handler */

   var bindArgs = {
            url: "employees.jsf?listEmployeeId=" + id,
            load: viewDetailsCallback,
            method: "GET"
   };

   dojo.io.bind(bindArgs); // sans error handling
}
```

The request is handled in a PhaseListener and a data-access object is used to retrieve the employee details from a database. The details are encoded in JSON and sent back to the browser via an HTTP response header:

```
public class EmployeeDetailsPhaseListener implements PhaseListener {

  public void beforePhase(PhaseEvent event) {

      FacesContext ctx = event.getFacesContext();

      ExternalContext external = ctx.getExternalContext();

      Map parameters = external.getRequestParameterMap();

      String id = (String) parameters.get("listEmployeeId");

      if (id != null) {

          Employee employee = new EmployeeDAO().findById(new Long(id));

    HttpServletResponse response =
                                            (HttpServletResponse)external.getResponse();

          response.addHeader("response", employee.toJSON());

          ctx.responseComplete();

      }

  }

  /* sans other methods */
}
```

The response is sent with a status code of 200, the status code designated by the HTTP specification for success. The response data is transferred via an HTTP response header, leaving the body empty. There is nothing wrong with bodyless HTTP responses per se, but such responses should be sent with a status code of 204.

The `viewDetailsCallback` function reads and evaluates JSON from the response header. If the response is successful, the event handler displays the details in a pop-up box:

```
/* client side response handler */

function viewDetailsCallback(type, data, xhr){

            var response = xhr.getResponseHeader('response');

            var employee = eval('(' + response + ')');

            renderEmployeePopup(employee);

}
```

This implementation is less than perfect. Using response headers as a poor man's map is a convenient way to do AJAX for many developers. However, the HTTP specification is silent on response header size; the limit is up to the servlet container implementation.

Large response header values are likely to be silently truncated. You can avoid this problem by moving the data to the body of the response:

```
public class EmployeeDetailsPhaseListenerRefactored implements
   PhaseListener {

    public void beforePhase(PhaseEvent event) {

      FacesContext ctx = event.getFacesContext();

      final ExternalContext external = ctx.getExternalContext();

      Map parameters = external.getRequestParameterMap();

      String id = (String) parameters.get("listEmployeeId");

      if (id != null) {

          Employee employee = new EmployeeDAO().findById(new Long(id));

          HttpServletResponse response = (HttpServletResponse)
                                         external.getResponse();

          try {

              response.getWriter().print(employee.toJSON());

          } catch (IOException e) {

              handleError();

          }

          ctx.responseComplete();

      }

  }

  /* sans other methods */

}
```

```
        /* client side response handler */

        function viewDetailsCallbackRefactored(type, data, xhr){

                var employee = eval('(' + data + ')');

                renderEmployeePopup(employee);

}
```

The viewDetails function also uses a GET request to retrieve the employee details. The HTTP specification allows GET responses to be cached by browsers and intermediary HTTP proxies. If the employee details change in the database, the browser can miss this on subsequent page visits, because it simply won't bother requesting a cached resource. There are many valid ways to prevent this caching. One way is to intercept requests like this with a filter that programmatically forces each response to be noncacheable:

```
public class ExpirationFilter implements Filter {

   public void doFilter(ServletRequest request,
ServletResponse response, FilterChain chain)
throws IOException, ServletException {

      HttpServletResponse res = (HttpServletResponse) response;

      res.setHeader("Expires", "Sat, 6 May 1978 12:00:00 GMT"); // past
      res.setHeader("Pragma", "no-cache");
      res.setHeader("Cache-Control", "no-store, no-cache, must-revalidate");

      // for MS IE
      res.addHeader("Cache-Control", "post-check=0, pre-check=0");
      chain.doFilter(request, response);

   }

   public void destroy() { }

   public void init(FilterConfig config) throws ServletException { }

}
```

Another approach is to use dynamic URLs for all dynamic resources—append a timestamp. As far as the browser is concerned, the employee details resource is different each time (pun intended):

```
/* client side event handler */

            function viewDetailsRefactored(id) {

                        var url = "employees.jsf?listEmployeeId=" + id;
                        url += "&nocache=" + new Date().getTime();

                        var bindArgs = {
                            url: url,
                            load: viewDetailsCallbackRefactored,
                            method: "GET"
                  };

               dojo.io.bind(bindArgs); // sans error handling
            }
```

Now, let's take it to a higher level of abstraction: partial page rendering. Using just a few components from the Trinidad library (see Chapter 4), we can implement the same solution without any JavaScript and with less Java code. First, comment out the "view details" anchor tag of the second column and replace it with a Trinidad `commandLink`. Next, comment out the `employeeDetails` `div` tag and replace it with a Trinidad `panelGroupLayout` tag:

```
<h:dataTable value="#{employeeBean.employees}" var="employee">
            <h:column>
<a onclick="deleteEmployee(#{employee.id}); return false;"
                  href="." >delete</a>
            </h:column>
            <h:column>
                        <!--
                          <a onclick="viewDetails(#{employee.id}); return false;"
                                    href="." >view details</a>
                        -->
                        <tr:commandLink partialSubmit="true"

actionListener="#{employeeBean.viewDetailsClicked}">
                                          view details
<tr:setActionListener to="#{employeeBean.selected}"
            from="#{employee}"/>
                            </tr:commandLink>
            </h:column>
            <h:column>
                        <f:facet name="header">First Name</f:facet>
                        #{employee.firstName}
            </h:column>
            <h:column>
                        <f:facet name="header">Last Name</f:facet>
                        #{employee.lastName}
            </h:column>
</h:dataTable>
```

```
<!-- <div id="employeeDetails" /> -->
<tr:panelGroupLayout id="employeeDetails"
             binding="#{employeeBean.panelGroupLayout}" partialTriggers="">

          <h:panelGroup rendered="#{employeeBean.selected != null}">
                      <span class="header">Employee Details</span><br/>
                      First Name : #{employeeBean.selected.firstName}<br/>
                      Middle Name : #{employeeBean.selected.middleName}<br/>
                      Last Name : #{employeeBean.selected.lastName}<br/>
                      Salary : #{employeeBean.selected.salary}<br/>
                      Department : #{employeeBean.selected.department}<br/>
                      Supervisor : #{employeeBean.selected.supervisor}<br/>
                      Hire Date : #{employeeBean.selected.hireDate}<br/>
                      Birth Date : #{employeeBean.selected.birthDate}<br/>
                      Office : #{employeeBean.selected.office}<br/>
          </h:panelGroup>

</tr:panelGroupLayout>
```

Let's take a closer look at the template changes, as well as the `EmployeeBean` managed bean class. The new `commandLink` tag has a `setActionListener` child. The `to` and `from` attributes behave just as you would expect: the selected property of the `EmployeeBean` managed bean is set to the selected `Employee` instance.

Pay close attention to each attribute of the new `commandLink`. The `partialSubmit` attribute indicates that the postback for this `commandLink` is an AJAX request; the DOM stays intact. It also tells the web application to render part of the page. Which part? This question is answered by the `actionListener` attribute and the managed bean method it evaluates to.

The `viewDetails` action listener method grabs a reference to `RequestContext`, a special class found in the Trinidad library. The `CorePanelGroupLayout` instance is then passed to the `addPartialTarget` method of `RequestContext`, telling MyFaces Trinidad to render the `CorePanelGroupLayout`. The rendered output of the `CorePanelGroupLayout` fills the response, and the employee details are dynamically updated in the browser. The rest of the page remains the same.

```
public class EmployeeBean {

     private List<Employee> employees = new LinkedList<Employee>();

     private Employee selected;

     private CorePanelGroupLayout panelGroupLayout;

     /**
      * @see the 'actionListener' attribute of tr:commandLink
      */

     public void viewDetailsClicked(ActionEvent event) {
```

```
            RequestContext ctx = RequestContext.getCurrentInstance();

            ctx.addPartialTarget(panelGroupLayout);

        }

        /**
         * @see the 'to' attribute of tr:setActionListener
         */

        public void setSelected(Employee selectedEmployee) {
                        this.selectedEmployee = selectedEmployee;
        }

        /**
              * @see the 'binding' attribute of tr:panelGroupLayout
              */

        public CorePanelGroupLayout getPanelGroupLayout() {
    return panelGroupLayout;
        }

        // sans other getters and setters
    }
```

We recommend MyFaces Trinidad for your knowledge portfolio. There is a lot of grunt work associated with raw AJAX, because so much code must be written to deal with the underlying protocol, HTTP. Trinidad does the heavy lifting for JSF AJAX development and allows web application developers to use Java instead of JavaScript. The end result is a cleaner solution that is easier to test with fewer lines of code.

Code to Interface

JSF was designed to encourage an "embrace and extend" mindset. The JSF component model is consequently driven largely by interfaces. `ImplementationDependentManagedBean` is an example of what happens when these interfaces are not observed:

```
import org.apache.myfaces.component.html.ext.HtmlInputHidden;
import org.apache.myfaces.component.html.ext.HtmlInputText;
import org.apache.myfaces.component.html.ext.HtmlOutputText;

public class ImplementationDependentManagedBean {

            private HtmlInputText input ;
            private HtmlInputHidden hidden ;
            private HtmlOutputText output ;
```

```
        /* getters & setters ommitted */

        public boolean recordTotal(ActionEvent event) {

                long total = ((Long)input.getValue()).longValue();
                total += ((Long)hidden.getValue()).longValue();
                total += ((Long)output.getValue()).longValue();

                return new JmsUtil().broadcastTotal(total);
        }

}
```

This managed bean has three component binding properties. Business logic is applied to each component in an action listener. Three classes from a MyFaces Tomahawk package have been imported. Notice that the business logic only invokes the getValue method of each component. The getValue method is inherited from a superclass found in the core JSF API. By replacing these imports, the class becomes interoperable:

```
import javax.faces.component.ValueHolder;

public class RefactoredManagedBean {

   private ValueHolder input ;
   private ValueHolder hidden ;
   private ValueHolder output ;

   /* getters & setters ommitted */

   public boolean recordTotal(ActionEvent event) {

    long total = 0;

    for(ValueHolder valued : new ValueHolder[] {input, hidden, output})
         total += ((Long)valued.getValue()).longValue();

    return new JmsUtil().broadcastTotal(total);

   }
}
```

ValueHolder is an interface implemented by a superclass of HtmlInputText, HtmlInputHidden, and HtmlOutputText. By refactoring the class to use the ValueHolder interface, the managed bean can be used with different JSF implementations as well as different ValueHolder component bindings (e.g., HtmlOutputText, HtmlInputText, and HtmlInputHidden). Polymorphism is used to clean up the business logic.

Remember, one of the beautiful things JSF provides above and beyond other MVC frameworks is the freedom to express logic in POJOs (plain old Java objects). Application developers don't have to implement an interface or extend a class provided by the container. This doesn't mean it is all right to drop the principles of object-oriented programming. When we see an opportunity to program to a standardized interface, we do it.

Did you notice anything peculiar about the `recordTotal` action listener method? The JSF specification defines the return type of action listener methods to be `void`, but the action listener has a return type of `boolean`. MyFaces allows this code, because it ignores the method return type. Try to avoid this style of coding—it is acceptable for other JSF implementations to throw an exception.

View State Encryption

A common misconception is that SSL does not need the view state encryption. Likewise, many developers assume using view state encryption means they have no need of SSL. We want to be very clear: SSL and view state encryption have no common ground. They solve completely separate problems at different layers of the network protocol stack.

Consider the classic man in the middle attack. Manfred works at a bank; Sean is an online customer, and Mike is an intermediary (see Figure 7-2). If Manfred and Sean are using plain HTTP, Mike can intercept the request from Sean, record Sean's password, and forward the request on to Manfred, unbeknownst to the party at each end.

Figure 7-2. *The classic man in the middle attack*

By working at the transport layer of the network protocol stack, Manfred and Sean can use SSL to prevent Mike from using the intercepted information.

SSL provides point-to-point security, keeping Sean and Manfred safe from Mike; it does not keep Manfred safe from Sean if the application saves the state on the client side. In the client-side state saving, MyFaces builds a data structure to represent the component tree during the response rendering phase. This data structure is called the view state. When state is saved on the client side, the view state is serialized, possibly compressed, encoded, and slipped into the response via a hidden HTML field in the form.

When the HTML form is submitted, it carries the view state value back to the server in the form of an HTTP parameter. MyFaces uses the value of this parameter to reconstruct the view during the view restoration phase. The view is restored by reversing the process used to obtain the view state: it is decoded, possibly decompressed, and deserialized. This poses a major security challenge to any JSF implementation, because Sean has the freedom to change the view state. He can toggle the `rendered` attribute of UI controls that are not supposed to be available to him. He can point a `commandButton` to a method on any managed bean in the application. He can circumvent an action listener.

We strongly recommend view-state encryption for public-facing JSF applications saving state on the client side in production. We recommend disabling encryption for development and functional testing.

```
<context-param>
    <param-name>org.apache.myfaces.USE_ENCRYPTION</param-name>
    <param-value>false</param-value>
</context-param>
```

See Appendix B to learn more about the details of view state encryption.

Regardless of state-saving method or SSL, the main threats to your application are in the daily ins and outs of software development. Let's look at the following view template. The entity identifier is used to keep track of which database record to update and is maintained with an `inputHidden` field. This leaves the application vulnerable.

```
<h:form id="form">

        <h:inputHidden id="danger" value="#{userBean.id}" />

        <h:panelGrid columns="2">
                <span>First Name</span>
                <h:inputText value="#{userBean.firstName}"/>
                <span>Last Name</span>
                <h:inputText value="#{userBean.lastName}"/>
                <span>Admin Privileges</span>
                <h:selectBooleanCheckbox value="#{userBean.admin}"/>
        </h:panelGrid>

        <h:commandButton value="Update" action="#{userBean.update}"/>

</h:form>
```

Nothing stops the end user from changing the value of the `id` parameter on the client side, which can be done using a program such as Firefox. Locate the DOM Inspector under the Tools menu. If this menu item is missing, the DOM Inspector plug-in needs to be installed (see Figure 7-3).

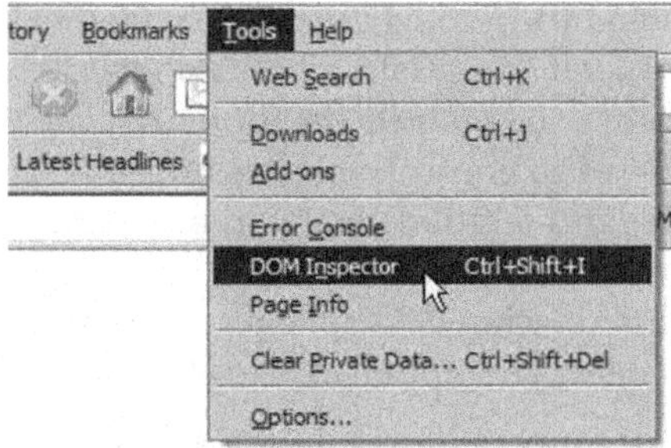

Figure 7-3. *Launching the Firefox DOM Inspector*

Locate the hidden input control after you launch the DOM Inspector. Right-click the control, and choose the Edit option (see Figure 7-4).

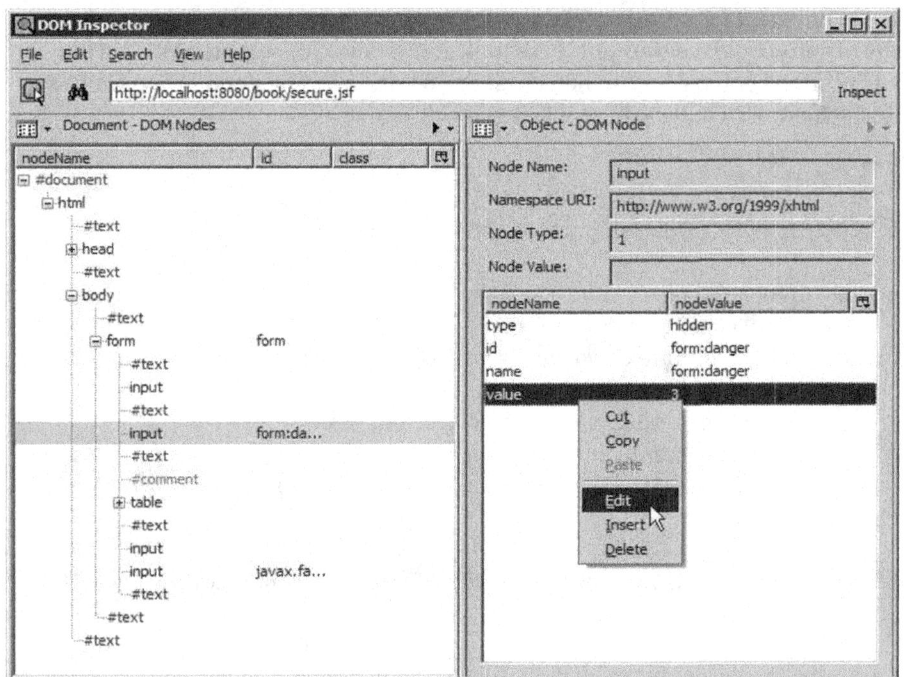

Figure 7-4. *Choosing the Edit option*

Specify any value via the Edit Attribute pop-up window (see Figure 7-5) and submit the form.

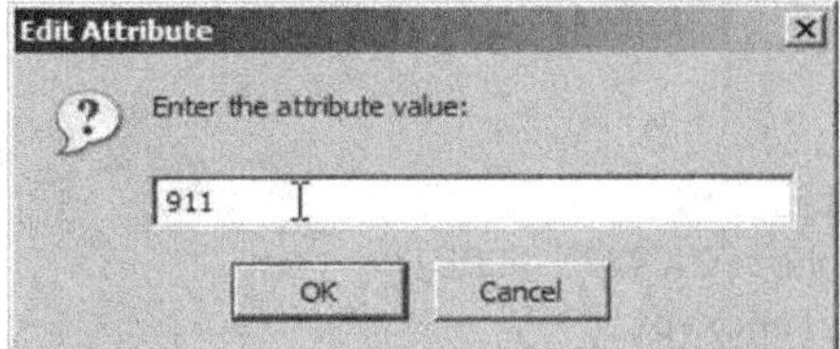

Figure 7-5. *Updating the attribute value*

When the form is submitted, the 911 row will be updated. The value comes in through the request, and it is passed to the managed bean. When the update action method is invoked, the database row is updated.

There are two ways to eliminate this threat. The `saveState` tag in MyFaces Tomahawk can be used to replace the `inputHidden` tag. The `saveState` tag will keep the identifier in conversation scope. View state encryption is used to keep the conversation between the browser and server confidential.

```
<!-- <h:inputHidden id="danger" value="#{userBean.id}" /> -->
<t:saveState value="#{userBean.id}" />
```

A second approach is to use a custom converter. For example, `SecureLongConverter` encrypts the `id` value each time the response is rendered and decrypts it each time the value is submitted:

```
<h:inputHidden id="safe" value="#{userBean.id}"
                       converter="#{userBean.converter}"/>

public class SecureLongConverter implements Converter {

    public Object getAsObject(FacesContext ctx,
        UIComponent component, String string) {

        Long object = null;

        if (string != null) {
           byte[] decoded = new Base64().decode(string.getBytes());
           byte[] decrypted = symmetric(decoded, Cipher.DECRYPT_MODE);
           object = Long.parseLong(new String(decrypted));
       }

       return object;
    }

    public String getAsString(FacesContext ctx,
            UIComponent component, Object object) {
```

```
        String string = null;

        if (object != null) {
            byte[] bytes = object.toString().getBytes();
            byte[] encrypted = symmetric(bytes, Cipher.ENCRYPT_MODE);
            string = new String(new Base64().encode(encrypted));
        }

        return string;
    }

    private byte[] symmetric(byte[] data, int mode) {

        // in production this would be hidden
        byte[] password = new byte[]{ 0, 1, 2, 3, 4, 5, 6, 7};
        // in production this would be cached
        SecretKey secretKey = new SecretKeySpec(password, "DES");

        try {
            Cipher cipher = Cipher.getInstance("DES/ECB/PKCS5Padding");
            cipher.init(mode, secretKey);
            return cipher.doFinal(data);

        } catch (Exception e) {
            throw new FacesException(e);
        }
    }
}
```

Portlet Issues

Some parts of the JSF API behave differently when inside a portlet application. If your code is to run within a portlet application and a regular servlet container, a few assumptions need to be avoided. Some of these assumptions are made in the examples of this chapter.

For example, the following code assumes it will always run in a servlet container.

```
FacesContext ctx = FacesContext.getCurrentInstance();
ExternalContext externalContext = ctx.getExternalContext();
ServletRequest request = (ServletRequest) externalContext.getRequest();
String id = request.getParameter("id");
```

If your code will run in a portlet application, you must not make explicit casts to `javax.servlet.ServletRequest` or `javax.servlet.ServletResponse`. If this code were used in a portlet application, `ExternalContext.getRequest` would return a `javax.portlet.PortletRequest`, causing a `ClassCastException`. An interoperable way to obtain a value of a request attribute is to do the following:

```
FacesContext ctx = FacesContext.getCurrentInstance();
ExternalContext externalContext = ctx.getExternalContext();
externalContext.getRequestParameterMap().get("id");
```

In some cases, you cannot avoid invoking methods that are servlet- or portlet-specific. If you must do so, the MyFaces utility class called `PortletUtil` will help you in these situations:

```
FacesContext ctx = FacesContext.getCurrentInstance();
ExternalContext external = ctx.getExternalContext();

if(PortletUtil.isPortletRequest(ctx)) {

    PortletRequest request = (PortletRequest) external.getRequest();
    PortletResponse response = (PortletResponse)external.getResponse();

    // do something with request and response

} else {

    ServletRequest request = (ServletRequest) external.getRequest();
    ServletResponse resopnse = (ServletResponse)external.getResponse();

    // do something with request and response
}
```

The Validating Setter

Constructors are generally a good place to perform validation logic for a domain model. In a perfect world, every XML marshalling framework, every ORM framework, and every dependency injection framework would support constructor injection—our domain models would not need setters for each field. As it turns out, we do not live in a perfect world.

The JSF specification defines a dependency injection mechanism for managed bean construction: constructor injection is not part of the specification, only setter injection. This is understandable, considering that JSF is a standard for Java MVC web development, not dependency injection. Unfortunately, this limitation gave rise to a whole slew of workarounds for application developers who want to perform domain validation and bean initialization logic, something that you would normally put in a constructor.

The Validating Setter antipattern involves taking code that would normally be in the constructor of a managed bean and moving it to the setter that would be invoked last by JSF dependency injection. How does one know which setter will be called last? The specification states that a JSF implementation must inject the dependencies of a managed bean in the order in which they are configured:

```
<managed-bean>
    <managed-bean-name>iteration</managed-bean-name>
    <managed-bean-class>
            org.apache.myfaces.book.agile.Iteration
    </managed-bean-class>
    <managed-bean-scope>request</managed-bean-scope>
    <managed-property> <!-- setStart called first -->
          <property-name>start</property-name>
                <value>#{projectBean.currentStart}</value>
    </managed-property>
    <managed-property>
          <property-name>end</property-name>
                <value>#{projectBean.currentEnd}</value>
    </managed-property>
    <managed-property>
          <property-name>stories</property-name>
                <value>#{projectBean.currentStories}</value>
    </managed-property>
    <managed-property><!-- setLast called last -->
          <property-name>last</property-name>
                <value>hack</value>
    </managed-property>
</managed-bean>
```

The Iteration class follows, and it states that the start, end, and stories fields should be mandatory: an Iteration without these values is invalid. Furthermore, start should never precede end.

```
public class Iteration {

  private Calendar start;              // injected
  private Calendar end;                        // injected
  private Story[] stories;             // injected

  // sans setters and getters for start, end & stories

  public void setLast(String last) {

    if(start == null)
            throw new NullPointerException("start");

    if(end == null)
            throw new NullPointerException("end");

    if(start.after(end))
            throw new IllegalStateException("start cannot be after end");
```

```
    if(stories == null || stories.length == 0)
            throw new IllegalStateException(
                        "An " + Iteration.class.getName() + " must have stories");
  }

}
```

Let's look at solutions. Applications that are using JSF 1.2 can take advantage of the PostConstruct annotation. In the following code, the PostConstruct annotation instructs MyFaces to invoke the initialize method after the managed bean has been created:

```
import javax.annotation.PostConstruct;

public class Iteration {

    private Calendar start;              // injected
    private Calendar end;            // injected
    private Story[] stories;            // injected

    public Iteration() { initialize(); }

    @PostConstruct
    public void initialize() {
            // sans domain validation logic here ...
    }
}
```

The PostConstruct approach is in vogue now, when much of the Java community is revolting against XML in favor of annotations. But it doesn't quite solve the problem; the Iteration author wants every Iteration to have a start, end, and at least one Story. The PostConstruct annotation insures that MyFaces will not hand you an invalid Iteration, but there is no way to make sure MyFaces has exclusive access to the no-arguments constructor (and the setters).

You could give MyFaces exclusive access to the no-arguments constructor of the Iteration class by scoping the constructor to package visibility and moving the class to the org.apache.myfaces.config package.

The PostConstruct approach is not bad, but a better approach would be to ditch the dependency injection capabilities that come with any JSF implementation and to use a full-blown dependency injection framework.

Summary

Sometimes, a single architectural mistake can cost us more than all that we gain from a handful of well-placed design patterns. This chapter has presented you with more than a dozen mistakes that can easily fall under this description. Perhaps the most important idea to take away from this chapter is that JSF encourages good design but cannot create it from nothing—good design is still the responsibility of the developer.

APPENDIX A

Facelets Tag Reference

This appendix describes all of the tags available in the Facelets library and explains each one's attributes.

<ui:component/>

The `ui:component` tag inserts a new `UIComponent` instance into the JavaServer Faces tree as the root of all the components or content fragments it contains. Table A-1 shows its attributes.

Table A-1. *UI Component Attributes*

Attribute Name	Required	Description
`id`	No	As with any component, an `id` can be provided. If none is present, Facelets will create an `id` following the JavaServer Specification rules.
`binding`	No	Following the JavaServer Faces Specification, this attribute can be used to reference a `UIComponent` instance by pointing to a property of managed bean. The instance will be lazily created if the property did not have an instance assigned already.

Everything outside of this component's tags will be ignored by the compiler and won't appear on the rendered view:

```
This and everything before this will be ignored.
<ui:component binding="#{backingBean.myComponent}">
  <div>The directory contains #{totalBirds} birds!</div>
</ui:component>
This and everything after this will be ignored.
```

The preceding code will produce this HTML output:

```
<div>The directory contains 214 birds!</div>
```

<ui:composition/>

The `ui:composition` tag is a templating tag used to encapsulate content that can be included in other Facelets pages. Table A-2 shows its attribute.

Table A-2. *UI Composition Attribute*

Attribute Name	Required	Description
`template`	No	The path to the template that will be populated by the content between the starting and ending composition tag.

This tag is a fundamental piece in Facelets and is based in the idea of compositions. The `UIComponent` tree may be formed by compositions described in different pages across the application. Like the `ui:component` tag, everything before and after the composition tag will be removed; the difference between these two tags is that `ui:composition` does not create a component in the tree. The `ui:composition` content can be included in your view or other compositions, and when this happens, all the components contained by the composition will be added directly to the component tree.

```
This and everything before this will be ignored.
<ui:composition>
  <h:outputText value="#{bird.lifeExpectancy}" />
</ui:composition>

This and everything after this will be ignored.
```

We can use the composition tag to populate a template, as shown in the example from the "Creating JSF Views" section in Chapter 3. We could use something like this:

```
<ui:composition template="bird-template.xhtml">
     <ui:define name="summary">
         <h:panelGrid columns="2">
             <h:outputText value="Bird Name"/>
             <h:outputText value="#{bird.name}"/>
             <h:outputText value="Life expectancy"/>
        <h:outputText
           value="#{bird.lifeExpectancy}"/>
         </h:panelGrid>
     </ui:define>
 </ui:composition>
```

The content within the `composition` tag would be used to populate the `ui:insert` tag with name `"summary"` from the `bird-template.xhtml` template.

The key components where creating composite views with Facelets are the `ui:composition`, `ui:define`, and `ui:insert` tags. The latter two are explained later in this appendix.

<ui:debug/>

The debug tag is a very useful tool when developing an application. It can be launched using the combination Ctrl + Shift + <hotkey> (D, by default) while browsing your Facelets application. It will display a pop-up window that shows the component tree and the scoped variables. Table A-3 shows its attributes.

Table A-3. *UI Debug Attributes*

Attribute Name	Required	Description
hotkey	No	Pressing Ctrl + Shift + <hotkey> will display the Facelets debug window. This attribute cannot be an EL expression. The default value is d.
rendered	No	Following the JavaServer Faces Specification, this attribute must evaluate to a Boolean value. If it is false, the script needed to launch the debug window won't be present in the page.

Conventionally, the debug tag can be found at the end of the pages, but it can be used anywhere. We can use the debug tag as follows:

```
<ui:debug hotkey="g"
    rendered="#{initParam['apress.DEBUG_MODE']}"/>
```

In this case, the debug window will be launched when pressing Ctrl + Shift + G and would be rendered if our init parameter with name apress.DEBUG_MODE is set to true. Usually, we don't want the debug script rendered when in production, so it is convenient to have a single point of configuration (like in the previous example), so we can enable or disable all debug tags.

<ui:decorate/>

The ui:decorate tag is similar to the ui:composition tag, the only difference being that the decorate tag does not remove everything outside of it. As its name implies, you can use this tag to add some content around the decorated section by using a template. Table A-4 shows its attribute.

Table A-4. *UI Decorate Attribute*

Attribute Name	Required	Description
template	Yes	The path to the template that will be populated by the content between the start and end of the decorate tag

For instance, we would have a template that wraps the content of the decorate tag in a box creating using div elements, like the one in Listing A-1.

Listing A-1. *box-template.xhtml*

```
<!DOCTYPE html PUBLIC "-//W3C//DTD ➥
XHTML 1.0 Transitional//EN"
        "http://www.w3.org/TR/xhtml1/DTD/ ➥
xhtml1-transitional.dtd">
<html xmlns="http://www.w3.org/1999/xhtml"
      xmlns:ui="http://java.sun.com/jsf/facelets">
<body>

<ui:composition>
    <div style="border: 1px solid black; display:block">
       <ui:insert name="header"/>
    </div>
    <div style="border: 1px solid black; display:block">
       <ui:insert name="content"/>
    </div>
</ui:composition>
</body>
</html>
```

Once we have the template, we could use the decorate tag as shown in Listing A-2.

Listing A-2. *decorate-example.xhtml*

```
<!DOCTYPE html
     PUBLIC "-//W3C//DTD XHTML 1.0 Transitional//EN"
     "http://www.w3.org/TR/xhtml1/DTD/ ➥
xhtml1-transitional.dtd">
<html xmlns="http://www.w3.org/1999/xhtml"
        xmlns:ui="http://java.sun.com/jsf/facelets"
        xmlns:h="http://java.sun.com/jsf/html">
  <head>
        <title>Decorate example</title>
  </head>
  <body>

  <p>These are the birds in today's menu:</p>

  <ui:decorate template="box-template.xhtml">
      <ui:define name="header">
          Happy Parrot
      </ui:define>
      <ui:define name="content">
          How many parrots do you want?
          <h:inputText value="3"/>
      </ui:define>
  </ui:decorate>
  <br/>
```

```
  <ui:decorate template="box-template.xhtml">
      <ui:define name="header">
          Mighty Eagle
      </ui:define>
      <ui:define name="content">
          Eagles are not available now.
      </ui:define>
  </ui:decorate>
  </body>
</html>
```

In the preceding listing, we would create a page and include two boxes with bird information. Everything outside the page will be rendered in the final page, and we would end up with HTML output like the following:

```
<html xmlns="http://www.w3.org/1999/xhtml">
  <head>
        <title>Decorate example</title>
  </head>
  <body>

  <p>These are the birds in today's menu:</p>
    <div style="border: 1px solid black; display:block">

          Happy Parrot
    </div>
    <div style="border: 1px solid black; display:block">
          How many parrots do you want?
      <input id="_id6" name="_id6"
          type="text" value="3" />
    </div>

  <br/>
    <div style="border: 1px solid black; display:block">
          Mighty Eagle
    </div>

    <div style="border: 1px solid black; display:block">
          Eagles are not available now.
    </div>
```

As you can see in the rendered page, the `div` elements that create the boxes frame the content defined in the `decorate` tag.

Note too that the template uses `ui:composition` tags to trim everything outside them. Otherwise, when we used this template with a `decorate` tag, the HTML and body tags would be repeated in the final output.

<ui:define/>

The ui:define templating tag can be used to insert named content into a template. It can be used within tags that allow templating, such as the ui:composition and ui:decorate tags. The names used in the define tag must match the names used in the ui:insert tags in the target template. Table A-5 shows its attribute.

Table A-5. *UI Define Attribute*

Attribute Name	Required	Description
name	Yes	This mandatory attribute specifies the literal name of the definition. It must match with the name of a ui:insert tag in the target template.

Let's take a look at the following snippet:

```
<ui:decorate template="box-template.xhtml">
      <ui:define name="header">
          Happy Parrot
      </ui:define>

     this will be removed

      <ui:define name="content">
          How many parrots do you want?
      </ui:define>
  </ui:decorate>
```

The template used by this snippet contains insert tags, named "header" and "content". The code within the define tags will be inserted in those areas, matching by name.

The content outside the define tags will be ignored by the Facelets compiler.

Listing A-3 illustrates the define tag in action.

Listing A-3. *define-template.xhtml*

```
<h:outputText value="Which bird sings like this? "/>
<ui:insert name="song"/>
define-example.xhtml
This will be ignored
<ui:composition template="define-template.xhtml">
       <ui:define name="song">
<h:outputText value="cock-a-doodle-doo"/>
       </ui:define>
</ui:composition>
```

This example will render:

```
Which bird sings like this? cock-a-doodle-doo
```

<ui:fragment/>

The `ui:fragment` tag is similar to the `ui:component` tag, but the `fragment` tag does not trim the content outside itself. Table A-6 shows its attributes.

Table A-6. *UI Fragment Attributes*

Attribute Name	Required	Description
`id`	No	As with any component, an `id` can be provided. If none is present, Facelets will create an `id` following the JavaServer Faces Specification rules.
`binding`	No	Following the JavaServer Specification, this attribute can be used to reference a `UIComponent` instance by pointing to a property of managed bean. The instance will be lazily created if the property did not have an instance assigned already.

The `fragment` tag inserts a new `UIComponent` instance into the component tree, and any other components or content fragments outside the tag will still be included at compile time. All elements with the `fragment` tag will be added as children of the component instance.

```
This will be ignored
<ui:fragment>
    <div>
         <h:outputText
             value="I want #{eagle.total} eagles."/>
    </div>
</ui:fragment>
This will be ignored
```

This will create the following output:

```
This will be ignored
    <div>I want 3 eagles.</div>
This will be ignored
```

<ui:include/>

The `ui:include` tag can be used to include another Facelets file into your document. It simply includes whatever source file you specify. You can include any Facelets file that has `ui:component` or `ui:composition` tags (which trim the content outside themselves) or a fragment of XHTML or XML. Table A-7 shows its attribute.

Table A-7. *UI Include Attribute*

Attribute Name	Required	Description
`src`	Yes	This attribute can be a literal value or an EL expression that declares the target Facelets to be included in the document.

The path in the src attribute can be absolute or relative. If it is relative, it will be resolved against the original Facelets instance that was requested.

```
<div>
  <ui:include src="#{backingBean.currentMenu}"/>
</div>
```

In this example, the expression #{backingBean.currentMenu} will be resolved to a file path. This can be used to include content dynamically depending on the context.

<ui:insert/>

The ui:insert tag is used to specify in a template those areas that can be replaced by ui:define tags declared in the client template. Table A-8 shows its attribute.

Table A-8. *UI Insert Attribute*

Attribute Name	Required	Description
name	No	This name will be use to match the insert tag with the same name in the client for the template. If no name is specified, the whole client template will be inserted.

The insert tag can contain nested content. If it does, and no define tag is specified in the client that matches the name of the insert tag, the nested content will be inserted. It can be used to insert default content when the define tag is not specified.

Let's take a look at the example in Listing A-4.

Listing A-4. *insert-template.xhtml*

```
<!DOCTYPE html PUBLIC "-//W3C//DTD XHTML 1.0 Transitional//EN"
        "http://www.w3.org/TR/xhtml1/DTD/ ➥
xhtml1-transitional.dtd">
<html xmlns="http://www.w3.org/1999/xhtml"
      xmlns:ui="http://java.sun.com/jsf/facelets">
<body>
    <h1>
        <ui:insert name="title">
            No title
        </ui:insert>
    </h1>

    <div>
        <ui:insert name="content">
            No content is defined
        </ui:insert>
    </div>
</body>
</html>
```

We'll need a client for this template; see Listing A-5.

Listing A-5. *insert-client.xhtml*

```
<ui:composition template="insert-template.xhtml">
        <ui:define name="title">
            The Parrot Quest
        </ui:define>
    </ui:composition>
```

In this client Facelets application, we have only defined the "title", so the "content" will be the default value. Given that, we expect the following output:

```
<h1>
       The Parrot Quest
 </h1>
<div>
        No content is defined
</div>
```

The name attribute of the insert tag is optional. When it is not present, the whole client template will be inserted, so it is not necessary to use define tags in the client. Let's see this with the new example in Listings A-6 and A-7.

Listing A-6 contains the code for a template that contains a ui:insert tag without attributes or children.

Listing A-6. *insert-template2.xhtml*

```
<!DOCTYPE html PUBLIC "-//W3C//DTD ➥
HTML 1.0 Transitional//EN"
        "http://www.w3.org/TR/xhtml1/DTD/ ➥
xhtml1-transitional.dtd">
<html xmlns="http://www.w3.org/1999/xhtml"
      xmlns:ui="http://java.sun.com/jsf/facelets">
<body>
    <div>
        <h1>One story of Birds</h1>
        <ui:insert/>
    </div>
</body>
</html>
```

In Listing A-7, we show how to use the previous template to include some content.

Listing A-7. *insert-client2.xhtml*

```
<ui:composition template="insert-template2.xhtml">
        One day I decided to start counting
        the number of parrots in the world,
        just to find that...
        <br/>
        <h:inputTextarea value="#{backingBean.story}"/>
 </ui:composition>
```

In this case, the whole content of the composition in `insert-client2.xhtml` will be inserted where the `insert` tag has been placed in the template. The output will be as follows:

```
<div>
        <h1>One story of Birds</h1>
        One day I decided to start counting
        the number of parrots in the world,
        just to find that...
        <br />
       <textarea name="_id3"></textarea>
</div>
```

<ui:param/>

Until now, we have been looking at how Facelets can pass fragments of code between documents. But we can also pass objects using the `ui:param` tag. This tag is used to pass objects as named variables between Facelets. Table A-9 shows its attributes.

Table A-9. *UI Param Attributes*

Attribute Name	Required	Description
`name`	Yes	The name of the variable to pass to the included Facelets instance
`value`	Yes	The literal or EL expression value to assign to the named variable

The `name` attribute of the `ui:param` tag must match the name of a `ui:define` tag contained in the template defined in the `ui:composition` or `ui:decorate` tag. Listing A-8 shows an example.

Listing A-8. *param-details.xhtml*

```
<!DOCTYPE html PUBLIC "-//W3C//DTD XHTML 1.0 Transitional//EN"
        "http://www.w3.org/TR/xhtml1/DTD/xhtml1-transitional.dtd">
<html xmlns="http://www.w3.org/1999/xhtml"
      xmlns:ui="http://java.sun.com/jsf/facelets">
```

```
<body>
    <ui:composition>
        <div>
            <h3>#{birdName}</h3>
            Order: #{birdOrder}
            <br/>
            Family: #{birdFamily}
        </div>
    </ui:composition>
</body>
</html>
```

We use the previous Facelets file in the application in Listing A-9.

Listing A-9. *param-example.xhtml*

```
<!DOCTYPE html PUBLIC "-//W3C//DTD ➥
XHTML 1.0 Transitional//EN"
        "http://www.w3.org/TR/xhtml1/DTD/ ➥
xhtml1-transitional.dtd">
<html xmlns="http://www.w3.org/1999/xhtml"
      xmlns:ui="http://java.sun.com/jsf/facelets">
<body>
    <ui:include src="param-details.xhtml">
        <ui:param name="birdName" value="Parrot"/>
        <ui:param name="birdOrder"
                  value="Psittaciformes"/>
        <ui:param name="birdFamily"
                  value="Psittacidae"/>
    </ui:include>

    <ui:decorate template="param-details.xhtml">
        <ui:param name="birdName" value="Eagle"/>
        <ui:param name="birdOrder"
                  value="Falconiformes"/>
        <ui:param name="birdFamily"
                  value="Accipitridae"/>
    </ui:decorate>
</body>
</html>
```

In this example, we are using `ui:param` to pass several literals (we could have referred to other objects using EL expressions) to the included document or to a template (in our example, both point to the same Facelets file: `param.details.xhtml`). The relevant portion of the resulting output follows:

```
<div>
            <h3>Parrot</h3>
            Order: Psittaciformes
            <br />
            Family: Psittacidae
</div>
 <div>
            <h3>Eagle</h3>
            Order: Falconiformes
            <br />
            Family: Accipitridae
</div>
```

<ui:remove/>

The `ui:remove` tag is used to remove blocks of code at compilation time. It has no attributes, though you can use this tag in conjunction with the `jsfc` attribute.

This tag provides a way to remove parts of the document used during development or testing when the application goes into production, allowing to retain the bits of code for use later if further development or bug fixes are needed.

```
<ui:remove>
       This will be removed.
</ui:remove>
This will survive
<div jsfc="ui:remove">
This will be removed too
<h:outputText value="#{backingBean.andThisToo}"/>
</div>
And this will survive too!
```

Most of the content of the previous snippet won't appear in the final output:

```
This will survive
This will survive too!
```

You may wonder why we are not using normal HTML comments (starting the commented section with the characters `<!--` and ending it with `-->`) to remove the content from the final page, as what we put between the comment characters won't be visible to the user. Facelets will interpret the EL expressions within the comments unless the context parameter `facelets.SKIP_COMMENTS` is set to `true` in the `web.xml` file. In that case, the behavior would be similar.

<ui:repeat/>

The ui:repeat tag is used to iterate over a list of objects, and we always recommend its use instead of c:forEach from the JSTL Code tag library. Table A-10 shows its attributes.

Table A-10. *UI Repeat Attributes*

Attribute Name	Required	Description
value	Yes	EL expression that resolves to the list of objects to be iterated over
var	Yes	The literal name of the variable used to iterate over the collection

As an example, take a look at Listing A-10, where we use the repeat tag to iterate over a list of birds provided by a backing bean.

Listing A-10. *repeat-example.xhtml*

```
...
    <ul>
        <ui:repeat var="bird"
                   value="#{birdDirectory.birds}">
            <li>#{bird.name}</li>
        </ui:repeat>
    </ul>
...
```

The relevant resulting output follows:

```
<ul>
      <li>Parrot</li>
     <li>Eagle</li>
</ul>
```

You can also use the ui:repeat tag with the jsfc attribute. The snippet in Listing A-11 will produce the same output as in Listing A-10:

Listing A-11. *repeat-jsfc-example.xhtml*

```
...
    <ul>
        <li jsfc="ui:repeat"
            var="bird"
            value="#{birdDirectory.birds}">
         #{bird.name}
        </li>
    </ul>
...
```

Caution `ui:repeat` and `c:forEach` are different. `ui:repeat` is a render-time evaluation, whereas `c:forEach` is a build-time evaluation. `c:forEach` does not represent a component in Facelets (it is a `TagHandler`) and will never become part of the component tree. It is used to create the tree when the page is first referenced (when the request is not a postback), but after that, `c:forEach` will not do anything else. On the other hand, `ui:repeat` is implemented as a component in Facelets and is part of the component tree. As an example, you could develop a list of elements with a button to add more elements. If you used `forEach` for the iteration, the new elements would never be added when the button is clicked (which is a postback).

APPENDIX B

View State Encryption

View state encryption with version 1.2 of MyFaces requires no assembly. By default, MyFaces will generate a random password at startup and use the Data Encryption Standard (DES) encryption algorithm. DES is usually sufficient, but stronger encryption algorithms can be configured using context parameters in the deployment descriptor. The following code snippet shows how to configure an application to use the Blowfish encryption algorithm with a secret of size 16:

```
<context-param>
    <param-name>org.apache.myfaces.ALGORITHM</param-name>
    <param-value>Blowfish</param-value>
</context-param>
<context-param>
    <param-name>org.apache.myfaces.SECRET</param-name>
    <param-value>NzY1NDMyMTA3NjU0MzIxMA</param-value>
</context-param>
```

Using stronger forms of view state encryption may result in the following exceptions:

- `java.security.InvalidKeyException`: Illegal key size or default parameters
- `java.lang.SecurityException`: Unsupported key size or algorithm parameters

These exceptions mean few JARs under `<JAVA_HOME>jre\lib\security` need to be replaced with unlimited strength policy JAR files. The replacement JARs can be downloaded from `http://java.sun.com/j2se/1.4.2/download.html`. Consult international cryptography laws if you plan on distributing your JSF application across international boundaries.

The `org.apache.myfaces.SECRET` context parameter is the second hurdle for stronger view state encryption. This parameter is the base-64–encoded form of the password, or secret. Base 64 encoding is used in order to allow applications to use passwords composed of nonprintable characters. There is a command line utility class in MyFaces for encoding passwords of printable characters. Using this command may require Jakarta commons-logging and Jakarta commons-codec to be in the `classpath`:

```
commandPropt$ java org.apache.myfaces.util.StateUtils abcd1234
```

Here is how to use the Triple DES encryption algorithm with a secret of size 24:

```
<context-param>
    <param-name>org.apache.myfaces.ALGORITHM</param-name>
    <param-value>DESede</param-value>
</context-param>
<context-param>
    <param-name>org.apache.myfaces.SECRET</param-name>
    <param-value>MDEyMzQ1Njc4OTAxMjM0NTY3ODkwMTIz</param-value>
</context-param>
```

The following example uses the Advanced Encryption Standard (AES) encryption in Cipher Block Chaining (CBC) mode with a secret of size 24:

```
<context-param>
    <param-name>org.apache.myfaces.ALGORITHM</param-name>
    <param-value>AES</param-value>
</context-param>
<context-param>
    <param-name>
          org.apache.myfaces.ALGORITHM.PARAMETERS
   </param-name>
    <param-value>CBC/PKCS5Padding</param-value>
</context-param>
<context-param>
    <param-name>org.apache.myfaces.ALGORITHM.IV</param-name>
    <param-value>NzY1NDMyMTA3NjU0MzIxMA==</param-value>
</context-param>
<context-param>
    <param-name>org.apache.myfaces.SECRET</param-name>
    <param-value>MDEyMzQ1Njc4OTAxMjM0NTY3ODkwMTIz</param-value>
</context-param>
```

The `org.apache.myfaces.ALGORITHM.PARAMETERS` context parameter can be used to configure encryption mode. We don't recommend tinkering with this parameter unless you are comfortable with the low-level specifics of encryption. The default encryption mode is Electronic Codebook (ECB). CBC mode is generally regarded as better than ECB (for reasons beyond the scope of this book) and requires what is known as an initialization vector (IV). The IV, like the secret, is base 64 encoded.

The JSF 1.1 specification does not require view state encryption, but MyFaces has provided it since the 1.1.2 release. By default, the MyFaces JSF 1.1 implementation does not encrypt the view state in order to maintain backward compatibility with earlier versions of MyFaces core; versions 1.1.2 and 1.1.3 of MyFaces recognize these security context parameter names in lowercase.

APPENDIX C

Custom Dependency Injection

The most popular way to override JSF dependency injection is to use Spring. This is done using a custom EL VariableResolver that comes with the Spring framework. The following lines of JSF configuration code instruct MyFaces to delegate all managed bean construction to Spring:

```
<application>
    <variable-resolver>
       org.springframework.web.jsf.DelegatingVariableResolver
    </variable-resolver>
</application>
```

Spring has added value to the Java community, and it clearly has market penetration, but one limitation of Spring dependency injection is that it currently does not support annotations. This means you are jumping from one XML file (faces-config.xml) to another (application-context.xml). If you feel a strongly typed approach to dependency injection is more attractive, MyFaces 1.2.2 also integrates with Guice using a custom EL Resolver:

```
<application>
    <el-resolver>
           org.apache.myfaces.el.unified.resolver.GuiceResolver
    </el-resolver>
</application>
```

The GuiceResolver looks to application scope for the Guice Injector, which is typically placed in application scope via ServletContextListener. You can configure ServletContextListener by placing the following code in your /WEB-INF/web.xml file:

```
<listener>
     <listener-class>
          org.apache.myfaces.book.GuiceContextListener
     </listener-class>
</listener>
```

In the ServletContextListener implementation, you then configure dependency injection the way anyone in the Guice community would want it—in plain Java:

```
public class GuiceContextListener implements ServletContextListener {
   /* Occurs once, at startup */
   public void contextInitialized(ServletContextEvent event) {
        ServletContext ctx = event.getServletContext();
        Injector injector = Guice.createInjector(new ShoppingModule());
        // place the Injector where the Resolver can find it
        ctx.setAttribute(GuiceResolver.KEY, injector);

   }

   public void contextDestroyed(ServletContextEvent event) {
        ServletContext ctx = event.getServletContext();
        ctx.removeAttribute(GuiceResolver.KEY);
   }

}
public class ShoppingModule implements com.google.inject.Module{

   public void configure(Binder binder) {

       binder.bind(Order.class).to(BulkOrder.class);

   }

}
```

MyFaces Guice integration will mean far less configuration code but has drawbacks as well. Guice has nowhere near the market penetration of Spring. GuiceResolver can only be used in JSF 1.2 applications, because the el-resolver element was not available in JSF 1.1. The GuiceResolver class is also tied to the MyFaces implementation; it will not work with Sun's RI. Finally, GuiceResolver still requires you to "name" your managed bean the old-fashioned way—in a JSF configuration file, so you still have to declare your managed bean in JSF configuration file, specifying its name and scope just as you normally would. Its dependencies, however, are configured via annotations.

Index

B

D

E

F

G

J

N

O

W

X